The Channel Islands Pilot; or sailing directions for Guernsey, Serk, Alderney, and Jersey. By ... J. Richards.

Anonymous, John Richards

The BiblioLife Network

This project was made possible in part by the BiblioLife Network (BLN), a project aimed at addressing some of the huge challenges facing book preservationists around the world. The BLN includes libraries, library networks, archives, subject matter experts, online communities and library service providers. We believe every book ever published should be available as a high-quality print reproduction; printed on- demand anywhere in the world. This insures the ongoing accessibility of the content and helps generate sustainable revenue for the libraries and organizations that work to preserve these important materials.

The following book is in the "public domain" and represents an authentic reproduction of the text as printed by the original publisher. While we have attempted to accurately maintain the integrity of the original work, there are sometimes problems with the original book or micro-film from which the books were digitized. This can result in minor errors in reproduction. Possible imperfections include missing and blurred pages, poor pictures, markings and other reproduction issues beyond our control. Because this work is culturally important, we have made it available as part of our commitment to protecting, preserving, and promoting the world's literature.

GUIDE TO FOLD-OUTS, MAPS and OVERSIZED IMAGES

In an online database, page images do not need to conform to the size restrictions found in a printed book. When converting these images back into a printed bound book, the page sizes are standardized in ways that maintain the detail of the original. For large images, such as fold-out maps, the original page image is split into two or more pages.

Guidelines used to determine the split of oversize pages:

• Some images are split vertically; large images require vertical and horizontal splits.
• For horizontal splits, the content is split left to right.
• For vertical splits, the content is split from top to bottom.
• For both vertical and horizontal splits, the image is processed from top left to bottom right.

lough f. 25.*

THE CHANNEL ISLANDS PILOT

OR

SAILING DIRECTIONS

FOR

GUERNSEY, SERK, ALDERNEY, AND JERSEY

BY

Staff-Commander JOHN RICHARDS, R.N.

PUBLISHED BY ORDER OF THE LORDS COMMISSIONERS OF THE ADMIRALTY.

LONDON:
PRINTED FOR THE HYDROGRAPHIC OFFICE, ADMIRALTY,
AND SOLD BY
J. D. POTTER, *Agent for the Admiralty Charts,*
31 POULTRY, AND 11 KING STREET, TOWER HILL.
1870.

Price 2s. 6d.

25017.

ADVERTISEMENT.

The Channel Islands Pilot contains a description of, and Sailing Directions for the islands of Guernsey, Serk, Alderney, and Jersey; with the outlying islets and adjacent channels. The work has been prepared by Staff-Commander John Richards, R.N., during the Admiralty Survey of these islands in the years 1859–70, and includes the latest information.

G. H. R.

Hydrographic Office, Admiralty, London,
March, 1870.

GLOSSARY OF WORDS PECULIAR TO GUERNSEY.

Amfroques......(Amphes roques), called by pilots and fishermen the Humphs.

Amont............Up the stream; Vent d'Amont, northerly, or easterly wind.

Aval ....Down the stream; Vent d'Aval, southerly, or westerly wind.

Bec..... ....A beak ; a narrow point of precipitous land jutting out into the sea, as Bec du Nez at Serk.

Becquet.. ....A diminutive of Bec.

Boue......... .... A sunken rock causing an overfall or breaker.

Col................A neck ; a ridge connecting a rock with the mainland or one rock with another, as Col du Homptol.

Corbière..........Headlands bearing this name occur in the Channel islands and on the French coast.

Demies........ ...Rocks that uncover at half tide.

Fourquie.........Meaning forked (a rock with two heads), as Fourquie du Becquet.

Grève............A beach, as Belle Grève.

Grune ....A name frequently applied to rocks which are rather flat on top, as Les Grunes off Jerbourg point, and La Grune off north point of Serk.

Houmet, or Hommet. — This word is used to describe low islets lying near the shore, and eminences on the land rising in the midst of marshes, as Houmet Paradis, Houmet fort, Houmet mill.

Kaines............Denotes long reefs of rocks linked as it were together, as Les Boues des Kaines, Les Kaines d'Amont.

L'Etac...........A name applied to high isolated rocks, as L'Etac de Serk.

Moulière.........A rock where muscles are found.

Moye, or Moie — A steep rocky promontory ; occasionally a detached islet, as Pointe La Moye on south coast of Guernsey, and Grande and Petite Moie at Serk.

Pièce.............A name applied to rocks too small or insignificant to have acquired a distinguishing name.

Plat..............(in the feminine platte) signifies flat. Thus Platte roque means flat rock.

Pleinmont........in Jersey Plémont—a bluff headland.

Tas de Pois......from a supposed resemblance of rocks so named to a stack of peas.

CONTENTS.

CHAPTER I.

	Page
General remarks on the appearance of the islands of Guernsey and Jersey, as seen from the westward; refraction - - - - -	1, 2
Prevailing winds among the Channel islands; soundings - -	3, 4
Tidal stream in the offing; caution - - - - -	5, 6
Guernsey island; St. Peter Port; supplies - - - -	7, 8
St. Peter Port road; lights; caution; anchorage - - -	9, 10
Pilotage - - - - - - - -	11
Tidal stream through the channels - - - - -	12–14
Dangers off N.W., south and east coasts. The great bank -	15–17
Directions for approaching St. Peter Port by day and night -	18
St. Sampson and Bordeaux harbours. L'Ancresse bay and Grande Havre - - - - - - - - -	19, 20
Rocks off coast between Grande Havre and Grand Roque point; anchorage - - - - - - -	21
Cobo, Vazon, Perelle and Rocquaine bays and outlying rocks. Icart and Petit Port bays - - - - - -	22–24
Herm and Jethon islands; the Amfroques and other rocks off them -	25
Hayes channel and Passe de la Percée; anchorage; directions -	26, 27
Little Russel channel, directions for - - - -	28–30
Great Russel channel, directions for - - - -	31, 32
Serk island, general description of - - - -	33, 34
Islets and rocks round Serk. Blanchard rock - -	35
Baleine bay; Grève la Ville; anchorage off N.E. side of Serk -	36, 37
Banquette bay. La Grande Grève - - - -	38, 39
Tidal stream round Serk - - - - - -	40–42

CHAPTER II.

The Casquets islets and rocks; anchorage; lights; caution -	43, 44
Ortac channel, dangers in; Ortac rock - - -	45–47
Casquet banks; anchorage on in fine weather - -	48, 49
Tidal stream round the Casquets - - - -	50

Page

Burhou island and outlying rocks   -   -   -   -   -   51, 52

The Swinge channel, dangers in ; tides   -   -   -   -   53, 54

Alderney island; harbour of refuge; dangers; lights; old Braye and
Craby harbours   -   -   -   -   -   -   -   55–58

Rocks and dangers round Alderney   -   -   -   -   59–65

Directions for approaching Alderney, by day and night   -   -   66–68

Tidal stream round Alderney   -   .   -   -   -   69–71

Race of Alderney, dangers in ; caution   -   -   -   72

Bearings and distances   -   -   -   -   -   73

Banc de la Schole ; directions ; oyster ground   -   -   -   74

CHAPTER III.

Jersey, general description of ; pilots; outlying rocks and dangers on
the approach to Jersey from the northward   -   -   -   -   78

Appearance of Jersey from the westward   -   -   -   -   79

St. Ouen bay, and dangers off ; anchorage.   Frouquie pass   -   80–82

Corbiere rock, and dangers off   -   -   -   -   -   83

St. Brelade bay ; dangers in and near it   -   -   -   -   84

Directions for rounding the Corbiere, and approaching St. Brelade
bay ; anchorage in and off it.   Portelet bay.   Portelet ledge ;
anchorage off   -   -   -   -   -   -   -   85, 86

St. Aubin bay.   St. Helier and St. Aubin harbours ; lights   -   87, 88

Dangers off St. Aubin bay on the western, southern, and eastern
approaches ; dangers in St. Aubin bay, and at the entrance of
the Little road of St. Helier   -   -   -   -   -   89–93

Anchorage in the Little road and in St. Aubin bay -   -   -   94

Passages into St. Aubin bay ; directions for north-west, western,
south-west, Sillette, Middle, Danger rock, Hinguette, south, and
eastern passages   -   -   -   -   -   -   -   95–99

St. Helier Little road, passages into and directions for, by day and
night ; caution   -   -   -   -   -   -   -   100, 101

General directions.   Coast eastward of St. Helier, Violet bank.
Rocks and dangers off the coast E. of St. Helier   -   -   102–104

Icho bank.   Violet and Anquette channels ; rocks and dangers in
them, and directions   -   -   -   -   -   -   105–109

Grouville bay.   Gorey harbour ; rocks and dangers off Banc du
Chateau ; anchorage in Gorey roads, and directions   -   -   110–116

Anneport bay and dangers off.   St. Catherine's bay and dangers off
and in ; anchorage ; directions   -   -   -   -   -   117–120

Coupe point.   Fliquet bay ; anchorage in ; telegraphic cable.   Rozel
bay and harbour ; directions for   -   -   -   -   121, 122

Bouley bay ; anchorage and directions.   Belle Hougue point   -   123

CONTENTS.

Page

Giffard and Bonne Nuit bays; anchorage. Shamrock bank.
St. John bay. Ronez, Sorel, and Plemont points - - 124

Grève de Lecq bay; anchorage in and dangers off. Grève au
Lancon; anchorage in; caution - - - - 125

Ecrehos rocks. Banc de L'Ecreviere; anchorage south of Maitre ile - 126, 127

Drouilles rocks and dangers; directions for clearing them. Le Ruau
channel; dangers in and directions for. Passe L'Etoc - - 128-130

Jersey, bearings and distances - - - - - - 131

General directions for approaching Jersey by night. Light on
Roches Douvres - - - - - - - 132-134

Tidal stream round Jersey - - - - - - 135, 136

IN THIS WORK THE BEARINGS ARE ALL MAGNETIC,
EXCEPT WHERE MARKED AS TRUE.

THE DISTANCES ARE EXPRESSED IN SEA MILES OF
60 TO A DEGREE OF LATITUDE.

A CABLE'S LENGTH IS ASSUMED TO BE EQUAL TO
100 FATHOMS.

THE SOUNDINGS ARE REDUCED TO LOW WATER OF
ORDINARY SPRING TIDES.

THE CHANNEL ISLANDS PILOT.

CHAPTER I.

THE ISLANDS OF GUERNSEY, HERM, AND SERK, WITH THE RUSSEL CHANNELS.

Variation 21° West in 1870.

GENERAL REMARKS.—Though a section of Guernsey, if taken from south to north, would decline nearly in the form of a wedge, the highest part of which would be the southern shore, while a section of Jersey would decline in a contrary direction, or from north to south, yet these distinguishing features do not so immediately manifest themselves on first sighting these islands from the westward. Seen from a westerly direction, at any considerable distance, both Guernsey and Jersey appear level; the low land of Braye du Valle in the former island, and that of St. Clement in the latter, being yet in the horizon. The outline of Guernsey, however, is somewhat more irregular than that of Jersey; the western shore of the former is also clothed with more verdure than that of the latter, and appears of a deeper shade. St. Ouen bay, in Jersey, has suffered considerably from the encroachments of the sea-sand; so much so, that the whole of the western land between La Corbière point and L'Etac point appears identified with it.*

ASPECT of GUERNSEY.—The most remarkable objects which first present themselves when running for the south-west end of Guernsey, are the light-tower on the Hanois rocks, the white castellated tower of Fort Grey (in the centre of the sandy bay of Rocquaine), Pleinmont guard-house, Torteval church spire, and the Tower of L'Erée, on a hummock at the northern part of the above bay, near Lihou island. Pleinmont guard-

---

* _See_ Admiralty Charts :—Islands of Guernsey, Herm, and Serk, in 3 sheets, No. 61, scale, $m = 4$ inches; and France, North coast, Sheet 10, No. 2,669, scale, $m = 0\cdot5$ of an inch.

house is on the heights to the southward of the bay, near the apex of the bluff. Torteval church, with its round tower surmounted by a high steeple, stands at a little distance inland ; being as conspicuous in this quarter of the island as Câtel and Vale churches are in the northern part.

As the coast is approached, the declivity of the northern land begins gradually to rise from the horizon ; presenting a surface diversified with houses, churches, windmills, and groups of trees ; and which are still more conspicuous if seen from a north-westerly position.

All the western shore of Guernsey is studded with precipitous rocks, many of which are wholly detached from the land. On the high land above St. Martin point, at the south-east end of the island, a stone column, 96 feet high, having its apex 424 feet above the level of low water, ordinary springs, has been erected, in honour of Lieut.-General Sir John Doyle. Another remarkable, as well as beautiful object, is the Victoria tower (100 feet high, and 322 feet above low water), erected on the heights above the town of St. Peter Port ; to commemorate the visit of Her Majesty the Queen in 1846. It is a square tower, slightly tapering from its base, surmounted by a battlemented gallery, with square turrets at its angles.

ASPECT of JERSEY.—The approach to Jersey from the westward is marked nearly in a similar manner to that of Guernsey. The first objects seen are the churches of St. Peter and St. Ouen; St. Ouen windmill, with an extensive range of buildings on the sandy heights, called St. Ouen barracks ; and now and then the turret of St. Mary church together with that of Princes tower or Hougue Bie, will appear from among the trees in the interior of the island. St. Peter and St. Ouen churches stand high : the steeple of the former is lofty, that of the latter merely a turret. On a nearer view the six martello towers on the sandy beach in St. Ouen bay will present themselves, and also the Corbiére rock, with the declining land to the south-eastward ; the surface of which latter is covered with wood, and its base with sand and rock.

Such are the features which characterize Guernsey and Jersey, nor can they be mistaken even by a stranger. In clear weather these islands may be seen at the distance of 25 miles.

REFRACTION.—To show the strange effects of refraction, it may be noticed, that from a station near Verclut guard-house in Jersey, the top of the south-eastern battlement of Seymour tower exactly coincides with the line of the visible horizon at low water great spring tides ; sometimes however, when viewed from the same position, it has appeared consider-ably below that line, and in several instances above it. In this case the line of sight passes partially over the surface of the rocky ledge called the Violet bank, and over the sandy strand in its vicinity, as well as over the sea, and is at a mean height of 64 feet above it. Similar variations in the refraction have been observed on the French coast, between the steeple of Coutances and the summit of the trees in that neighbourhood, and also in the vicinity of Cancale.

As there is much low land about this part of the coast, and extensive outlying reefs which dry at low water, these occasional changes in the appearance of objects must be considered and allowed for.

WINDS and WEATHER.—The prevailing winds among the Channel islands in the winter are those between S.S.E., round by the south and W.N.W.; the latter, however, is most predominant: and it is fortunate that against the occasional furious effects of this wind Guernsey and Jersey should offer such good security for shipping. During the summer months, vernal and autumnal equinoxes, the winds appear variable and uncertain.

There is an opinion that easterly winds last longer when they set in, and set in with more uniformity in this neighbourhood than has been observed elsewhere during the winter season. Southerly and south-westerly winds during that period are almost universally accompanied with or followed by stormy weather, which seldom or ever clears up until the wind changes to the north-west, as it almost invariably does.

The state of the weather, as well as the direction and force of the wind, in the vicinity of Alderney, does not always correspond with that at Guernsey and Jersey ; being frequently local or peculiar to itself ; owing, perhaps, to the island being in the immediate vortex of the tides, which are in a constant state of rotation : and this more particularly during the new and full moon. At that period, a difference of four points has been experienced ; viz., the wind from E. by N. at Guernsey and Serk, and from N.E. by N. at Alderney, both blowing at the same time on a South-western tide, lightly or moderately in the neighbourhood of the former, while vessels near the latter were under double-reefed sails.

Upon a north-eastern stream the wind has often been found S.W. by W. at Alderney, while at Herm it blew West, with similar variety in strength ; and this without any perceptible cause (the attraction of the tides excepted) or any difference in the barometer at the two places. The southerly, south-easterly, northerly, and north-easterly winds, also invariably blow from Alderney in strong irregular gusts ; more particularly the first and last.

Gales of wind from S.W. and N.W. send in the heaviest sea amongst the islands, to which the strength of the tides greatly contribute ; the worst period is from half flood to half ebb, after which the westerly stream keeps much of the sea out in the offing.

SOUNDINGS.—Near the coasts of the Channel islands and between them there is nothing remarkable in the soundings (either in depth or quality of the ground) to assist the mariner uncertain of his position. But to vessels approaching from the westward in thick weather it may be useful to note the following facts ; namely,—That nothing less than 35 fathoms (at low water) will be obtained in the offing outside (or westward of) Roches, Douvres, and Guernsey ; nor less than 33 fathoms between Guernsey and the Casquets ; excepting on some of the very small gravel knolls near *Hurd Deep,* where as little as 20 fathoms may perhaps be found ; such *knolls,* however, may be easily distinguished from the large *banks* near and amongst the islands, by their very inferior size, as well as the greater depths by which they are surrounded.

An increase of depth from 40 to 50 and 60 fathoms would indicate a position N.W. of Guernsey, somewhere near the west end of Hurd Deep, and if between 70 and 100 fathoms such depths could only be obtained north of the Casquets and Alderney, near the east end of the *Deep.* The bottom of Hurd Deep is remarkable for large patches of black mud, although there is also much rocky ground there, and other substances. Between the *Deep* and the islands, as well as amongst them, the ground is all much of the same character ; consisting of rock, gravel, granitic sand, and coarse ground ; excepting near the banks, round the bases of which it is all fine sand.

Within the Channel islands, from Alderney down to Jersey, the soundings are a safe guide, in approaching the French coast to within a reasonable distance. A line drawn from the east end of one to the other of those islands would be nearly parallel to the French coast, and distant from it about 9 miles ; at the north part of this line near Alderney there is 25 fathoms over clean ground, and to the southward near Jersey 20 fathoms with coarse rotten ground, and occasionally oyster beds. Within this line the water shoals very gradually towards the coast. Southward of Jersey the numerous reefs render all approach to the coast by a stranger very hazardous.

Heavy gales of wind are found to cause very considerable alterations in the appearance of outlying sand-banks, as well of the exposed beaches of the islands ; south-westerly gales sending in and heaping up large quantities of sand and shingle, and those from north-east washing them away. It is well known that the *Chateau* and *Ecreviere* banks (eastward of Jersey) vary as much as 6 feet in height from this cause ; and it is probable, therefore, that the Banc la Schole, the Casquets, and other banks, also vary from similar causes.

All these variable banks, however, consist of fine sand and gravel, having sharp ridgey apexes, and are not, therefore, very dangerous to shipping, only for the confused sea occasioned by the tide rippling over them in bad weather.

TIDES.—Near Guernsey, and northward of that island, the true Channel stream prevails; the great body of the *flood* running about E. by N. whilst the tide is *rising* at Dover, and the *ebb* W.S.W. when it is *falling* at that place; but near Roches Douvres, and to the eastward, the flood stream sets S.E. into the Gulf of St. Malo, and the ebb N.W. out of it: the change in the latter section of the stream taking place an hour after high and low water by the shore respectively, and near the time of half flood and half ebb at Dover.

Thus what is called *tide and half tide* prevails at Guernsey and amongst the islands to the N.E., whilst at Jersey, and along the southern shore of the Gulf, as well as out to the westward near Roches Douvres, the stream is more regular: the former resulting from the *direct* action of the Channel stream, the latter from an interruption of the southern portion of that stream by the coast of France, and its diversion into the Gulf of St. Malo.

The centre of the Deroute Channel (between Roches Douvres and Guernsey) may be considered to mark the separating boundary of these two streams, for along this line and to the eastward they successively run side by side together, blend, and separate, in alternating direction and force, depending on the state of tide. It should here be noted that the tidal stream around and between the Channel islands has a rotary motion (caused by the differences in the action of the stream above described, and the peculiar form of the shores of the Gulf,) from right to left; going right round the compass in little more than 12 hours (an ebb and a flood). It is also worthy of remark that, in consequence of these differences, the action of the streams near the northern part of the Gulf, north of Cape La Hague and Alderney, and along its southern shore, out to Roches Douvres, are nearly the reverse of each other: there being slack tide at one of these places when the stream is running at its maximum rate at the other, and vice versâ.

About the time of half ebb at Dover and 1st quarter flood by the shore at Guernsey, the stream sets sharply into the Gulf on both sides and continues to run in, south-eastward, until half-flood by the shore and slack and change of stream in the offing, both of which occur nearly simultaneously with low water at Dover. A division of the Deroute stream now takes place: the northern part sweeping to the E.N.E., through the Russel's, Swinge, and Race channels, and then uniting with the *east* going Channel stream, northward of Alderney; the southern part near Roches Douvres setting into the depth of the Gulf to the S.E., past Jersey and the Minquiers, until near high water by the shore: after which, although the main body of the stream to the southward slacks, its northern border turns off past Jersey to the north-eastward and into the Deroute stream.

The ebb stream begins to run out to the westward *close in along the southern shore of the Gulf* soon after high water : out in the Channel within Roches Douvres an hour later : at a position 8 miles N.W. of Roches Douvres the stream changes at 2 hours ebb ; and farther to the northward near Guernsey, as already noticed, the slack and change of stream takes place soon after half ebb by the shore : at which period the Westerly stream also makes down through the Race, Swinge, and Russel channels.

It is high water at St. Helier, Jersey at 6.29, mean spring range 31¼ feet ; at Guernsey 6.37, mean spring range 26 feet ; and Alderney 6.46, mean spring range 17½ feet.* Out in the offing westward of Guernsey the stream seldom exceeds 3 knots, until the island is approached, near which it sometimes attains the rate of 4½ knots. In the Russel channels it exceeds 5 knots, and it runs about the same rate between Jersey and the Minquiers, and nearly 4 knots in the centre of the Deroute channel between Jersey and Serk. The Race and Swinge streams sometimes attain the rate of more than 7 knots.

The rapidity with which the tides rise and fall, and their velocity, are greatly influenced by strong north-eastern and south-western gales of wind ; the former retarding and the latter accelerating their progress in a very remarkable degree : the latter will also cause the Race stream to run three-quarters of an hour longer to the north-eastward than it otherwise would do, though the former has not a similar effect upon the stream when running to the south-westward.

The tides put in and take off in all this neighbourhood very suddenly, and the general run of the springs takes place about half an hour earlier than the neaps.

The approaches to the Channel Islands present peculiar difficulties to the stranger. The outlying rocks fronting their coasts ; the strength and ever varying direction of the tidal stream, and the rough sea occasioned by it in bad weather are all elements of danger : nevertheless most of these difficulties may be overcome by the skilful seaman, assisted by a careful study of the charts and sailing directions.

CAUTION.—A constant and careful allowance should always be made for the set of the stream. If approaching from the westward, and to the southward of Alderney a south-easterly set may certainly be expected, which will increase in intensity on nearing Guernsey ; and between that

---

* The average duration of the flood stream is 5¾ hours, and of the ebb 6¾ hours.

island and Roches Douvres a considerable indraught is always found, especially in N.W. gales.

If a vessel should happen to be near the islands during a long winter's night, but to the westward withal, the following observations may be worth consideration. With northerly, north-westerly, and westerly winds, it would not be prudent to lay her head to the north-eastward, between the periods of low water and half-flood, unless the depth of water exceeds 34 fathoms, because during that interval the wind and tide unite in driving the ship to the south-eastward. It is equally imprudent with southerly, south-westerly, and westerly winds, to lay a vessel's head to the south-eastward between half-flood and high water, for the same reason, the wind and tide contributing to drive her to the north-eastward.

With all easterly winds the islands become a weather shore, and may consequently be made free with as discretion may point out. Further : a position or departure taken before dark may, by attention to the set of the streams, be preserved within 3 or 4 miles, provided a vessel can carry close-reefed top-sails and fore-sail, as what may be lost on one tide will be nearly regained on the next, if the wind will enable her to lie across either. This calculation may be made with a degree of certainty off St. Malo, Granville, and Cape Flamanville.

When making the Casquets or any of the rocks or islands in thick foggy weather, never run close home *with the stream*, but wait until the turning of the stream would set you *off shore* in the event of getting into danger suddenly.

In westerly gales always avoid passing close to windward of any of the banks on a weather tide : and it will be as well to remember, that on such occasions, whilst the western stream is running in the offing, there is a very heavy sea to the westward of the islands and comparatively smooth water within them, and along the coast of France : so that a small vessel leaving Alderney at 2 hours ebb, and pushing through the Race *before* the W.S.W. stream makes down, could run a considerable distance towards Jersey in smooth water.

On entering or leaving any of the narrow channels between the islands be careful to make early allowance for the different sets of tide, sure to be met with at such places.

GUERNSEY is nearly in the form of a right-angled triangle, the north-west side forming the hypothenuse, the length of which is about 8 miles. The land on the south side is comparatively high and steep, its general elevation being about 300 feet, (the highest part of the island is Hautnez, over Icart bay, which is 363 feet above the level of low water,) but it gradually lowers towards the north, where in some places it is little above the sea. The island is encompassed with many dangerous rocks, the principal of which are the Hanois, Sambule, and Grunes, on the west and north-west sides ; the Braye rocks with several others on the north side ; and on the north-east and east sides lie the Amfroque rocks, together with the islands of Herm and Jethou, which are also surrounded by numerous rocks and ledges.

Guernsey contains 16,000 acres of land, which is fertile and highly cultivated, but having a population (in 1861) of 29,800, it does not grow grain enough, nor raise sufficient number of cattle to supply its inhabitants.

ST. PETER PORT, the capital of the island, stands on the eastern shore, and its population numbers about 16,000. From the sea it has rather an imposing appearance, but is irregularly built. It is the seat of government of the northern division of the Channel islands, or Bailiwick as it is termed; which includes Alderney, Serk, Herm, and Jethou. Its small tidal harbour, carrying a depth of 20 feet alongside quays at high water springs, and 10 feet at neaps, is now enclosed by a new harbour formed between two breakwaters, with an average depth in it of 10 feet at low water of mean springs.

The principal articles of export are cider, apples, potatoes, wines, and building stone, and granite in a broken state for the repair of roads. The imports are British manufactures, wine, sugar, coffee, grain, and cattle ; the two latter are chiefly from France. In the year 1862 the number of vessels belonging to the port was 128, their total registered tonnage 19,679 tons, and they were manned by 1,053 seamen. At the same period 2,261 vessels, of 256,290 tonnage, entered inwards, and 2,185, of 254,288 tonnage, cleared outwards.

Supplies.—Though Guernsey abounds with springs, the only accessible watering place for vessels has hitherto been on its eastern side, at Fermain bay, about a mile northward of St. Martin point; where (with the wind from N.N.E., round westerly to S.W.) boats provided with long hoses may fill at pleasure almost any quantity. Pipes are now laid down from the large reservoir at Havelet to the harbours; where water is supplied at a shilling a ton. St. Peter Port market furnishes fresh meat, fish, vegetables, and fruit in abundance at a cheap rate.

ST. PETER PORT HARBOURS.—The small tidal harbour of St. Peter Port, 4¼ acres in area, is enclosed by piers of masonry 35 feet high, with an entrance 80 feet wide, facing the east. The depth at high water springs between the pier heads is 24¾ feet, and 14¾ feet at neaps ; the average depth along the quays on the same tides being respectively 20 and 10 feet. To the south-eastward of the harbour stands castle Cornet, which is now connected with the mainland by a massive granite causeway.

The new harbour works comprise two esplanades, one on each side of the old harbour, running parallel with the sea front of the town, and averaging together 2,500 feet in length and 150 in breadth. From these esplanades spring two breakwaters, one on either side, and equidistant from the old harbour; being 2,500 feet apart at the base, and projecting to the eastward, so as to enclose the natural sandy bay in front of the town.

The south or Castle breakwater is carried across the rocky isthmus, by which, at low water springs, castle Cornet is connected with the main, and terminates at the north-west bastion of the castle, being 1,900 feet in length. The southern face of this breakwater consists of an upright wall and parapet, constructed of rough masonry, and carried to a height of 15 feet above the highest tides. Along this is constructed a level roadway and footpath 40 feet wide. On the north side and under the lee of this arm it is proposed to construct a floating dock. Farther, on this side, a rough stone breakwater projects 600 feet eastward from the north-east salient angle of castle Cornet; its end marked by a handsome stone building, from which is exhibited a powerful (white) light. These works effectually screen the entrance of the harbour from the most exposed quarter (the southward), and add greatly to the security of the anchorage in the road.

The north, or St. Julien's, breakwater (and landing pier) begins on the north side of the old harbour, at the extremity of the new esplanade, and extends in an easterly direction about 1,400 feet, or as far as the head of the *Blanche* rock; from whence it changes to a southerly direction (or a little outside the line of Castle Cornet) for nearly 900 feet, leaving an entrance between the pier end and the rocks off Castle Cornet of only 370 feet in width, and completely sheltering the pool within. Within and alongside the outer part of this pier are three capital landing stages for steamers, having 9, 8, and 3 feet respectively at the lowest spring tides,* at which period there is 10 feet at the entrance, near the end of the pier, and 6 feet near the middle of the pool within. From the middle of the pool the water shoals gradually and regularly towards the shore. The bottom of the harbour is nearly altogether fine sand.

The whole space enclosed by the works above described (exclusive of the areas of floating dock, old harbour, carcenage, &c.) amounts to about 57 acres, of which, however, only about 23 acres are covered with water at the lowest tides.

---

* The depths as well as heights, &c., appearing in Chapter I. of this work, and the new Admiralty Chart of Guernsey generally, are reckoned from a zero *near* mean springs. The lowest tide registered at Guernsey from 1858 to 1868 fell 3 feet 9 inches *below* that zero.

ST. PETER PORT ROAD is in front of the town, and to the north-eastward of castle Cornet. The ground is excellent for holding, and the road affords good shelter against all winds, except those from between S.S.W. and S.E., which send in much swell and sea, especially on the ebb tide. Under such circumstances it is highly probable that smoother water will be found under the lee of the Great bank, where a vessel will be much safer than in the road, as in the event of parting from her anchors she might easily run through the Little Russel and anchor off Fort Doyle, or in L'Ancresse bay.

A vessel should moor in St. Peter Port road, with open hawse, to the S. by E., and within the following limits :—southern limit, St. Peter Port church in line with the end of the breakwater off castle Cornet: northern limit, the beacon on the Sardrette rock and Victoria tower in line : western limit, the outer angle of castle Cornet in one with the white beacon on Fermain point ; and eastern limit, the Anfré beacon in line with left extreme of buildings on high land over St. Martin point. Here there are from 5 to 11 fathoms water, fine sand ; but farther southward the bottom is coarse, and the depth increases to 20 fathoms. There is a government mooring $2\frac{1}{4}$ inch chain laid down in 5 fathoms, at the distance of about a cable north-eastward of castle Cornet breakwater lighthouse.

LIGHTS.—The light tower on the south-western rock of the Hanois group, one mile off the west end of Guernsey, exhibits, at 100 feet above the level of high water, a quick *revolving red* light of the first order, which attains its greatest brilliancy every *forty-five seconds*, and should be seen in clear weather at a distance of 12 to 14 miles. The light is visible all round the western horizon, and obscured only to the eastward by the island of Guernsey, from its north point, which bears E. by N. from the light, to the southward as far as Pleinmont point, which bears S.E. from the light; the line of eclipse in this latter direction passes $3\frac{1}{4}$ miles south-westward of L'Etac de Serk, and over the Pierres de Lecq rocks. The light tower is of gray granite, and 117 feet high from base to vane ; the Casquets bear from it N.E. by E. $\frac{1}{6}$ E., distant $21\frac{1}{3}$ miles ; the Corbière rock, Jersey, S.S.E. $\frac{1}{2}$ E., $23\frac{1}{2}$ miles ; and the Roches Douvres, S.W. $\frac{3}{4}$ S., 20 miles.

On the outer or eastern extreme of castle Cornet breakwater, at the south side of entrance to the outer harbour of St. Peter Port, is a *fixed* white light at an elevation of 46 feet above high water, and visible at a distance of 9 miles. It shows as a *bright* light from north round by east to south, and as a *dim* light landward, from south round by west to north. From the lighthouse the Longue Pierre rock off St. Martin point bears S.S.W. distant 2 miles nearly ; Lower Heads rocks buoy S.E. by S. $2\frac{1}{8}$

miles ; Rousse rock E. by N. $\frac{3}{4}$ N. $2\frac{1}{2}$ miles ; Platte rock N.E. by E. northerly $2\frac{1}{8}$ miles ; and the Roustel rock N.E. by E. $\frac{1}{2}$ E. $2\frac{1}{2}$ miles.

A *fixed red* light is exhibited from a wooden building (painted white) on the south pier-head of the old harbour of St. Peter Port, for the convenience of vessels approaching the roadstead or harbour. The light is elevated 35 feet above high water, and may be seen when coming through the Little Russel from the northward, the Great Russel from the eastward, and also from the southward when St. Martin point is rounded.

CAUTION.—Vessels bound to Guernsey from the westward should not approach the island in thick weather within the depth of 40 or 38 fathoms, unless their position has been previously well ascertained. Careful allowance should also be made for the flood stream setting in for the island.

The water is deep at a quarter of a mile westward of the Hanois lighthouse, but dangerous rocks extend to the S.S.W. for a third of a mile, to the N.N.W. three-quarters of a mile, and to the northward one mile from the lighthouse. The Grune de l'Ouest, or du Nord-Ouai, (a rock that dries 10 feet at low water springs, and which has hitherto been considered the northernmost danger off Guernsey,) bears N.E. by E., nearly 5 miles from the lighthouse; but as several dangerous sunken rocks have lately been discovered outside it, (the outer of which, the Boue Blondel, has only 5 fathoms on it, and bears from the lighthouse N.N.E. $3\frac{1}{2}$ miles,) it is recommended that, to clear all these dangers, vessels passing westward of Guernsey at night, should not bring the Hanois light westward of South until the Casquets lights bear E.N.E.

ANCHORAGE.—There are several anchorages on the south side of Guernsey, where, with the wind off the land, a vessel may stop a tide ; but as they would not be safe for a stranger to approach, a vessel not having a pilot should not close the coast so as to shut in the north point of Serk with Jerbourg bluff.

St. Peter Port road, as already noticed, affords good shelter, except with the wind between S.S.W. and S.E. ; and the anchorage is excellent.

There is good anchorage at the north end of the Great bank, on the east side of the island, as well as in Petit Port, on the south coast ; also on the north coast off Fort Doyle, and at L'Ancresse, Grand Havre, Cobo and Vazon bays ; but at most of these places it would be necessary to employ a pilot. Rocquaine and Perelle bays are very dangerous, and, together with the intermediate coast, quite unfit for any but the smallest vessels to approach.

PILOTAGE.—By ordinance of the Royal Court of Guernsey it is enacted, that every pilot boat shall carry a flag, half red and half white, the white part being placed uppermost; the letter P shall be marked in black on the white part, and the pilot's number in white on the red parts near the centre of the flag:—the whole under the penalty of a fine, at the discretion of the court.   And that every ship or vessel of above 50 tons burthen, new admeasurement, shall be bound to take a pilot, both on her arrival in this island and on her departure, on pain of paying the usual pilotage to the pilot who shall first have presented himself for the purpose of undertaking the conduct or pilotage thereof.

Steam boats and yachts are excepted, as are also ships or vessels putting into the roads in consequence of stress of weather or contrary winds, and putting to sea again; provided they do not load or unload either merchandise or ballast.   In case of a pilot being prevented by tempestuous weather from getting on board a ship or vessel at sea, such ship or vessel and the pilot boat shall so manage as to enable the pilot boat to take the lead and serve as a guide; and such ship or vessel shall pay the same pilotage as if the pilot had actually gone on board.

Rates of Pilotage.

—	Vessels above 50 tons burthen and under 80 tons.	Vessels of 80 tons and up to 100 tons.	Vessels of 100 tons and up to 250 tons.	Vessels of 250 tons and upwards.
	£ s. d.	£ s. d.	£ s. d.	£ s. d.
To the pilot who shall have brought a vessel from sea into the roads.	0 10 6	1 0 0	1 5 0	1 10 0
To the pilot of the harbour of St. Peter Port, for bringing a vessel into the said harbour.	0 7 0	0 10 0	0 15 0	1 0 0
	0 17 6	1 10 0	2 0 0	2 10 0

TIDAL STREAMS.—It is high water, full and change, in St. Peter Port harbour at 6h. 37m.; great springs rise 33 feet, ordinary springs 26 feet, neaps $18\frac{1}{2}$ feet, and neaps range $11\frac{1}{4}$ ft.   The general level of the sea is liable to be depressed or elevated, between 2 and 3 feet, by strong easterly or westerly winds.

The eastern stream or flood makes close in shore, along the south and north-western coast of Guernsey, soon after low water; whilst the south-western stream is still running at its strength in the offing 4 miles westward of the island; between these positions the streams vary in strength and direction as one or the other is approached.

The flood stream between Guernsey and the rocks projecting from the south-west end of Jethou island, takes two different directions; one part runs directly through the Great road and thence into the Little Russel; another branches off nearly at right angles from the former and runs to the eastward, towards Jethou, and through the before mentioned rocks, into the Great Russel. The ebb stream runs directly the reverse; the stream from the Great Russel uniting with that in the road, after it has passed the rocks at Jethou, from whence they both set to the south-westward. By bringing the Grande Braye rock a boat's length open westward of Brehon tower, a vessel will keep in the former draught, or road-tide, and the said rock, if brought in one with Brehon tower, will place her in the latter, or indraught of the Great Russel. A vessel working into Guernsey road from the southward, will derive great advantage by paying attention to this division of the stream.

It is high water in the Great and Little Russel channels at the same time as at St. Peter Port, and the streams run nearly $5\frac{1}{2}$ hours on each tide, allowing better than half an hour for high and low water slack. In the Great Russel the strength of the flood stream runs E.N.E., and the ebb W.S.W., and in the Little Russel the strength of the flood runs N.E. $\frac{1}{2}$ E., and the ebb S.W. $\frac{1}{2}$ W., nearly. At the north-eastern entrance, however, of the Little Russel, between the Braye and the Amfroque rocks, the stream takes the direction of that in the offing, viz., the first two hours of the flood sets directly for the north end of Herm island, gradually joining the south-western stream in the Russel, and the last hour of the flood as well as the first of the ebb.

To understand the various sets of the tides in the Russel channels, as well as all round the outer shores of this group of islands, it is necessary to refer to their governing cause, namely, the rotary motion of the offing stream, which in one tide runs in regular succession from every point of the compass.

At high water, by the shore, the flood stream sets E.N.E. fairly through the Russel channels, and is then at its greatest strength, coinciding nearly with the general direction of the offing stream; which at this time, to the westward of Guernsey, is running E. by N., and to the eastward of Serk N.N.E. The direction of the offing stream in its progressive change from North to West, &c., sets about N.W. by N., 3 hours after high water, or at half ebb, which a glance at the chart will show to be right across the Russel channels; producing, as might be expected, a slack tide in the Great Russel, under the lee of Serk, and especially in the Little Russel, protected as it is by Herm and Jethou and the numerous rocks to the northward and southward of those islands. At low water, the offing stream has got round to W.S.W., and as this is about the direction of the Russel channels, the ebb stream, at this time, attains its greatest strength.

After low water the island of Guernsey begins to obstruct the free course of the stream into the channels eastward of it; and at half flood, the pressure of the stream, setting in a south-easterly direction, is so divided by the island, that although there is a strong easterly tide along its north and south shores, there is slack water throughout the whole extent of the Russel channels. The offing stream, still revolving, gradually forces the flood to the north-eastward through these channels; attaining its greatest strength, as before stated, near high water.

A proper consideration of the foregoing general remarks is necessary to understand the cause of the inumerable sets of tide and eddies about these islands. It must also be remembered, that a body of water once set in motion will continue to move onward for some time after the force which originated it has been removed; thus the Russel streams continue to run to the southward (after low water) for some time after the source of their supply has been cut off by the shutting in of the offing stream behind Guernsey; and these southerly streams being met off St. Martin point by the first of the eastern stream, they blend together and make a south-east tide, which at springs runs with considerable strength, from the north end of the Great bank to the S.E. for some distance outside the Têtes d'Aval, but is not felt *inside* the Great bank, or near St. Martin point.

An illustration of the value of a knowledge of the tides will be seen by following the track of the Guernsey boatman, on a trip to the east side of Serk and back. He will take a fair tide the whole distance. Leaving Guernsey road a little after low water, he proceeds with a fair tide to the S.E., outside the Têtes d'Aval, until he meets the eastern stream, with which he sails to the southward of Serk. Near L'Etac de Serk he meets a northerly tide, which accompanies him along the east side of the island as far as the Creux. On his return to Guernsey, he will be able to round the north point of Serk about an hour after high water (at which time the turning of the offing stream towards the north removes the pressure of the Great Russel stream from the Bec du Nez, and causes an eddy from it to the Givaude rock, off Brecqhou,) and carry an eddy or counter stream as far as the Givaude rock; outside of which he will meet the true stream setting to the N.W., at 2 hours after high water. Going with this stream, he will pass through the Passe de la Percée, and crossing the Little Russel arrive at St. Peter Port before the south-western stream has fairly made.

It appears that the general *drift* of the tidal stream corresponds with its rotary motion from right to left, close to the coasts of the Channel Islands as well as in the offing outside of them; for it has frequently happened that floating objects near the shore have been seen successively on their northern, western, southern, and eastern coasts. Moreover part of a wrecked vessel, having been drifted from a rock near the Casquets during calm weather, was known to take a south-westerly course, and to drift (with a rotary motion through a succession of parabolic tidal curves) at the rate of about 4 miles per day, round the western and southern coasts of Guernsey (several miles distant from the island) and up the Deroute and Race streams ; whilst other parts of the same wreck (having probably drifted off the rock at the *commencement* of the western stream and thereby got set farther out to the westward) were met with about the same time several miles within and to the eastward of Roches Douvres.

These last examples prove the existence of a *current* whose drift coincides with the shifting movement of the tidal stream ; south-westerly from the Casquets, southerly past Guernsey, and easterly and southerly between Guernsey and Roches Douvres. The easterly or main branch of this current, as already noticed, passes up the Deroute and Race channels, and it seems highly probable that after clearing the Race of Alderney it turns off to the westward past that island, to reunite with its own stream again off the Casquets, and repeat the same round as before in endless succession. This current (hitherto known under the name of "indraught of the Gulf of St. Malo"), it is generally believed, only exists during fresh westerly breezes, and doubtless its strength is greatly increased at such times, but there is no doubt it runs continuously between the Casquets and Roches Douvres, and with a rate proportioned to the strength of the tidal stream.

A little consideration of the facts stated above will serve to show, that vessels going round the islands, as well as those navigating the channels between them, may occasionally shorten their passages materially by following the curves of the tidal streams instead of taking direct courses.

CAUTION.—Although the flood stream begins to set through the Little Russel at the same time that it does in the Great Russel, viz., at half tide, yet there is no northern inclination round St. Martin point, until 4 hours flood ; care must therefore be taken that the first of the eastern stream does not draw the vessel into the Great Russel, or among the rocks in the vicinity of the Têtes d'Aval.

DANGERS off N.W. COAST.—The north-west side of Guernsey should not be approached nearer than 3½ miles, there being several dangerous rocky ledges lying off it; those most to be feared are the Grunes de l'Ouest, or du Nord-Ouai, Sambule, Soufleuresse, Boin, and Grand Etacre. *The Grunes de l'Ouest dry 10 feet at low water spring tides ; the

---

* To reduce all the depths and heights given in Part I. of this work (as well as in the new Admiralty Chart of Guernsey) to the *lowest* tides, subtract 3 feet 9 inches from the depths and add that quantity to the heights.

Sambule 16 feet; the Soufleuresse 10 feet; the Boin 3 feet; and the Grand Etacre 19 feet. The positions of the outer rocks of the Banc du Hanois, Banc Bisé, and other dangers off them have been briefly described in page 10.

From the outer head of the Grune de l'Ouest, Câtel church spire appears *just* open eastward of Guet du Câtel, S. by E. ¾ E., and Hanois lighthouse is in line with the rock off the west end of Lihou island, next within Corner rock, S.W. by W.

From the Sambule, Câtel church is in line with Vazon tower, S.E.; St. Saviour church is in line with the Conchée rock; and the Hanois lighthouse is just open westward of Corner rock, S.W. ¾ W.

The Grand Etacre lies with the church of St. Pierre du Bois (without a spire) over the west part of Lihou island, S.S.E. ¼ E.; Vazon tower touching the south side of Gros Pont, E.S.E., easterly; and Hanois lighthouse just open eastward of the Pendante, S.W., westerly.

There are also several dangerous sunken rocks, on which the sea breaks heavily in bad weather, considerably outside these dangers; as the Boue Blondel, of 5¼ fathoms water, lying with Torteval church in line with west extreme of Lihou island, S. by E. ½ E., distant 2¼ miles from the latter; the inner head of the Roches de l'Ouest of 5¾ fathoms, lying with Câtel church, the Guet du Câtel, and the outer and highest head of the Grunes in line S. by E. ¾ E., three-quarters of a mile outside the latter; and the outer head of the Frettes of 5½ fathoms, lying with Câtel church just open eastward of Grand Roque tower, S. ⅓ W. 2¾ miles from the tower.

The Hanois lighthouse kept just open westward of the Pendante (the outer rock of the Trois Pères group, S.W. ¼ S. (until Vale church comes in line with the Grand Saut Roquier, S.E. ¾ E.), will lead inside the above sunken rocks and outside the Etacre, the Sambule, the Boin, and the Grunes de l'Ouest.

CAUTION.—Unless a vessel is quite under command, and in charge of a pilot, she should not approach these rocks nearer than 2 miles; also if proceeding round the south side of the island to St. Peter Port; Corbière point, Moye point (two remarkable headlands on the south coast between Pleinmont and Icart points), and the land to the eastward, should always be kept open of Pleinmont point.

DANGERS off SOUTH COAST.—Pleinmont ledge has 9 feet water on the shoalest part; which spot lies S.S.W. ¼ W. nearly two-thirds of a mile from Pleinmont Guet, but only one-third of a mile outside the Herpin rock.

The Boue Baker of 16 feet water, lies with the Round rock just shut in with Pleinmont point, N. by W. ¼ W.; and Torteval church spire on with the north part of a remarkable projecting bluff (marked by a white spot) in the bay under, N.E. ½ E.

The Boues des Kaines, of 29 feet water, lie with the extreme of the Moye point in line with the inner guard-house on Icart point, E. ¾ S.; Torteval church spire just in sight above the cliff, and open westward of Guet du Tielle, N. ¾ E.; and the Grand Hanois within the Tas de Pois and in line with Pleinmont point, N.W. by N.

Within these rocks there are many others, some of which uncover at or near low water; as the Kaines d'Amont, lying S.W. from the Guet du Tielle, and nearly half a mile from the land: the Lieuses, lying S.W. from Corbière point, and nearly half a mile from the land, dry 8 feet at low water; and Les Sept Boues, nearly a quarter of a mile within it, dry 10 feet.

DANGERS off EAST COAST.—The dangers to be avoided in rounding St. Martin point, the south-east extreme of Guernsey, are the Grunes de Jerbourg, described at page 18, the Longue Pierre and Gabrielle rocks, as well as the shoal part of the Great bank. The Longue Pierre dries 19 feet at low water springs, and is marked by a black staff and ball *beacon*. The Gabrielle dries 4 feet at low water, at which period there are 23 feet on the south end, 19 feet on the middle, and 17 feet on the north part of the Great bank.

A vessel, to pass eastward of these rocks and westward of the shoal part of the bank, should keep Delancy mill (ruin) in line with, or a little open of, the end of the breakwater off castle Cornet, bearing N. by E. ¾ E.; this mark will also lead outside the Anfré rock, and between the Ferico and Oyster rocks, right up to the Tremies. From the Gabrielle rock, Delancy mill is just shut in with north-east angle of castle Cornet.

THE GREAT BANK, within the 5 fathoms line at low water springs, is 1½ miles long and 2 cables broad. From its southern limit, St. Peter Port church is in line with the Anfré beacon; and from its northern limit, the north angle of castle Cornet, the old harbour lighthouse, and Elizabeth college tower are in one. The shoalest part, 17 feet, lies 2 cables southward of this latter line of direction, and from it the above church is just open of south angle of castle Cornet; the Anfré beacon, and the white stone beacon on the top of Fermain point in line, leads northward of it, and crosses the north end of the bank in 20 feet at low water.

Several dangerous rocks lying in the vicinity of castle Cornet must be carefully avoided when running for St. Peter Port road, viz.:—the Tremies to the north-east of the castle and south nearly half a cable from the breakwater lighthouse, the Ferico to the east, the Oyster rock to the south-east, and the Moulinet to the south-west, which latter is marked by a *pole* and bird *beacon*.

FERICO is a dangerous rock with only 9 feet on it at low water, lying nearly a quarter of a mile eastward of the castle, and in the fairway of vessels bound to St. Peter Port from the southward. To pass eastward of it, keep St. Martin barracks open south-east of the Anfré beacon until Salerie point opens of the end of castle Cornet breakwater, or bring castle Cornet breakwater light to bear N.N.W. The Forein rock, of 38 feet water, lies a little outside the Ferico, and will be cleared to the eastward by the same marks. The Oyster rock dries 12 feet at low water.

DIRECTIONS.—A vessel bound from the westward to the anchorage off the eastern side of Guernsey, and intending to pass southward of the island, should, as before stated, make a careful allowance for the flood stream if it is running, as it sets in towards the land. Rounding Pleinmont point, give the lighthouse on the Hanois rocks a berth of at least 1½ miles, to avoid the Hanois and Bise banks; and to clear the Hanois rocks, keep Corbière point, or Moye point, open of Pleinmont point, bearing S.E. by E. ¼ E.

To clear Pleinmont ledge and the other dangers between it and Moye point, do not shut in Lihou island with Pleinmont point until Serk church (which stands northward of the mill) comes open of Jerbourg point. When abreast La Moye point, open the north point of Serk with Jerbourg point, or keep Pleinmont bluff open of Corbière point, to avoid the Balliene rock, which lies W.S.W. a quarter of a mile from Icart point, and is awash at low water. After passing this point, keep Sommeilleuse guardhouse (a ruin standing on the edge of a remarkable high cliff a short distance eastward of Moye point) a little open southward of Icart low point until Brehon tower opens eastward of the Longue Pierre, or until Herm mill (ruin) touches the north side of the high land of Jethou. These marks will lead outside the Grunes de Jerbourg, which are a dangerous cluster of rocks lying a quarter of a mile from the shore, and in a south-west direction from St. Martin point; they are covered at one quarter flood, and have 26 fathoms close to their south side.

Rounding St. Martin point, when Delancy mill (ruin) comes on with the end of castle Cornet breakwater, proceed with this mark on, between the Anfré rock and Great bank, keeping St. Martin barracks open southward of the Anfré beacon until Salerie battery opens of castle Cornet breakwater, or the breakwater lighthouse bears N.N.W. When the town church comes open of the breakwater, anchor in the road as convenient, or run into the harbour.

To pass eastward of the Great bank, keep Vale mill, about midway between Mont Crevelt tower and Vale castle, and touching the east end of the breakwater off St. Sampson harbour, N. ½ E.; and when the town church is shut in behind castle Cornet haul in for the anchorage.

At night, when running for this anchorage from the northward and eastward, through the Great Russel, steer to the south-westward till the *red* light on the south pier head of St. Peter Port *old* harbour bears N.W. by N., or opens southward of castle Cornet, which mark leads southward of the Têtes d'Aval, and over the north end of the Great bank, in 22 feet at low water. On nearing the castle and running for the harbour, bring the light to bear W. by N., which is also the best line to anchor on in the road. The light open and shut of the south part of castle Cornet leads only 150 feet southward of the Têtes d'Aval, and across the Great bank in 21 feet at low water.

Steering for the Little Russel from the northward, keep the Casquets lights on a N.E. ¾ N. bearing until castle Cornet breakwater light bears S.W. by W. ½ W.; this being the line of bearing for the central track. This passage, however, should never be attempted at night by a stranger, nor even by a person acquainted with the place, unless in a steamer of light draught, at or near high water.

From the westward and southward, after passing St. Martin point, steer to the eastward until the old harbour red light is seen clear of Terres point, bearing N. ⅓ E.; keep it in sight on this line, and it will lead a quarter of a mile eastward of the Longue Pierre. When St. Martin point bears S.W. ½ W. steer N.E. by N., to pass between the Anfré rock and the Great bank, and when castle Cornet breakwater light bears N.N.W. steer N. by E. until the red light bears W. by N., after which proceed as before directed.

ST. SAMPSON HARBOUR is on the eastern side of Guernsey, between Vale castle and Mont Crevelt, but vessels lie aground in it at low water. The site now occupied by this harbour was originally the eastern entrance creek to an arm of the sea, which severed the northern portion of Guernsey from the main island. About 60 years since this strait was embanked at each end, and since that period the intervening land has been reclaimed.

The harbour may be termed rectangular in form; its extreme length being about 1,900 feet N.W. and S.E., by an average width of 500 feet, and containing a water area of 22 acres at high water springs. At low water springs this space is dry, and the tide ebbs for a considerable distance outside the pier heads. The entrance between the pier heads is 120 feet wide, and the depth there 15 feet at high water ordinary neaps. At this time, there are 12 feet along the south pier, and 11 feet for a length of 150 feet along the south quay, the remainder of which gradually shoals to its western end.

DIRECTIONS.—The approach to this harbour is difficult, being athwart the tidal streams ; and on account of the Crabière, Grunette, and Grande Demie rocks, which lie off the entrance. The most dangerous of these is the Crabière, in the fairway of the entrance, and distant about 200 yards from the head of Mont Crevelt breakwater; it has however been lately reduced in height, having now 9 feet on it at half tide.

The best entrance into the harbour is between the Crabiere and the Grunette, (which passage, however, is not above half a cable wide,) and the leading mark is the white, or south-western, house on Jethou island wholly open to the northward of the battery on Brehon rock, but nearly touching it, which will lead to the outer warping buoy; then steer in between the pier head. The bottom is blue clay covered with a layer of sand.

A Lifeboat is stationed at St. Sampsons.

BORDEAUX HARBOUR, to the northward of St. Sampson, is used only by fishermen. Here vessels must lie aground the same as at St. Sampson ; and as the entrance to the harbour will not admit of larger vessels than those of 10 tons burthen, a further description is needless.

L'ANCRESSE BAY, on the north side of Guernsey, to the westward of Fort Le Marchant, affords good shelter for small craft against south-easterly, southerly, and westerly winds, in 6 to 2 fathoms water. The bottom is muddy sand, and excellent for holding.

GRAND HAVRE, to the westward of Ancresse bay, and north-westward of Vale church, has its entrance between the martello tower on Mont Guet to the north, and the martello tower on Rousse point to the south. It affords excellent anchorage for small vessels, in 14 to 9 feet water, with good shelter against southerly and all easterly winds, over a bottom of sand and grass : north-westerly winds, however, send in a heavy swell and sea, between half flood and half ebb ; though there is little danger to be apprehended if the ground tackling be good. For vessels capable of taking the ground, there is a safe place for that purpose on the south-eastern side of Rousse point. A dangerous rock lies in the fairway of the entrance, called the Rousse de Mer, which appears at a quarter ebb ; and on each side of it there are several other rocks. The marks for this rock are Delancy mill (ruin) just shut in with the south-western angle of Vale church, S. by E., and the house on the highest part of Lihou island in line with the highest part of the Grand Saut Roquier, W. by S. $\frac{1}{2}$ S.

DIRECTIONS.—From the numerous dangers that lie off the entrance to Grand Havre there is only one channel by which it can be safely approached by a stranger. This channel lies between the Rousse de Mer and Main rocks; the former rock dries 20 feet, and the latter 5 feet, at low water springs.

Bring Victoria tower in line with the rocky point just eastward of the tower on Rousse point, bearing S. by W., and run in on this line until Delancy mill opens south-west of Vale church; then steer for the high rocky bluff near the middle of the bay, and anchor when about midway between the towers on entrance points, in 10 feet at low water. A vessel of only 6 feet draught may anchor with Noirmont house in line with the tower on Rousse point, and Victoria tower about midway between Rousse point and the rocky bluff near the middle of the bay to the eastward of it.

The **ROQUE NOIRE, BOUE CORNEILLE, L'ETAC,** and **SAUT ROQUIER ROCKS,** (extending three-quarters of a mile in a W. by S. direction) front the coast between Grand Havre and Grand Roque point, at the distance of three quarters of a mile from the land. They are always above water, and serve to distinguish this part of the coast at high water, when the dangerous rocks around them are covered. Grand Roque point has a rocky hummock on it (from which it takes its name), surmounted by a small fort and watch tower.

The **HOFFETS** are dangerous rocks, most of which uncover only at low tide. The outer head, awash at low water, bears N.N.E. three-quarters of a mile from the Roque Noire. Victoria tower in line with the tower on Rousse point, S. by W., leads a quarter of a mile eastward of them; the Petite Braye open northward of Roque au Nord clears them to the northward; and Torteval church in line with Houmet fort S.W. ¼ W., clears them a quarter of a mile to the westward.

There are some dangerous rocks, awash at low water, extending W.N.W. an eighth of a mile from the Grand Saut Roquier; and others a little outside of them to the northward always covered, the outer of which has 27 feet on it, and lies N.W. by N., nearly half a mile from the Grand Saut Roquier. There is a good channel inside all these rocks; the middle of which lies with the lower house on Lihou island, touching the outer corner of the Mouillière rock W. by S. ¼ S.: there is also a channel between the inner head of the Hoffets and the Boue Corneille, but neither should be attempted without a pilot.

PLAQUIERS ROCKS, with 8 feet water over them, lie half a mile westward of the Grand Saut Roquier, with Victoria tower just open south-west of Grand Roque tower. They will be cleared by opening Victoria tower one side or the other of Grand Roque tower.

ANCHORAGE, secure from easterly winds, will be found inside the Grand Saut Roquier.

COBO and **VAZON BAYS** have also good anchorage in easterly winds, but with westerly winds there is generally a rolling swell along this part of the coast on the flood tide ; and this, together with the numerous outlying rocks, render these bays dangerous for strangers to approach.

The principal dangers off these bays inside the Grunes de l'Ouest, described in pages 15, 16, are the Susanne, which dries 7 feet at low water, S.E. by E. a quarter of a mile from the Grunes ; the Grunette dries 3 feet, S. by E. ½ E., half a mile from the Grunes ; the Boue Auber dries 8 feet, E.S.E. nearly half a mile from the Sambule ; the Flabet dries one foot, about midway between the Grand Etacre and Sambule ; the Colombelle dries 2 feet, N.W, nearly half a mile outside the Conchée ; the Messellettes, awash at low water, lies N.N.E., half a mile from the Conchée ; the Boue Vazon dries 7 feet, and lies with St George tower (white) in line with south-west angle of Houmet fort, and the upper house on Lihou island, just open inside the Conchée ; the Fourquies, awash at low water, lies S.W. a quarter of a mile from the Boue Vazon ; the Petit Etat dries 20 feet, N.N.W., a quarter of a mile from Houmet fort ; and the Gros Etat, 34 feet high, lies an eighth of a mile within it, at the outer extremity of the rocks of Houmet fort.

The Mouillière, lying N. by E. five-eighths of a mile from Houmet fort, is 4 feet above high water springs. It is surrounded by rocks, many of which uncover at low water, extending rather more than a cable to the westward, but not more than three-quarters of a cable to the northward. The large lower house on Lihou island in line with the Conchée, W. by S. ½ S., will clear these rocks to the northward.

DIRECTIONS.—To approach Vazon bay from the north-eastward, bring Torteval church open westward of Houmet fort, and run in ; being careful to have Torteval church in line with Richmont fort, S.W. ¾ S., before passing the Grand Saut Roquier ; which mark will lead midway between the Grunettes and Mouillière, and nearly a cable's length eastward of the Boue Vazon ; within which anchor as convenient, in 6 to 8 fathoms, sand.

To run out of the bay between the Grunettes and Boue Auber, bring St. George turret in line with east side of Houmet fort. The large lower house on Lihou island in line with the Conchée, leads nearly a cable's length northward of the Boue Vazon ; and St. Matthew church on with south-west end of Houmet fort leads out between the Sambule and Colombelle.

PERELLE BAY affords good shelter to fishing boats at low water, but is only safe for such as can take the beach, in the event of a westerly gale setting in.

To clear the sunken rocks extending from the Grand Etacre towards Lihou island, when passing between it and Lihou, keep the Hanois lighthouse open a little eastward of the Trois Pères, or pass through about mid-channel.

ROCQUAINE BAY is fronted by numerous groups of rocks as well as isolated ones, many of which are always above water; a far greater number uncover with the falling tide, whilst those that are always hidden below low water are still more numerous.

The anchorage in this bay is well sheltered from northerly, easterly, and southerly winds; but westerly winds send in such a heavy sea, especially between half-flood and half-ebb, that a sailing vessel caught in the bay under such circumstances could not possibly get out. The holding ground, consisting generally of fine gravel and sand covered with grass and seaweed, is not good. It is only frequented by fishermen resident in the neighbourhood, or occasionally by vessels calculated to take the beach: nevertheless Staff Commander Richards is of opinion that, at the anchorage in the south-west part of the bay off Pezerie point, a vessel of not more than 12 or 13 feet draught, *well* moored, would ride securely all the year round, and under any circumstances of wind and weather.

The most remarkable rocks, bounding Rocquaine bay to the westward and southward, that never cover with the tide are, the Mauve, 40 feet high *above low water*; the Bisé, on which the Hanois lighthouse stands; Grand Hanois, 70 feet high; Petit Hanois; Hayes rock, 30 feet high; Percée, 32 feet high; Round rock, 51 feet high; Grosse rock, 69 feet high; and Tas de Pois d'Aval, 69 feet high.

Banc des Trois Pères.—The largest and most conspicuous rocky group in the northern part of Rocquaine bay is called the Banc des Trois Pères, the outer rock of which, named the Pendante, is 48 feet above low water, and lies West one mile from Lihou upper house. The Trois Pères rocks are about the same height, on the same line of bearing, but nearly a cable's length within the Pendante. There are also other rocks nearly the same height, fronting this reef to the eastward.

There is a passage between the Trois Pères bank and Lihou island, with a depth through of not less than 15 feet at low water, the marks for which are given at page 24; but neither this nor any other passage into Rocquaine bay should be attempted without a pilot, unless under most urgent circumstances.

Banc des Hanois lies three quarter of a mile westward of the Pendante rock. It extends N.N.W. and S.S.E. about half a mile, and the highest rock, called the Haut Fourquie, is on its inner part, and dries 10 feet at low water; there are also two rocks which dry 5 feet near its outer extremity. The outer sunken rock of the bank has 6 feet on it at low water ; the marks for it are, Tas de Pois d'Aval on with the inner part of the Percée rock S.S.E. ; and the Guet du Câtel just to the southward of the lower house on Lihou island, and on the same side of the rock next within the Grand Battue, E. $\frac{1}{8}$ S. Guet du Câtel in line with Lihou upper house, E. $\frac{1}{2}$ S., leads $1\frac{1}{4}$ cables northward of the bank.

Banc Bisé, the westernmost danger off Guernsey, lies rather more than a third of a mile outside the Mauve, which rock is 10 feet above high water springs. This bank is connected with the Mauve by a chain of sunken rocks, as the Mauve is with the Bisé, the rock on which the Hanois lighthouse is built. The outer sunken rock of the bank is three-quarters of a mile N.N.W. from the lighthouse, and has 15 feet on it at low water ; it lies with the lighthouse just open westward of the head of the Mauve S.S.E. ; and Lihou upper house over the middle of the Trois Pères E. $\frac{1}{2}$ N.

DIRECTIONS.—To enter Rocquaine bay from the southward, inside the Hayes rock, bring the outer high water rock (called Corner rock) off Lihou island in line with Nipple rock (which dries 26 feet at low water), bearing N.E. by N. and run in until abreast the Percée rock ; within which, Black rock will soon come in line with a remarkable rock on Lihou saddle ; this mark will lead into a good anchorage a little beyond the Nipple rock in 4 fathoms at low water.

Should it be desired to go into the anchorage off the Torquetil rock in $2\frac{1}{2}$ fathoms at low water ; Cacquerau house on with the north side of the Torquetil E. $\frac{1}{4}$ N. will be the leading mark, until Fort Grey comes in line with the Braye rock ; when Cacquerau house must be opened a little northward of the Torquetil, to clear a rock with only 4 feet on it at low water ; after passing which, anchor as convenient. Marks are given on the Admiralty chart for entering the inner anchorage off Pezerie point, but being useless to strangers on account of the narrowness of the channel, they are not repeated here.

The passage into Rocquaine bay, between Lihou island and the Trois Pères bank, may be entered by bringing Torteval church in line with the north-east corner of Fort Grey S. by E. $\frac{1}{2}$ E. ; this mark will lead safely as far as the Fourquie, (a rock which dries 17 feet at low water, and which must be passed rather close to the westward,) within which, as directions to the stranger would be useless, we must refer him to the chart.

By bringing Torteval church in line with the south-west side of Round rock S.E. $\frac{1}{4}$ E., a vessel could pass safely between the Banc des Hanois and the Aiguillons ; and by opening Torteval church a little to the south-west of Round rock, after passing the Aiguillons, she could enter Rocquaine bay to the south-west of the Round rock.

There is no channel for ships into Rocquaine bay between the Trois Pères and the Banc des Hanois.

ICART BAY and PETIT PORT BAY, on the south side of Guernsey, afford good anchorage and shelter in easterly and northerly winds. Petit port being larger and easier of access, is by far the best bay of the two : the ground is clean, fine white sand, and any depth of water may be chosen from 5 to 9 fathoms, but a sailing vessel at anchor here should be in readiness to put to sea immediately a shift of wind renders it necessary.

The only danger in entering Petit Port bay is the Banc du Petit Port, with 12 feet on it at low water. It lies W. $\frac{1}{2}$ S. a quarter of a mile from Jerbourg point, and to clear it in entering, do not shut in the Goubinière rock with St. Martin point until Doyle column opens westward of a remarkably high rocky bluff on the east side of the sandy bay under it. The column on with peak of rocky bluff, N.E. by E. $\frac{3}{4}$ E. is the leading mark in.

HERM and JETHOU ISLANDS, together with Amfroque rocks on the north, and Ferrière rocks on the south, extend rather more than 5 miles in a N.E. $\frac{1}{2}$ N. and S.W. $\frac{1}{2}$ S. direction, and divide the Great and Little Russel channels from each other. Herm is $1\frac{1}{4}$ miles long, half a mile wide, elevated 232 feet above the level of low water, and its centre bears E. by S. $\frac{1}{4}$ S. $3\frac{1}{4}$ miles from St. Peter Port. The little island of Jethou lies S.W. half-a-mile from Herm, and is 16 feet higher than it. The rocky islets, Crevichon and Fauconnière, are connected with Jethou at low water, the former to its north side and the latter to its south ; they are each marked on their conical summits by white stone *beacons.*

The Ferrières are most conspicuous rocks to the southward of Jethou, that never cover with the tide. The north head of the outer or western rock, called the Barbes, lies S.W. nearly three-quarters of a mile from Jethou, and is marked by a *beacon*, consisting of a staff and barrel. There are good ship channels between these rocks, and especially between the Ferrières rocks and the Têtes d'Aval, but they should not be attempted without a pilot.

Amfroque rocks extend from Herm to the north-eastward for rather more than 2 miles. The outermost rock, called the Grande Amfroque, has two peaks, is nearly three-quarters of a cable in diameter and 78 feet above low water; it is surrounded by dangerous rocks, of which the easternmost is the Bonne Grune, with 14 feet over it at low water, bearing from the Grande Amfroque E. $\frac{3}{4}$ S. $1\frac{1}{4}$ miles. The Selle d'Amfroque, bearing N.W. by W. $\frac{1}{4}$ W., half a mile from the Bonne Grune, has 17 feet over it; and within it to the westward lie the Demies du Nord, and the Petite Amfroque, which uncover with the tide.

At rather more than half a mile West from the Grande Amfroque, lies a table rock elevated 56 feet, called Cul de l'Autel; and between the Cul de l'Autel and the north point of Herm, at nearly equal distances, and about the same height (70 feet), lie the Longue Pierre and Traiffe rocks, also Godin islet; which, as well as the Longue Pierre, is covered with a light soil, on which grow a variety of wild flowers; the Traiffe lies near the south-east side of the Longue Pierre and resembles a ship under sail. Besides these are others of minor importance that the tide never covers, as well as numerous rocks and ledges that are alternately covered and uncovered, and many which never appear at all.

Plat Boue rock, lying three-quarters of a mile northward of the Grande Amfroque, is the northernmost danger off Herm, at the eastern side of the entrance to the Little Russel. It is about 20 feet in diameter, dries 3 feet at low water, and is steep-to all round except to the E.N.E., in which direction, at the distance of 500 feet, there is a rock with 15 feet over it at low water.

The marks for the Plat Boue are Câtel church spire in line with the Canteen house at the gate at Vale castle (showing on its south-east angle), bearing W. by S., and the Grande Moie, the highest detached rock on the east side of Serk, just open eastward of the Grande Amfroque S. $\frac{3}{4}$ E. A *chequered black* and *white* buoy, has lately been placed in 6 fathoms, N. $\frac{1}{2}$ E. 66 feet from the Plat Boue, but it is washed away so frequently that no dependence can be placed on seeing it at any time.

HAYES CHANNEL and PASSE de la PERCÉE.—The channels between the above rocks and islets are extremely intricate, and rendered even more dangerous by the rapidity and variety of the tides; two of them (Hayes channel, between Godin islet and the Longue Pierre rocks, and Passe de la Percée, between Herm and Jethou,) are nevertheless sometimes used for ships by the Guernsey pilots.

Hayes channel has a rock, awash at low water, at its eastern entrance on the line of the Longue Pierre and Godin. To sail southward of it, keep Vale mill in sight to the southward of the Pierre de la Moue until past that line. Pass a cable northward of the Pierre de la Moue, and then gradually haul to the southward until the high land of Serk at Banquette point comes over Godin. When the Grande Amfroque is in one with the Longue Pierre, keep it so, until the peak of Godin is nearly in line with the north extreme of Galeu, S.E.; which mark will lead into the

Little Russel, between the Tautenay ledge and the rocky bank extending from the north point of Herm.

ANCHORAGE, out of the strength of the tide, and with good holding ground, will be found South of Tautenay ledge, by bringing the peak of Godin between the two sharp-peaked rocks of Galeu, S.E. ⅓ E., and Brehon tower in line with the Rousse rock S.W. by W. ½ W.

There is good anchorage also S.W. of this, inside the Cavale rock, in 6 fathoms, sand; with the Pierre aux Rats (a small stone obelisk on Herm) in line with the Mouisonnière rock, bearing S.E. ¼ S., and Brehon tower between the Rousse rock and the Blanche.

Between Herm and Jethou, off the Mouette rock, is the *Rosiere* anchorage, where small vessels will find good shelter from all winds, excepting those from S.W., round by the south, to S.E. The best entrance into it is from the Great Russel channel.

There is one great convenience attending this latter anchorage, viz., that the tide runs 9 hours to the southward and only 3 to the northward; the former stream commencing when it is low water by the shore, and setting directly into the Great Russel during the whole of the flood, until half ebb, when the latter stream begins and runs faintly to the northward until low water. A vessel therefore, caught here by a southerly wind may always, at half ebb, run northward through the Passe de la Percée into the Little Russel channel, and thence to the anchorage inside the Cavale rock or into the Great road.

DIRECTIONS.—The dangers to be avoided in running for the Passe de la Percée from the eastward are, the Fourquies; a patch of rocks that uncover near low water, lying right in the fairway and north-eastward of the Goubinière rock, in the Great Russel; and farther in, the Mulet rock on the starboard, and the Tinker rocks on the port hand. Vale castle touching the south-west end of Herm, bearing N.W. ⅔ N., will lead eastward of the Fourquies; and Vale mill (the north-eastern mill on Guernsey,) touching the north-eastern side of Jethou, N.N.W. ¼ W., will lead considerably to the westward.

Mulet Rock lies about half a cable from the south point of Herm, and the Tinker about twice that distance to the eastward of Jethou. The west side of the Houmet rock in line with the highest part of the Mouette rock leads westward of the Mulet; and the west side of the little green plat on the Hermetier half a point open eastward of the highest part of the Mouette, leads eastward of the Tinker.

To run through the Passe de la Percée into the Little Russel, after clearing the Fourquies, bring Vale mill a little open westward of the Percée rock, and also a little open on the same side of the Corbette rock, (now marked by a beacon) N.N.W. ¾ W.; this latter mark will clear the outer point of the Percée rock, when it is covered, at half tide, at the distance of 60 yards, and lead through the middle of the channel, the narrowest part of which, and least depth (14 feet), will be found on a line between the north extreme of the rocky bank extending from Jethou and the Vermerette rock, which is marked by a staff and white beacon. When Delancy mill (ruin) comes open northward of Brehon tower (about the apparent breadth of the tower), take it as a leading mark to clear the Etacre rock : when abreast the Etacre, on this line, the Victoria tower will be seen in one with the Creux rock beacon (staff and truck), with which mark proceed up to the Creux rock, and round it to the southward at the distance of half a cable to get into the Little Russel.

LITTLE RUSSEL CHANNEL lies on the north-west side of Herm between it and Guernsey, and is much contracted by numerous rocks projecting off from both islands as far out as the *Roustel* and *Rousse* rocks, which are a little more than 3 cables apart. The wind northward of N.N.W., or eastward of S.E., will always prove a leading wind through this channel from the northward, without the *certainty* of which no square rigged vessel of large draught should attempt its navigation.

The entrance to the Little Russel from the northward is between the Braye rocks on the western side, and the Amfroque rocks on the eastern. The approach to both these groups is exceedingly dangerous, as well on account of the tides as from the numerous hidden and other rocks by which they are encompassed; the principal of which, and the most dangerous, are the Plat Boue and the Boufresse, in the neighbourhood of the Amfroque, and the Roques de Braye or Platte Fougére in the vicinity of the Braye.

Braye rocks.—The Grande and Petite Braye rocks lie about a mile off the north-east point of Guernsey ; they are within a quarter of a mile of each other, and both are encompassed with outlying dangerous rocks. The Grand Braye is elevated 10 feet above high water springs, and the Petit Braye is 2 or 3 feet lower.

The Roques de Braye or Platte Fougére, appear about half tide ; the ground is clean at the distance of a cable eastward of them. An iron frame beacon stands on the outermost or north-eastern rock of the group surmounted by a red cone 12 feet above the highest tides ; to guide vessels into the Little Russel.

Nearly midway between the Roques de Braye and Corbette rock (the latter is marked by *staff* and *red* ball) lie the Canupé rocks ; the outer of which appearing only after the last quarter ebb, is now the principal danger (not marked) on this side the Little Russel.

To clear the Braye rocks and all dangers eastward and southward of them, keep the south-western end of Little Serk a little open eastward of the low north-eastern sandy point of Herm, bearing S. by E. ; this mark will lead into the fairway of the Little Russel.

Platte Roque, lying S.W. by S. half a mile from the Corbette, is marked by a *beacon* mast painted with *black* and *white* bands. About a cable's length E.S.E. from the beacon, is a rock awash at low water ; and from this rock towards the Corbette, on a line convex towards the Russel, there are several dangerous rocks which strangers should carefully avoid when passing.

Boue Agenor, with only 4 feet on it at low water, is the south-western and innermost danger on this side the Little Russel, of which it is necessary to caution strangers. It lies with the Coal hole, under Vale castle, in line with the end of Sampson breakwater N. by E. $\frac{3}{4}$ E. ; and Hogue à la Pierre tower just open north-east of Ivy castle (a ruin) N.W. $\frac{1}{2}$ W. There are two rocks, one of 9 feet water, lying nearly a cable S.W. by W. $\frac{1}{2}$ W. of the Agenor ; another of 12 feet at nearly the same distance S.W. by S. ; and a third (the Trois Grunes), of 13 feet water, lying two cables to the N.E. by E. $\frac{1}{2}$ E. of it.

Rousse rock.—The following rocks are on the east side of the Little Russel :—The Plat Boue (described in page 26) ; the Boufresse dries 8 feet at low water ; the Tautenay is just awash at high water ; and the Cavale dries one foot at low water. The Rousse rock is 8 feet above high water springs, and is marked with an iron *beacon*, consisting of a cross with an anchor fluke at each point. A dangerous string of rocks, awash at low water, project in a W. by N. direction 60 yards from the Rousse.

To pass northward and westward of all these rocks, keep Câtel church spire a quarter of a point open westward of Vale castle, W. by S. ; and when the north-eastern end of Serk comes on with the middle of the Grande Amfroque, a vessel will be abreast the Plat Boue. The above mark (Câtel church open westward of Vale castle) will also lead into the fairway of the Little Russel.

Doyle column in line with Brehon tower is a good clearing mark for the rocks on the east side of the Little Russel, as far as the Cavale, to clear which, the column must be opened one side or the other of Brehon tower. The breast mark for the Cavale is the Pierre aux Rats obelisk in line with the Mouisonnière rock, S.E. $\frac{1}{4}$ S. Doyle column in line with Brehon tower will also clear the rocks extending from the Rousse and lead inside the Boues Genitales.

The Roustel is the most dangerous rock in the Little Russel, as it lies exactly in mid-channel, and does not appear until 4 hours ebb. The beacon on the Rousse bears from it S.S.E. ½ E., 3¼ cables; a sunken rock, connected with the Roustel, E.N.E., half a cable; the beacon on the Corbette rock, N. by W. ½ W. rather more than half a mile; the beacon on the Platte Roque, W. ½ N., half a mile; and the Grune au Rouge rock, S.W. by W. ⅓ W., nearly a mile.

A *black* buoy is moored about 20 yards S.W. of the Roustel; and a *red* buoy, 50 yards N.N.E. from the Grune au Rouge, which latter has only 3 feet on it at low water.

DIRECTIONS.—The best leading mark to the entrance and through the fairway of the Little Russel channel, when approaching it from the northward, is, St. Martin point just open westward of the battery on Brehon rock, bearing S.W. ½ W.; there is no other mark whatever so conspicuous, or which shows the alteration of the vessel's position so quickly. This mark will lead in through the fairway, and between the Roustel and Rousse rocks; and when either the high land at the north-east end of Serk begins to shut in with the northernmost bluff land of Herm, or when Delancy mill (ruin) appears within its breadth of Mont Crevelt tower, W. ¾ N., a vessel will be abreast the former rock as well as the latter. Near this position, Belvedere house (a large building on the bluff to the eastward of Fort George), will be seen in line with a white patch just within the east extreme of castle Cornet; which mark will lead more than half a cable eastward of the Grune au Rouge, about a cable eastward of the Agenor, and all other dangers, and up to the anchorage in the road. This latter mark will lead right up through the Little Russel, clear all the dangers in it, and, being the only line that is possible to answer this desirable purpose, is given here; but as it necessarily passes rather near some of the rocks, (the Grune au Rouge, for instance,) care must be taken at these parts to keep off a little one side or the other as necessary.

If intending to pass north-westward of the Roustel and Grune au Rouge, bring the near angle of castle Cornet, (marked with a vertical white stripe,) in line with Fort George signal post, and it will lead three-quarters of a cable westward of the Roustel, and a cable westward of the Grune au Rouge. When Brehon and Herm towers come in line, open the leading marks a little either way, as desirable, to clear the Trois Grunes and the Agenor, and proceed on until the town church opens southward of the old harbour lighthouse, then haul in for the anchorage.

If a vessel be compelled to beat through the Little Russel, it may be useful to note, that St. Martin point kept open eastward of the Brehonnet rock will clear the Roustel; and that St. Martin point open one side or the other of the Brehon rock will clear the Boues Genitales.

If intending to run through Doyle pass into the Little Russel, keep the windmill on the island of Great Serk, just open northward of the northernmost high land of Herm, and in one also with the Mouisonnière (a remarkable pointed rock on the sandy beach) bearing S.S.E. ½ E.; which mark will lead through the pass, between the Roque au Nord and the Grande Braye, inside the Grune Pierre, and between the Grune la Fosse and the Vraic, into the fairway of the Little Russel; but the greatest caution must be used, when near low water, to preserve the leading mark. The narrowest part of the channel is between the Grune Pierre and the rocks off Homptol; its width here being only 650 feet. The Pierre aux Rats obelisk on the north end of Herm, will appear a little to the left of the Mouisonnière.

GREAT RUSSEL CHANNEL lies between the islands of Herm and Jethou, and the clusters of rock, called the Amfroques, the Longue Pierre, the Godin, &c., to the north-west, and the islands of Serk and Brecqhou and the rocks in their vicinity to the south-east. This channel, which is the eastern passage to Guernsey, is above two miles wide, and easy of access, even to strangers. The following are the principal dangers in it :—

Bonne Grune Rock, with only 14 feet water on it, is the outer danger at the northern entrance of the Great Russel. It lies E. by N. ¼ N. 3 miles from the north end of Herm, and E. ½ S. rather more than a mile from the Grande Amfroque; and is cleared to the eastward by opening the west extreme of Little Serk of the east extreme of Brecqhou.

Noir Pute Rock, lying on the western side of the Great Russel, about a mile south-eastward from the mill on Herm, is never wholly covered, though at equinoctial tides it is sometimes nearly awash. A string of rocks awash at low water, extend from it to the north-eastward for nearly 1½ cables. From the Noire Pute, the Doyle column appears a quarter of a point open southward of the Fauconnière.

Fourquies Rocks, which dry 7 feet at low water, lie about three-quarters of a mile eastward of Jethou island, and from their centre St. Martin point is in one with the Goubinière rock, W. ½ S., and Vale castle in line with the sandy beach on the north-eastern side of Crevichon island, N.N.W. ¾ W.

Grands Bouillons rocks, having only 9 feet over them at low water, lie between the Noir Pute and the Fourquies. The Thwart mark for them is, the Caquorobert (a large rock in the form of a hay-stack, projecting from the eastern side of Herm,) in line with the north-eastern low sandy point of that island bearing North.

Goubiniere rock, elevated 10 feet above high-water springs, lies south, half a mile from Jethou.

Banc des Anons, with 18 feet over them at low water, lie about

S.W. by W., a third of a mile from the Goubinière; with Mont Crevelt tower in line with the eastern side of the Grosse Ferrière, bearing N.N.W.

Têtes d'Aval rocks lie about S.W., nearly 1½ miles from Jethou island, and dry at low water, great springs. The marks for them are, Herm mill, (without vanes) in one with a remarkable red-headed rock on the beach between the Grande Fauconnière and Jethou, called the Petite Fauconnière, bearing N.E. ½ E.; Vale mill, its apparent breadth open westward of Vale castle, North; and the lighthouse on south pier head of St. Peter Port old harbour, shut in with castle Cornet, N.W. ½ N.

A conical buoy, with black and white *horizontal* stripes, lies about 60 fathoms south-west of the middle head of the Têtes d'Aval.—Vessels should pass westward of the buoy.

Sardrière rock, with 8 feet water on it, lies south-eastward of the Tetes d'Aval; with St. Martin church spire on with the north side of Fermain beacon, N.W. by W. ½ W., and the Selle Roque twice its apparent breadth open westward of the Goubinière, N.E. ¾ E.

Givaude rock, about 70 feet high, forms the eastern boundary of the Great Russel channel. It lies off the west end of Brecqhou, and a reef extends from its north-west point to the distance of nearly half a cable. The Vesté, a pointed rock that dries 20 feet at low water, lies N.E. by N. one cable from the Givaude, on the outer edge of a reef extending from Brecqhou.

The Grune is a sunken rock, over which, however, there are never less than 36 feet water, lying about 1¼ miles westward of Brecqhou. The marks for it are, the Grande Amfroque in one with the Noire Pute N.N.E. ⅔ E., and Victoria tower half the breadth of castle Cornet open northward of it N.W. ¼ W.

DIRECTIONS.—The course to the northern entrance of the Great Russel channel, from the middle of Alderney Race, is about W.S.W., and the distance 21 miles. In proceeding, however, towards this channel from the north-eastward, great care must be taken to avoid the Banc de la Schôle (described at page 74), lying nearly in the direct line between Alderney Race and the entrance.

Having entered the channel, with the western extreme of Little Serk open eastward of the eastern extreme of Brecqhou, in order to avoid the Bonne Grune (the north-eastern danger on the western side of the channel), bring St. Martin point a quarter of a point open southward of the Goubinière rock, bearing W. ½ S.; this will lead southward of the Noire Pute, the Grands Bouillons, and the Fourquies. Continue to run with this mark on until the Grande Amfroque appears within its own apparent breadth of the Selle Roque (a rock near the south-east point of

Herm) bearing N.E. This latter mark must now be preserved until the lighthouse on the south pier head of St. Peter Port old harbour comes open southward of castle Cornet, or until St. Martin church steeple (seen over the trees) appears over the middle of Fermain sandy beach ; either of these two marks will lead southward of the Sardrière and the Têtes d'Aval ; after having rounded which, steer boldly for the Great road.

There is a good channel between the Têtes d'Aval and the Ferrière rocks, the middle of which lies with Victoria tower half-way between castle Cornet flag staff and the north angle of the castle wall bearing N.W. This channel, however, should not be attempted by a stranger unless in cases of emergency, the difficulty of the tides rendering its navigation hazardous.

When turning through the Great Russel, in standing to the south-eastward, the island of Serk may be approached to about half a mile without fear ; as between the Bec du Nez and Brecqhou island there are no rocks farther than a quarter of a mile from the shore ; but take care when standing towards the west point of Brecqhou, and to the south-ward of it, to keep the Grande Amfroque its own apparent length open westward of the Givaude rock, N. by E. $\frac{1}{2}$ E., to clear the Dents and Hautes Boues.

When standing northward towards Herm and Jethou, do not shut in St. Martin point with the Goubinière when to the eastward of the latter rock, but keep it a quarter of a point open southward of it, to avoid the Fourquies and the Bouillons ; and when to the southward of the Goubinière, keep the Grande Amfroque open eastward of the Selle Roque until the lighthouse on the south pier head of St. Peter Port old harbour appears a quarter of a point open southward of castle Cornet, or until St. Martin spire appears over the middle of Fermain sandy beach ; either of these two marks, as before stated, will lead southward of the Sardrière and the Têtes d'Aval.

The north-eastern stream of tide slacks half an hour sooner on the south-eastern side of the Great Russel, that is under Serk, than on its north-western side.

SERK lies $3\frac{1}{4}$ miles S.E. by S. from Herm, and divides the Great Russel. from the Deroute channel. The island is $1\frac{1}{2}$ miles broad, and nearly $2\frac{3}{4}$ miles long, including Little Serk, with which it communicates by an isthmus or very narrow causeway, called La Coupée. It is lofty and precipitous in all its extent, and its highest part, at the base of the windmill near the centre of the island, is 375 feet above the level of low water. The small island of Brecqhou lies on its western side, being separated from it by a narrow channel only 70 yards wide, named by the islanders Gouliôt pass, through which the tides run with great velocity.

There is no town in Serk; there is however a hamlet or group of cottages, called La Ville, on the north-east side of the island. The island constitutes one Royal Fief or Manor, held direct from the Crown, of which the Rev. W. T. Collings, M.A., is the present Lord or Seigneur. There are forty original copyhold farms, averaging 15 acres each, the title to which descends in succession to the eldest sons or (if no sons) to the eldest daughters of their occupants ; the junior members of the different families are therefore frequently compelled to emigrate.

The island is fertile, highly cultivated, and besides supplying all the wants of its inhabitants it exports largely in cereals and vegetables to Guernsey. Its rocky coasts abound with fish, particularly with crabs and lobsters. All able-bodied men belonging to the island are organized as militia, of which there are 140 of all arms. In 1861 the population was registered at 586. There is a church where the Anglican service is regularly conducted in French. There are also two endowed schools.

The approach to Serk on the north-eastern, eastern, south-eastern, and south-western sides, is difficult by reason of the numerous rocks which encompass it, as well as by the rapidity and irregularities of the tide in its immediate vicinity. These difficulties, however, may be easily over-come, if common attention be paid to the leading marks and run of the stream ; and the island will afford good security against almost all winds, as will be shown in the description of the different bays.

There are several small inlets in various parts of the rocky coasts of the island, where the inhabitants haul up and secure their boats in stormy weather; the most noted and frequented of which is Le Creux, so called from a subterraneous passage in its neighbourhood. It lies on the eastern side of the island, and is the general rendezvous for landing and shipping, when the weather will permit, as well as the principal resort of the fishing and other island boats. The small harbour here situated has lately been enlarged, and now affords perfect security to small craft ; its entrance is, however, only 60 feet wide, and dries at low water of spring tides.

Water.—There is a tolerable run of water on the north side of Baleine bay, to the westward of Château point, on the south-west side of Serk : the stream from it during the winter season is very copious, and may be procured with off-shore winds without difficulty. It is the only acces-sible watering place round the island, with the exception of an inconsiderable drain in Port du Moulin, on its north-west side, and another of similar character at the Creux harbour.

ISLETS and ROCKS around SERK.—The following islets and rocks above *high water*, lie off the coasts of Serk.

The Noire Pierre, lying off Banquette point, on the north-east coast, is a small square rock, 11 feet high and steep-to all round.

The Petite Moie, 57 feet high, is a rocky clump steep-to except at its north point, off which, at the distance of 60 feet, there is a sunken rock.

The Grande Moie, lying off Robert point, is a large rocky clump, 91 feet high, dangerous to approach, especially on its eastern side.

The Burons, are a cluster of cragged rocks 66 feet high, in the form of half a moon, rising nearly perpendicular from the sea, steep-to on their south-eastern side, but dangerous to approach from any other quarter. They lie about E.S.E., a quarter of a mile from Le Creux; and between them and Serk is the Goulet pass, which dries half-way across at low water springs; the deepest water, 4 feet, being towards Le Creux. Through this pass the tides run with great strength, both ways, but especially about half flood; setting right for and over the Fournier and Grune de Nord rocks, on the north side, and the Pierre Carrée rock on the south side; this pass therefore should not be attempted in a sailing vessel, but on the greatest emergency.

The Conchée, lying about half a mile southward of the Burons, is a square rock, 11 feet high, whitened at the top, having sunken rocks close to all around.

The Baleine rock, in Baleine bay, is 20 feet high, and has a rocky reef extending 70 feet from its north-east side.

Pierre du Cours is a small rock awash at high water, and very steep-to on its south-east side. It is useful as a guide, (as its name implies,) to vessels passing inside L'Etac de Serk.

L'Etac de Serk is a rocky islet about 200 feet high, lying off the south end of Little Serk. In form it resembles a hay-stack, and is very conspicuous, both from its appearance and position.

On the south-west side of Little Serk are numerous rocks, the most conspicuous of which are the Moie du Port Goury, a square topped rock, 62 feet high; the Moie de la Bretagne, a peaked rock, 57 feet high; and the Moie de la Fontaine, 57 feet high.

The Givaude rock, about 42 feet high, and lying off the west end of Brecqhou, has a reef extending nearly half a cable from its north-west point.

The Moie de Batardes, a square rock of a whitish colour, about 20 feet high, lies off the north-west coast of Brecqhou.

BLANCHARD ROCK, lying nearly 1¾ miles eastward of Serk, has only 3 feet over it at the lowest equinoctial spring tides. The marks for it are, the Conchée rock in one with a remarkable cavity, or chasm, called the Convache, to the northward of La Coupée, bearing W. by N. ⅓ N., and the Corbée du Nez just open southward of the Gorge, (a rock at the south-west end of the Petit Moie,) N.W. ¾ N.

Chateau point open southward of the Conchée, N.W. by W. ½ W. leads southward of the Blanchard; the Corbière rock, off the south-west point of Jersey, touching the land about Cape Grosnez, S. by W. ½ W., leads half a mile eastward; and the northern bluff land on Herm in sight to the north-eastward of the Bec du Nez, N.W. ¼ N., leads to the northward.

Many rocks lie within the Blanchard and to the eastward of the Burons, and between them are several navigable channels, of 10 to 26 fathoms water; they are, however, seldom frequented but by the island boats on account of the impetuous whirl of the tides.

BALEINE BAY, on the south-eastern side of Serk, between the Baleine and the Conchée rocks, may be resorted to with great advantage in winter as well as in summer, as it affords excellent anchorage in from 3 to 7 fathoms, over sand, fine gravel and broken shells, and shelter from all winds from N.N.E., round by the North, to West.

Notwithstanding the numerous overfalls and various discolourations of the water, which appear on all sides on approaching this bay, the only **dangers** are, the Têtes de la Conchée, the Gripe, the Vingt Clos, the Balmée, and the Demie Balmée.

The Têtes de la Conchée have never less than 6 fathoms water over them.

The Gripe, lying directly in the fairway of the entrance to the bay, has only 6 feet on it at low water springs, from which the Conchée is in line with the Goulet rock, N.E. by N., and the Balmée is in line with the Pignon, W. ¼ N.

The Balmée, which appears at a quarter ebb, lies within and to the westward of the Gripe, with the Baleine in line with La Coupée, N. ½ W., and the western side of the Burons touching the outer or north-eastern part of Terrible point, N.E. by E. On this latter line of bearing at the distance of three-quarters of a cable from the Balmée, there is also a small rock called Demie de Balmée, which dries 9 feet at low water.

Vingt Clos bank, lies 4 cables southward of the Balmée, between it and L'Etac de Serk, and consists of sand and shingle interspersed with rocks: one of these, at the north end of the bank, dries 3 feet at low water springs, at which time two others to the southward have only 3 feet water over them. The south end of La Coupée in line with the Baleine, N. by W. ¼ W., leads nearly 2 cables north-eastward of the bank; and the Doyle column, on Guernsey, in sight to the southward of L'Etac de Serk, N.W. by W., leads southward. The sand and shingle of this bank is continually shifting; its inclination being entirely governed by the tide and wind.

DIRECTIONS.—Château point kept open southward of the Conchée will lead into the anchorage of Baleine bay, to the northward of the Gripe; and Serk mill just open West of Château point N. ¼ W., will lead in to the southward of it: in both cases anchor when the west extreme of the Burons comes on with Terrible point.

LA GREVE de la VILLE, on the north-eastern side of Serk, gives its name to an anchorage affording good shelter for small vessels from westerly and southerly winds, in from 6 to 9 fathoms water; but the ground being sand and rock the anchor is likely to come home, unless riding with a long scope of cable. It has also this inconvenience attending it, that should the wind suddenly shift to the northward or north-eastward at low water, (the tide running for 3 hours to the southward after that period,) a sailing vessel could not possibly weather the strong indraught of the Goulet pass (the effects of which are sensibly felt half a mile north-eastward of it), and must therefore ride until the offing tide slacks, or at least, if hard pressed, until there is water enough over the neck of the Goulet.

Dangers off La Grève de la Ville:—The Sardrière rock, with 29 feet over it at low water, lies East a quarter of a mile from Bec du Nez. The Jolicot rock, which dries 5 feet at low water, lies S.W. three-quarters of a cable from the Sardrière; and the Moulinet rock, which dries 8 feet, lies just eastward of Bec du Nez, and only 150 feet off shore. The Jolicot and the Moulinet lie East and West of each other, rather more than an eighth of a mile apart; there is a safe channel of 6 fathoms water between them, in entering which from the westward be careful to have the peak of the Grande Moie well in sight eastward of Banquette point before hauling in. The peak of the Grande Moie in line with Banquette point clears the Moulinet; and the same peak over the middle of the Pêcheresse rock leads *over* the Jolicot.

The Pêcheresse, lying about East, nearly a quarter of a mile from the rifle target, on the summit of La Grune, covers at high water, but only to the depth of 2 feet; its inshore point is long and straggling, narrowing the channel between it and the island to a cable's length.

There is a rock with 7 feet on it lying E. ½ N. nearly a cable's length from the Pêcheresse; and another, which dries 3 feet, called the Grande Boue, lying E. by S. ½ S. rather more than a cable from it.

The Pavlaison rock, just awash at low water, lies N.E. ¼ E. nearly a quarter of a mile from the Noire Pierre.

DIRECTIONS.—There are two entrances into La Grève de la Ville; one from the northward, between the island and the Noire Pierre, and one from the southward (which is very narrow) between the island and the Grande Moie. The marks to lead in from the northward are, the Noire Pierre in one with a remarkable hollowed rock on the shore, the upper part of which has been whitewashed, called La Chapelle, bearing S.S.W. ½ W., or La Chapelle half a point open eastward of Banquette point, S. ½ W.; between these limits a vessel may also work in. The Noire Pierre is steep-to on all sides but the south.

No particular marks can be given to lead into this anchorage from the southward, that is, between the Grande Moie and the island. There is never less than 3 fathoms in this channel, but as a rock, awash at low water, lies within the Grande Moie, and connected with it under water at a distance of 150 feet, care must be taken to pass through nearer to Robert point, which is steep-to, rather than in mid-channel. There is also at the distance of a cable northward of Robert point, a dangerous rocky reef extending half a cable from the shore; and a half tide rock at half a cable S.W. from the Petite Moie.

The mark for anchoring is, the east extreme of the Burons just open of Robert point, and midway between the Petite Moie and the island, S. by E. ¼ E.: outside, or eastward of this mark, the stream runs strong; within or to the westward it is scarcely perceptible.

ANCHORAGE.—There is good anchorage on the north-eastern side of Serk, outside all the rocks, in 14 to 19 fathoms water, fine clean sand, with St. Martin point, Guernsey, in line with the Corbée du Nez, bearing W. by N., and the Chapelle rock midway between the Noire rock and Banquette point, S. by W. ½ W. This anchorage, however, unless in fine weather, is only tenable with the wind between West and S.S.W.

BANQUETTE BAY, on the north-western side of Serk, affords good shelter against easterly, south-easterly, and southerly winds, in 5 to 10 fathoms water, over coarse sand interspersed with small black stones and pieces of sea-weed. Should the wind chop round to the westward, a vessel at anchor here, would even then be able to weather the Bec du Nez; and may from thence push to sea, or haul under the lee of the island.

Dangers in this bay are, the Epissures rock, with 13 feet on it at low water springs, lying N.W. a quarter of a mile from the Autelêts rocks. Between the Epissures and Port du Moulin there are several dangerous rocks.

The Guillaumez rock, which covers 6 feet at high water, lies E. by N., rather more than a quarter of a mile from the Epissures, and about half a cable off shore.

The Grune de Gouliot, with 6 feet over it at low water, lies North a quarter of a mile from the east end of Brecqhou.

The Petite Banquette is a narrow bank of fine sand with a sharp ridgy apex. It is about a quarter of a mile in extent, north and south, and has 16 feet on the shoalest part near the middle, from which the Platte Roque, off Port du Moulin, bears E. ½ S. distant 2 cables. In heavy gales from the north-eastward or westward, this bank has been reported to shift a cable's length or more in one tide, which here runs to the south-eastward from low water till half flood, and to the south-westward from half-ebb till low water.

ANCHORAGE.—The best deep water berth in Banquette bay is in 9 fathoms, with Givaude rock in line with Moie de Batardes, S.W. by W. ¾ W. ; Little Serk mill (without vanes) in line with west side of Gouliot island, S. by W. ; and Manor tower and north cliff of Port du Moulin in line, S.E. ¾ E.

LA GRANDE GREVE is the name applied to the anchorage on the south-western side of Serk, between Brecqhou and Little Serk. It takes its name from the great beach of fine white sand under La Coupée, uniting Great with Little Serk. The approach to it is much encumbered with rocks, but there is plenty of room notwithstanding, and good shelter from S.S.E., East, and N.E. winds, in 7 to 11 fathoms water, fine sandy bottom with pieces of shells : it would not, however, be prudent for a sailing vessel to remain at anchor here should the wind shift either to the northward or southward of the points above specified; for the W.S.W. wind, from the long fetch it commands, brings in a heavy swell ; and the obstruction caused by the weather tide coming through the Gouliot pass, raises it to such a height, as to preclude the possibility of a vessel riding out even a moderate gale.

Should a vessel, therefore, be unavoidably caught by a westerly wind at this anchorage, she should immediately endeavour to get out either to the westward, or through the Gouliot pass, which latter may with confidence be attempted at half flood.

Dangers off La Grande Grève :—The Hautes Boues are a group of rocks lying off the north-west side of Little Serk. The outer, north-west rock of the group dries 4 feet at low water, and lies N.W. by W., three-eighths of a mile from the Moie de la Fontaine : there is deep water close to this rock to the northward and westward, but a string of dangerous rocks extend from it in a S.S.W. direction, to the distance of nearly half a mile ; there are also numerous rocks within this line to the eastward, five of which dry at low water.

There is no safe channel for large vessels inside the Hautes Boues.

The Dents, a rocky clump off the south-west end off Brecqhou, are awash at high water ordinary spring tides. They are steep-to and safe of approach from the southward.

The Baveuse is a large rocky clump lying N. by E. rather more than a cable from the Moie de la Fontaine. It covers 4 feet at high water.

From the Baveuse in the direction of the Gouliot pass, there are several dangerous rocks, the chief of which, the Boue de Baie, has only 3 feet on it at low water, from which the Baveuse bears S.S.W. ¼ W., distant 1½ cables ; the Chapelle (a large rock to the northward of Le Jeu point) is in line with that point ; and the Pierre au Norman appears in the middle of the chasm between the Moie du Gouliot and the islet called La Tour.

DIRECTIONS.—The mark to lead to the inner anchorage in La Grande Grève, northward of the Hautes Boues, and southward of Boue de la Baie, is the south end of La Coupée in line with Le Jeu point. Serk mill in line with the gap in the outer part of Longue point bearing East, will lead southward of the Dents and northward of all the dangers in Grande Grève, until the Pierre au Norman comes in line with the east end of Brecqhou, which mark will lead to the southward into the anchorage. The best mark for anchoring is with the Pierre au Norman in line with the east point of Brecqhou ; and about two-thirds of La Coupée roadway open southward of the south-east point of Great Serk. Should it be desired to anchor farther out, a good position will be obtained by bringing Serk mill in line with Longue point, bearing East, and the Givaude between Brecqhou and the Dents.

It should however be observed that as Serk mill will be hid behind the intervening high land of Longue point before a vessel arrives abreast of the Dents, it will be necessary to look out in time for another object on the same line of direction.

TIDES around SERK.—It is high water, full and change, at Serk, at the same time as at St. Peter Port, that is at 6 h. 37 m., and there is about the same rise and fall. The streams in the immediate vicinity of the island are subject to a great variety of courses during the twelve hours; their direction being governed by the peculiar configuration of the land. On its north-eastern side there is a tract of water in which a perpetual eddy or slack tide exists, during the six hours that the stream occupies in running to the north-eastward in the Great Russel and the Déroute channels, extending nearly 3 miles from the land, and gradually contracting in breadth as it increases its distance from the shore. The marks for its north-western and south-eastern limits are, the west end of Brecqhou island in one with the Corbée du Nez ; and L'Etac de Serk just appearing to the eastward of the land at Le Creux. Outside of the intersection of these marks, even at a cable's length, run the true Russel and Déroute streams.

The streams in Baleine bay, in Terrible bay, and in the neighbourhood of the Conchée, Baleine, and Balmée rocks, runs $7\frac{1}{2}$ hours to the eastward, and only $4\frac{1}{2}$ hours to the south-westward. The former stream begins an hour after low water by the shore and runs until $2\frac{1}{2}$ hours ebb, when the south-western stream commences and runs faintly for the remaining $4\frac{1}{2}$ hours or until an hour after low water again.

The streams on the north-eastern side of Serk, in La Grève de la Ville and in the neighbourhood of the Grande and Petite Moie rocks, &c., run $8\frac{1}{2}$ hours to the S. by E. and only $3\frac{1}{2}$ hours to the N. by W. The southern stream commences at 4 hours flood and runs until half an hour after low water, when the northern stream commences and runs faintly for the remaining $3\frac{1}{2}$ hours, or until 4 hours flood again.

The southern stream above-mentioned, on the north-eastern side of Serk, and the northern one on the south-eastern side, branch off circuitously to the eastward of the Burons, where they meet and unite with the Déroute stream, which sets directly both ways, and runs for equal spaces of time. A curved line drawn from the Grune Noire towards L'Etac de Serk to the southward, and to the point of intersection* before mentioned, on the north-eastern side of the island, will divide the irregular streams (in shore) from that of the Déroute ; and this line continued from the above point of intersection close round the Bec du Nez towards the Givaude rock, and thence to within 4 cables of L'Etac again, will divide the regular Russel stream from the irregular one within it.

The stream on the north-western side of Serk begins to run to the southward at the Bec du Nez, and thence along the land towards Brecqhou island at three-quarters flood, near which it meets with the stream from the Gouliot pass : which latter prevailing over the former, carries it circuitously into the Great Russel to the north-westward, where it unites with the regular stream. The stream begins to run to the north-eastward, along the shore of the Moie du Gouliot towards the Bec du Nez, at three-quarters ebb, and so continues until three-quarters flood again.

The stream on the south-western side of Serk in the neighbourhood of the rocks called the Hautes Boues, Bretagne, Sercul, &c., runs $4\frac{1}{2}$ hours to the northward, and anly $1\frac{1}{2}$ hours to the southward : the former stream commences at half-flood and runs for one hour ; it then suddenly turns and runs to the south-eastward for $1\frac{1}{2}$ hours, or until half an hour before high water by the shore, at which time it again as suddenly veers to the northward, and sets in that direction for the remaining $3\frac{1}{2}$ hours, or until half ebb.

---

* These two marks do not exactly intersect each other until considerably beyond the eddy here alluded to. Vale mill, however, in line with the Sardinière rock—on the east side of Herm—terminates its boundary.

The stream in the Gouliot pass runs for equal spaces of time, similar to that in the Great Russel, and does not partake of the apparent irregularity which governs the tides in its vicinity. On the contrary, the force and shape of the flood stream, acquired by the contracted and peculiar form of the channel between Serk and Brecqhou, is continued until it falls into the Russel channel ; the same is the case with the ebb until it unites with the stream to the south-westward of the Hautes Boues.

CHAPTER II.

THE CASQUETS ISLETS; BURHOU ISLAND; ALDERNEY ISLAND AND RACE; AND BANC DE LA SCHÔLE.

Variation 21° West in 1870.

THE islands and rocks which occupy a large portion of the space between Bréhat island and Cape de la Hague, extend to the northward as far as the parallel of that Cape, where they form a sort of chain 9 miles long from west to east, and 3 miles wide from north to south. This chain forms three distinct groups, namely, the Casquets islets and rocks lying at its western extremity, the island of Alderney at the eastern, and Burhou island occupying the centre position. They are separated from the coast of France by a channel 8 miles wide, called the Race of Alderney, and in a similar manner from the island of Guernsey and its islets by a space of about 12 miles.

The CASQUETS ISLETS and ROCKS (so named, probably, from their remarkable helmet or cap-like appearance) lie N.W. by W. ¼ W., 6 miles from Alderney telegraph, and form an isolated group half a mile in length W.N.W. and E.S.E. by one to two cables in breadth. The largest and highest of the rocks form a clump near the centre of the group (on which the lighthouses are built); they are elevated 90 feet above high water, and at low water are all connected together, extending 3 cables W.N.W. and E.S.E. by 1¼ cables across their widest part, which lies N.N.E. and S.S.W. from the lighthouses. From this central mass to the eastward for 1½ cables lie six high rocks detached from each other at low water by narrow gullies, through which the tide rushes with great velocity; the easternmost rock is called Colotte, it is elevated 33 feet above high water, it is very steep-to, and safe of approach.

The entire group above described is as steep as a wall to the southward, and also to the eastward, but on the north side, between point Colotte and the lighthouses, are two small detached heads that uncover at low water, they are, however, only a quarter of a cable distant from the main clump.

The little Casquet rock, situated three-quarters of a cable to the southward of the lighthouses, and elevated 53 feet above high water, shelters a landing-place for boats on the main rock, at an inlet called Petit Havre;

there is also a landing-place on the east side of the little Casquet rock, and another in a rocky bight on the north side of the main group.

The possibility of safe landing at either of these places is communicated to a vessel approaching, by the hoisting of a flag on the platform staff between the lighthouses. When landing can be effected at Petit Havre (or S.W. cove) a blue flag is hoisted; when at south cove, St. George's Ensign; and a red flag for the N.E. landing-place in north-east cove. When no flag is shown the landing is not considered to be safe.

L'AUQUIÈRE ROCK, lying three-quarters of a cable W.N.W. from the west end of the main group, is one-third of a cable in diameter, and elevated 44 feet above high water. Sunken rocks extend to the distance of a third of a cable to the north of L'Auquière, as well as to the westward and southward of it. There is a boat channel between it and the Casquets, but it is very narrow, owing to a ledge of sunken rocks extending nearly half-way across from west point of Casquet group, and rendered further dangerous by other rocks to the southward, which dry at low water; it should never be used, therefore, except in cases of urgent necessity.

NOIRE ROQUE, or Black rock, lies West $3\frac{1}{2}$ cables from the Casquet lighthouses, and W. by S. $\frac{3}{4}$ S., nearly two cables from L'Auquière; it is a quarter of a cable in diameter, and elevated 12 feet only above high water; it is craggy and unapproachable.

NOIRE ROQUE LEDGE, having only 8 feet over it at low water, lies N.W. $\frac{1}{2}$ W., a cable and a quarter from Noire Roque. Its position is generally pointed out by a strong ripple, and with any swell the sea breaks furiously over it.

There is a sunken rock with only 4 feet over it, midway between Noire Roque and L'Auquière; no vessel ought, therefore, to attempt to pass between them.

Excepting the dangers just noticed and above, the Casquets are very steep-to on all sides.

ANCHORAGE can only be safely attempted on the south-east side of the Casquets by a *steamer;* and in her only while the south-western stream is running. The best spot is in 15 fathoms, fine sand, the north-east lighthouse bearing N. by W., and with Fort Albert in line with Ortac and between L'Equêt and Fourquie rocks.

This position, although only $1\frac{1}{4}$ cables from the rocks, its quite safe (in fine weather) when carefully taken up; it is sheltered from the tide by the Casquet rocks. At the distance of 50 fathoms within it there is 8 fathoms, and at the same distance outside 23 fathoms.

LIGHTS. — Three stone lighthouses (coloured white) stand, in a triangular position with respect to each other, on the largest and highest of the Casquets, and exhibit *revolving* lights, each being eclipsed at intervals of 20 seconds. The height of one lighthouse from base to vane is 30 feet, and of the two others 50 feet, and each are elevated 113 feet above high water; the lights are catoptric and of the first order, and visible in clear weather at the distance of 15 miles. A bell is sounded during foggy weather.

CAUTION.—The bearings of the lighthouses one from the other are as follows:—From the south-eastern to the north-western lighthouse N.W. ¾ W.; from the north-western to the north-eastern E. ¾ N.; and from the north-eastern to the south-eastern S.W. ½ W.; the mariner is specially warned that the three lights will consequently appear as but *two* when viewed in either of those three or in the opposite directions.

The great strength of the tidal stream near these rocks renders an incautious approach to them during foggy weather extremely hazardous; it is therefore recommended at such times *never* to run for them *with* the tide, but either to wait for slack water, or until the stream in its usual rotary course turns from the desired direction, or by altering the position of the vessel, astream of the rocks to leeward, so as to approach them *against* the tide. Should a shoal cast be obtained when running for the Casquets in thick weather, the vessel's head should be *at once* turned against the tide; after which, haul out cautiously to the westward into deep water.

EIGHT FATHOMS LEDGE.—N.W. by W. ½ W., nearly three-quarters of a mile from L'Auquière, is a bank of sunken rocks, over which there is said to be as little as 8 fathoms water. The bank is from 40 to 50 yards in extent, and rises suddenly from soundings of 25 and 27 fathoms water, and although it cannot be touched upon by vessels of large draught, yet it is dangerous, for at all times it causes violent eddies, and during fresh winds the sea breaks upon it.

ORTAC CHANNEL is bounded on its eastern side by Ortac ledge, and the rocks extending from Renonquet and Verte Tête, with Speedy rock on the same side as its northern boundary; and on its western side by the eastern Pommier bank, Danger rocks and L'Equêt reef. There is a rock near the middle of this channel (called Dasher rock), with 6¾ fathoms over it; vessels may pass on either side of this rock, but that to the eastward is preferable. The northern entrance of the Ortac channel, between the eastern Pommier bank and Speedy rock, is rather more than a mile wide; its narrowest part (to the eastward of Dasher rock) is nearly three-quarters of a mile; at this part the Great Nannel appears a little open on the north side of the high head of Renonquet, bearing E. by S. ¼ S., this mark will lead *over* the Dasher rock; on the top of which the outer high rock Les Etacs is seen touching the north-east side of Ortac.

The general depth in this channel is about 15 fathoms, with tolerably regular soundings, but the bottom is rocky and foul throughout; anchorage, therefore, except in cases of most urgent necessity, is not to be thought of.

The tides here run with great strength, especially when near high or low water; at springs they attain a velocity of more than 7 knots; in the course of their rotary motion they set *across* the channel, and although when running in this direction their strength decreases, an incautious pilot might soon be taken amongst dangerous rocks. From these and previous remarks it will be seen that these channels are at all times very dangerous for sailing vessels, and even to steamers, without the persons navigating them possess considerable local knowledge.

DIRECTIONS. — To pass through the Ortac channel from the northward, bring Ortac to bear S. ¼ E., and steer direct for it on this line of bearing; and when the Great Nannel comes in line with Verte Tête E. by S. ¾ S., steer S.S.W. ¾ W.; which course will lead through the channel about a third of a mile to the westward of the outer part of Ortac ledge. As stated before, when the Great Nannel comes nearly on with the north part of the highest head of Renonquet E. by S. ¾ S., you will be abreast of *Dasher* rock, to the southward of which the deep water channel is nearly 2 miles wide. When bordering on Ortac, you will clear the ledge off it, by not bringing the Great Nannel nearer to Burhou reef than the middle of the water gap, or channel, between it and Renonquet, until Fort Albert opens to the southward of Ortac. When Noire Houmet is seen to the southward of Ortac, you are clear of L'Equêt and all danger to the southward.

FOURQUIE and L'EQUET ROCKS.—A bank of pebbles, sand, and broken shells, with from 6 to 10 fathoms water over it, extends to the distance of nearly a mile E.S.E. from Colotte point; Fourquie is near the western end of this bank, and L'Equêt near its eastern end. L'Equêt is rather a long straggling and dangerous rock; its northern head is the highest part and dries 7 feet at low water; this head bears from the N.E. Casquet lighthouse S.E. by E. ¾ E., 1⅛ miles. There is a detached rocky bank at the distance of a third of a mile to the eastward of L'Equêt. Fourquie rock dries 13 feet at low water, and is steep-to, excepting to the eastward, where there is a detached sunken rock. Fourquie bears S.E. by E. ½ E. more than half a mile from the N.E. lighthouse, and S.E. ½ E. a third of a mile from Colotte point.

There is no safe channel between Fourquie and L'Equêt rocks, nor is it safe to approach the east side of the latter nearer than half a mile.

Whirling eddies, thrown up by the tide rushing over the rugged bottom at these parts, render a vessel involved in them quite unmanageable. The tide sets fairly through the channel between Fourquie and Colotte point, and there is 10 fathoms water over a tolerably even bottom in it ; therefore a *steamer* can safely pass through in fine weather ; but near spring tides, with any swell on, prudence would suggest not attempting it except in cases of urgent necessity.

POMMIER BANKS consist of two extensive and very dangerous groups of sunken rocks, divided by a narrow channel, having 12 fathoms in it. The highest head is situated near the west end of the westernmost group ; it has only 13 feet on it at low water, and lies E. by N. ¼ N., 1½ miles from the Casquets : on it Ortac appears midway between Alderney telegraph tower and the south-western brick kilns S.E. ½ E., and the north-eastern and south-western lighthouses are nearly in line, bearing W. by S. ⅙ S. From this 13 feet rock, the east end of the eastern bank bears E. ½ S. one mile. The least water found on this bank was 5 fathoms but there *may* be 2 or 3 feet less.

To clear the Pommier banks—The north-eastern and south-eastern lighthouses in line bearing S.W. ½ W., leads three-quarters of a mile outside, or to the northward. The Noires Putes midway between Ortac and Renonquet S.S.E., leads nearly half a mile to the eastward ; and St. Anne's Church (steeple) in line with Ortac S.E. by E. ⅜ E., clears them half a mile to the south-westward. This latter mark is also the best line to enter the Ortac channel with, between Pommier and L'Equêt rocks.

DANGER ROCKS, having 21 feet over them, lie three-quarters of a mile within the Pommier bank, and E. ¾ S. 2 miles from the Casquets. These rocks are very little more than half a cable in extent (in an east and west direction), but there *may* be a few feet less water over them than that given above ; they must therefore be approached with caution.

The channel between Danger rocks and L'Equêt bank has 15 fathoms in it, and is nearly three-quarters of a mile wide ; it is therefore quite safe to take in a vessel under perfect command, during fine weather ; but in bad weather, more especially if it happens near a spring tide, no vessel should attempt it ; indeed at such times, neither this nor any of the channels between the Casquets and Ortac should be used, for then the entire space is covered with tremendous overfalls, in which the largest vessels if involved would be quite unmanageable ; even during fine weather there are overfalls, but they are then confined to the shoalest parts over the high rocky heads, and thus marking their positions are easily avoided, and therefore at this time contribute to the safety of the navigation.

ORTAC ROCK, E. by S. ¾ S. 3⅓ miles from the Casquet lights, lies a remarkable huge nearly inaccessible rock, named Ortac, which rises 79 feet above high water, and may be seen in clear weather 9 or 10 miles. Its southern side is steep-to, having 8 fathoms within half a cable's length of the rock, but a sunken ledge with but 11 feet on it at its outer extreme extends to the distance of 2 cables to the westward of the rock. The highest part of this ledge to the south-westward (with 14 feet on it), lies with Fort Albert flagstaff just in sight to the southward of Ortac E. by S., three-quarters of a cable from the latter. The outer and shoalest spot to the westward of Ortac (11 feet), lies with the Clonque Fort just in sight to the southward of Ortac N.W. by W., 1¼ cables from it.   To clear the ledge to the westward, keep Fort Albert Flagstaff open South of Ortac until Verte Tête bears E.N.E.

Between Ortac, Verte Tête, and Burhou island, are scattered many dangerous sunken rocks and ledges, near and amongst which the streams run with great velocity.

SPEEDY ROCK. lying nearly half a mile due North of Vertetête, marks the northern boundary of the Ortac channel to the eastward ; the shoalest spot found is in 33 feet at low water ; at this position the outer high rock of Les Etacs is seen a little open to the westward of the high central rock of Renonquet S. by E. ½ E., and the whole of Fort Albert, its apparent breadth open to the southward of Great Nannel S.E. by E.

CASQUET S.W. BANK lies S.W. 4 miles from the Casquets lighthouses, and consists of a bank of fine gravel, sand, and shells ; 3¾ miles long (in a N.N.E. and S.S.W. drection) and nearly a mile wide.

The most elevated part of the bank lies close to its western side, near the middle ; the 10 fathoms contour line here includes a space just 2 miles long, and barely a ¼ of a mile wide ; the shoalest part on which (4 fathoms) lies a half a mile within, or to the north-eastward of its S.W. end.   At this position N.E. Casquet lighthouse bears N.E. ½ E., 4½ miles, Alderney telegraph tower E. ¼ S., Doyle Column in line with the N.E. extreme of Guernsey, S.W. ⅔ S.

Doyle Column in line with Vale Mill, S.W. by S., leads rather more than a mile to the westward of S.W. bank.   The channel between S.W. and S.S.W. banks is 2 miles wide, and has 22 to 29 fathoms in it.

CASQUET S.S.W. and S.S.E. BANKS, are steep ridgy banks of fine sand, lying within and to the eastward of S.W. bank and nearly across the Ortac channel to the south-west : all these banks are apparently formed by a deposit caused by the turning of the stream between low water and half flood ; for at this period near them the last of the westerly channel stream, after passing between Ortac and the Casquets, meets the south-easterly tide, then prevailing to the south-westward of the Casquets.

The north point of the S.S.W. bank (18 fathoms), bears S.W. $\frac{1}{2}$ S. $1\frac{1}{2}$ miles from the Casquet lights, and from this it extends due south rather more than $1\frac{1}{2}$ miles ; after which, the water deepens and the tail of the bank turns off to the eastward. This bank is a quarter of a mile broad, taking the 20 fathom line ; it has a sharp ridgy apex, fine white sand, having a depth of 12 to 13 fathoms over it, with 11 fathoms on the shoalest part near the middle.

Taking the 20 fathom line as a contour, the Casquet S.S.E. bank is rather more than three miles long (in a N.E. by E. and S.W. by W. direction) and $\frac{3}{4}$ of a mile wide : its south-west end (after the water deepens to 18 fathoms) turns off to the N.W., and unites with the S.S.W. bank. A narrow ridge of shoal water runs along the middle of the S.S.E. bank, a mile in extent ; having $4\frac{1}{2}$ fathoms at its east end, and only 4 fathoms at its west end ; with irregular soundings of 5 to 8 between. The Clonque and Tourgis forts beacons in line E. $\frac{3}{4}$ N. (the same mark as for Pierre au Vraie) passes over the top of the bank midway between the shoal spots at its extremes. At the N.E. extreme of the 10 fathoms contour the Casquet lighthouses bear N.N.W. $\frac{1}{2}$ W. $2\frac{3}{4}$ miles, and at the S.W. end of the 10 fathoms contour, the Casquets bear North $3\frac{3}{4}$ miles.

The shoal spots on the bank are difficult to pick up, they being generally the summits of sharp ridges of sand, and very steep ; these ridges appear to run rather across the bank, or in an E.S.E. and W.N.W. direction, but they shift in all probability with the turning of the tide.

ANCHORAGE should not be attempted on the S.S.W. bank, unless in a case of necessity, there being at all times a strong ripple over it ; but S.S.E. bank may in fine weather be used with great advantage by vessels cruising in the vicinity. The N.E. shoal spot on this bank (28 feet) lies with Tourgis beacon over the middle of Clonque Fort E. $\frac{1}{2}$ N. Ortac midway between Renonquet and Vertetête N.E. $\frac{1}{4}$ E., and Casquets N. by W. $\frac{3}{4}$ W. : the best anchorage will be found round this position in from 6 to 10 fathoms.

To clear the S.S.E. Casquet bank outside the 10 fathoms line, and to the southward, keep L'Etac de Quoire open to the southward of the Orboue rock E.NE. To the northward, the Great Coquelihou on the north side of the Coupè E. $\frac{1}{2}$ N., will lead clear in 10 fathoms, at the distance of more than half a mile from the shallowest spot on the bank.

Vertetête, behind the Ortac N.E. $\frac{1}{2}$ N., leads clear to the eastward ; and the west side of Renonquet in line with the east side of the Ortac N.E. by E., will clear to the westward.

CASQUET MIDDLE BANK lies about midway between the northern parts of S.S.W. and S.S.E. banks ; it is about a third of a mile in diameter, and has 15 to 20 fathoms on it, with gravel and broken shells.

The general depth of water round all the Casquet banks is 25 fathoms.

TIDES.—It is high water, full and change, at the Casquets and at the Ortac rock at 6h. 45m.; great springs rise 24 feet, ordinary springs 17 feet, and neaps 10 feet.

Although the tidal stream in the immediate neighbourhood of the Casquets preserves its rotary propensity, it varies much in strength and direction according to position. On their north side and to the eastward, for instance, outside the influence of the Ortac channel, the slack and change of stream takes place as in the offing; the great body of the flood setting E. by N. and the ebb W. by S.; but westward of the Casquets the strength of the stream is principally felt in three different directions, namely; at $2\frac{1}{2}$ hours flood south 3·7 knots, 1 hour ebb E.N.E. 3·0 knots, and an hour before low water W. by N. 3·1 knots: between these points a continuous stream of tide sets to the westward, southward, and eastward, the only slack occurring between 3 and 4 hours ebb.

On the south-western side of the Casquets, between the periods of half-ebb and low water, there is an eddy of nearly 2 miles in breadth and of considerable strength. Between low water and 2 hours flood this eddy revolves more to the eastward, as well as increases in breadth; the natural consequence of the obstruction which the Casquets present to the stream being in the latter case increased, because acted upon more directly than in the former; and this eddy continues until gradually weakened and destroyed by the current at half-flood. Similar eddies exist also on the north-eastern side of the Casquets, the effects of which are exactly the reverse of the preceding.

The stream in the Casquet channel, that is, in its immediate draft, begins to set to the south-westward at half-ebb exactly on the shore, and runs in that direction for 6 hours, or until half-flood, and the contrary with respect to the north-eastern stream, for there is neither high nor low water slack here. The stream which begins to run to the north-eastward at half-flood, after passing the Ortac, gradually veers to the northward and sets N.N.E. until it again unites with the stream flowing round the northern side of the Casquets. The south-western stream of this channel, which commences at half-ebb, sets right open the L'Equêt and the Fourquies; to avoid which the utmost care must be taken.

On the south-western side of the Ortac rock, there is an eddy of nearly $1\frac{1}{2}$ miles in extent, between half-ebb and one hour's flood; after which period the stream on the south side of Ortac gradually inclines to the westward, setting, at 2 hours flood, directly for the Casquets, until its progress is arrested by the last of the south-western stream in the Casquet channel.   There is no eddy of consequence on the north-eastern side of Ortac.

BURHOU ISLAND lies E. ½ S. 1½ miles from Ortac; it is rather level within, although huge rocks crop out near the extremes, and it is fringed with reef.   The western part of Burhou is cut off from the main island by the tide at high water; the portion thus detached is called Little Burhou. The two islands together are rather more than half a mile long in an east and west direction, and nearly two cables broad, their rocky peaks are about the same height (83 feet above high water).   The islands are covered with a light soil, on which grow coarse grasses and a variety of wild flowers, the soil is burrowed in every direction by rabbits, which animals, being now nearly extirpated by the fishermen of Alderney, their holes are frequently occupied by sea birds engaged in rearing their young; among others it is the resort of the stormy petrel during the breeding season.

There is a house of refuge for fishermen and shipwrecked mariners (built by the late Governor of Alderney), on the low saddle near the middle of the island, but it is now fast falling to ruin.   The landing places are in two small coves near the house, one on either side of the island. There is no fresh water on the island other than may be deposited by the rain in the interstices of the rocks.

The eastern side of Burhou is clear of danger to within half a cable from the shore, but a reef stretches out to the westward of Little Burhou for half a mile, and the whole of it, with the exception of a few elevated rocky heads, covers at high water.   There are also numerous detached rocks along the border of this reef to the southward, and also to the westward.

There is a 5 fathoms channel between Burhou reef and the rocks stretching out 3 cables to the eastward of Ortac; there is also a very narrow channel to the northward of Burhou reef leading into the little Swinge, but only the most expert pilots amongst the Alderney fishermen could navigate either of them with safety.

VERTE TÊTE REEF, lying to the north-eastward of Ortac, marks the north extreme of the dangerous rocks, stretching in a north-westerly direction to the distance of a mile from the west end of Little Burhou. There are three high rocks on this reef, of which the most remarkable, called Cone rock, lies to the westward; bearing N.E. by N., ⅚ of a mile from Ortac rock, and E. ¾ S., rather more than 3½ miles from the Casquets. It is of sugar-loaf form and elevated about 20 feet above high water; is detached from the main reef at all times of tide; very steep to the northward, but to the westward, at the distance of three-quarters of a cable, there is a small pointed rock that uncovers 6 feet at low water.

The main rock of the Verte Tête group is 13 feet higher and much larger than Cone rock; it has, moreover, two heads; the inner and highest is very flat on the top; the outer (situated to the north-eastward, at the distance of a quarter of a cable), lower, smaller, and peaked. A reef, dry at low water, extends nearly a cable to the eastward of the high head of Verte Tête; there is also a sunken rock, bearing E.N.E. about a cable from it; but with the exception of these dangers and the rock above described, situated to the westward of Cone rock, the Verte Tête rocks, *that are always above high water*, are very steep-to on the outside.

RENONQUET REEF, lying in an east and west direction, at a quarter of a mile within the Verte Tête, is nearly three-quarters of a mile long : its western end is low and covers with the tide for a third of a mile, but near the eastern end there is a group of high rocks, about $1\frac{1}{2}$ cables in diameter, that never cover. The highest rock of this group is elevated 40 feet above high water, and lies nearly a third of a mile within the high head of Verte Tête, on a line between it and the peak of Little Burhou.

WHITE ROCK is about 2 cables to the eastward of Renonquet; it is small and elevated 20 feet above high water; steep-to and safe of approach to the northward. There is only another rock situated to the eastward of this (near the Renonquet group) that is visible at high water, and this is a small head nearly awash lying S.E. at the distance of $1\frac{1}{2}$ cables from White rock; therefore, the White rock on the east, Verte Tête to the westward, with the Renonquet rock in the middle, together, form a remarkable group to guide the mariner set in here during foggy weather.

Les MAQUEREAUX ROCKS.—A sunken reef, 2 cables in extent north and south and 1 cable broad, lies half a mile East from the White rock : there are 3 heads near the middle of the reef with only 4 feet over them at low water : there is no proper channel for vessels between these rocks and Verte Tête. Outer L'Etac, in line with the saddle rock of Burhou (just to the westward of the house), bearing S. $\frac{1}{2}$ W. leads clear of Les Maquereaux rocks to the east, and the Casquets W. $\frac{3}{4}$ N. leads half a cable to the northward of them. The eastern clearing mark for these rocks is also the best line to run in for the anchorage on the north side of Burhou, should necessity compel a vessel to use it; in such a case, anchor with Outer L'Etac between the above leading line and the high western apex of Burhou; and Ortac in line or just within the northernmost high water head of Burhou reef; in 7 fathoms sand.

The NANNELS, said to be an English corruption of Les Nianaise, is a reef about a third of a mile long east and west, and a quarter of a mile wide : it may be said to form the eastern part of the Burhou group, and consists of enormous rocks, curiously shaped, some which are always above water and others that cover and uncover with the tide. The highest, called the Great Nannel, rises 58 feet above high water, and is situated near the middle of the south-western part of the reef : the next in magnitude, called the Little Nannel, is elevated only 12 feet above high water, and lies at the N.W. end of the reef, rather more than a cable's length from the Great Nannel.

Other rocks above high water, but of lesser magnitude, lie in an easterly direction from the Great Nannel for the distance of 2 cables : the extreme point of the group is called Pierre de Bût : this part of the rock covers with the tide near high water. There are also two sunken rocks, having 9 feet over them, lying a third of a cable to the eastward of Pierre de Bût.

Le CORDONNIER, a small rock drying 3 feet at low water, lies at the distance of a cable and a half, south of the Great Nannel.

The breadth of the channel between Burhou and the Nannels is exactly 2 cables, and it is further divided into two parts by a rock near the middle called L'Equêt, which dries 6 feet at low water. The tide rushes through this channel into the Little Swinge with great velocity.

L'EMPRONE REEF lies N.N.E. a third of a mile from the Great Nannel : it is nearly 1½ cables long east and west by three-quarters of a cable wide : there are 4 rocks which dry at low water ; the highest 2 feet, and others awash. The sea breaks furiously on this reef, especially with fresh north-westerly winds.

ROUND ROCK dries 9 feet at low water, and lies midway between the Nannels and L'Emprone.

Directions, to clear L'Emprone and the Nannels, to the northward and eastward, keep the Casquet lighthouses open to the northward of Verte Tête, W. ½ N., until Alderney mill opens to the eastward of the Grosse rock, S. ½ E.

The SWINGE CHANNEL divides Burhou island and its rocks from Alderney ; its narrowest part is included in the space, bounded by the rocks fringing the south shore of Burhou island on one side, and the Barsier and Corbet rocks to the southward. It is here three-quarters of a mile wide, but on either side of these points it soon widens. The bottom is rocky throughout, and very uneven ; the average depth at its narrowest part cannot be taken at more than 8 fathoms. There are several very dangerous rocks in the Swinge, some lately discovered, which will be noticed hereafter. This, like the Casquet channel, abounds with broken water, even during the calmest weather, caused by the rapidity of the stream and the rugged bottom. There are also two overfalls in it, caused solely by the tide, the dangers of which are of course much increased in bad weather. During easterly winds, on the north-east stream, overfalls extend nearly across the Swinge, from Burhou island to the outer end of Alderney breakwater. With westerly winds on the south-west stream, they extend from Ortac to Les Etacs. Both overfalls may be avoided by following the directions given hereafter.

DANGERS in the SWINGE.—Les Boues des Kaines, the outer head, is awash at low water, and lies S.W. by S., distant 3 cables from the high water rocky clump at the south-west end of Burhou reef; on it fort Albert flagstaff is seen just inside the outer end of Grosnez Fort, E. by S. $\frac{1}{2}$ S., and Long rock a little open westward of S.W. rocky clump of Burhou reef, N.N.E. $\frac{3}{4}$ E.

The channel inside these rocks is barely 1$\frac{1}{2}$ cables wide.

North Rock, 11 feet, lies a cable and a half to the S.E. of Noire Houmet, off Burhou island; on it the Great Nannel is seen in the gap just within the eastermost, high, semi-detached rock of Burhou, bearing N.N.E. $\frac{2}{3}$ E., and Ortac just open southward of the half tide reef, south-west of Noire Houmet W. by N. $\frac{1}{4}$ N.

South Rock, 5 fathoms, lies with the west end of Great Noire Pute, touching the east side of inner Les Etacs, S. $\frac{3}{4}$ E., and the outer or northern upper extreme of Fort Albert a little open to the southward of the inner part of Grosnez Fort, E. $\frac{3}{4}$ S. There is another head with 5$\frac{1}{2}$ fathoms over it, situated at the west end of this same rocky bank; it bears from south rock S.W. by W. $\frac{3}{4}$ W., 2$\frac{1}{2}$ cables.

Both of these heads *may* have less water than is here given; in approaching them from the westward, it will be useful to remember that you cannot touch the western head so long as the Great Noire Pute is in sight, westward of Les Etacs; and proceeding to the eastward, you are clear of the eastern head as soon as the whole of the Great Noire Pute is seen *clear* of the inner of Les Etacs.

Les Etacs Bank lies nearly half a mile W.N.W. from the Etacs; the least water found (26 feet) lies near the south end of it. This bank will be cleared outside by keeping the Great Noire Pute open to the westward of Coupé rock until Tourgis beacon comes near the north end of Clonque Fort.

Pierre au Vraic.—This dangerous rock (which dries 5 feet at low water) lies immediately in the stream of the Swinge channel, 4 miles S.E. $\frac{1}{4}$ ·S. from the Casquets, S. by W. nearly 1$\frac{3}{4}$ miles from Ortac, and west, exactly 1$\frac{3}{4}$ miles from Les Etacs, near the west end of Alderney. In form and size this rock is like a small boat bottom up; it is surrounded by very deep water; at the distance of a cable and a half to the southward and westward there are 26 fathoms, and within it 14 to 16 fathoms.

The marks for this rock are the inner peak of Great Coquelihou, in line with the Coupé rock, E. by S. ½ S., and the conical beacon on the slope of the high land just within Fort Tourgis, in line with the beacon in Clonque Fort, E. ¾ N. These marks are used to clear the rock on either side as necessary. Tourgis beacon, in line with north end of Clonque Fort, leads two cables to the northward of Pierre au Vraic. Cape La Hague light, open and shut of the south end of Alderney, leads *close* to the northward of it also.

Richards and Ellis Rocks are on a rocky bank lying rather more than half a mile to the S.E. of the Pierre au Vraic, at the distance of a quarter of a mile from each other. Richards rock has 5½ fathoms over it, and there is 23 fathoms within a cable's length to the southward ; on the rock, the outer Coquelihou appears a little open northwards of the inner Noire Pute, E. ⅞ S., and the Great Nannel seen just within the outer eastern high rock on Burhou, N.E. by N. Ellis rock lies nearly 3 cables north from Richards rock. The Great Nannel on with the east end of Burhou, will lead a third of a mile to the eastward of these rocks. No large ship should pass between Richards rock and the Pierre au Vraic.

TIDES.—The strength of the stream in the Swinge, that is, between Burhou island and the Corbet rock, sets straight through both ways at high and low water ; and, like the stream in the Casquet channel, begins to set to the south-westward at half-ebb exactly, and runs in that direction for 6 hours, or until half-flood ; and the contrary with respect to the north-eastern stream. One branch of the flood, to the westward of the Narrows, sets through between Burhou island and the Ortac, particularly after high water on the shore ; and, to the eastward of the Narrows, it veers and sets circuitously round the L'Emprone to the north-westward, and both uniting with the Casquets channel tides, and ultimately with that of the English Channel, again sets to the eastward. The last 2 hours of the south-western stream in the Swinge gradually veers towards the South, as it recedes from the draft of the former passage. The velocity of the north-eastern stream, during the springs, is 7¼ miles ; that of the south-western stream 6½ miles per hour.

ALDERNEY or AURIGNY ISLAND, is 3⅓ miles long, east and west, and 1⅓ miles wide where broadest, which is near the west end; the highest part is at the base of the windmill ; it is here 295 feet above the mean tide level ; at the telegraph, the island is about 9 feet lower. Alderney may be seen in clear weather at the distance of 22 miles ; its eastern extremity bears N.W. by W. ¾ W. nearly 8 miles from Cape La Hague lighthouse, and E.S.E. ⅛ E. 8½ miles from the Casquets. The appearance of the island from a distance is wild and gloomy, nor does its character improve on a nearer view : the southern and western coasts are high precipitous cliffs, intersected by narrow valleys, and fronted by outlying rocks ; the most conspicuous among which are the Coquelihou and Noire Putes groups to the southward, and Les Etacs and Clonques to the westward : the latter are now crowned with a battery, which commands the Swinge channel. The northern and eastern sides are much less elevated, and the coast there is formed by a series of bays of sand and gravel, separated from each other by steep projecting points, but with the exception of the small bays of Braye (now enclosed as a harbour of refuge), Plat Saline, and Corblets, the intervals of beach are inaccessible, on account of the outlying rocks, which forbid all approach. The heights along the south and western coasts are covered with heath and furze, but the land within is generally cultivated and fertile. There are but very few trees on the island, and they are only to be met with in the valleys near the town, where the neighbouring hills afford some shelter from the wind.

The town of Alderney (St. Anne) is situate near the middle of the island ; it is large, well built, paved, and lighted with gas ; it has a large and handsome church (St. Anne's) : there are besides several chapels.

Besides the town of St. Anne, villages have lately sprung up at Craby, Braye new town, and at Mannez, owing to their vicinity to the public works and quarries.

The island abounds with springs of excellent water. Wood and fuel are imported from England, and cattle, for fresh meat, from Cherbourg : these necessaries are nevertheless to be obtained almost at the same prices as at Guernsey ; the latter owing to the regular steam communication now existing between Alderney, Cherbourg, and Guernsey, which will probably cease with the stoppage of the Government works.

Until of late years Alderney possessed but two small insecure harbours, one called Longy bay, originally named Baie de Câtel, on the south-east side of the island ; and the other, the old artificial harbour of Braye, on the north side ; both of which dry at low water neaps.

Alderney forms part of the Bailiwick of Guernsey, and is included in the military command of the Lieutenant-Governor of that island ; it forms one parish, under the patronage of the Crown, named St. Anne, the area of which is 1,962 imperial acres at high water of spring tides. The land was originally divided into small parcels amongst the inhabitants, but of late years the Government have purchased about a third of it for their works.

The civil government or States consist of a Judge, appointed by the Crown, six jurats, and twelve douzeniers, who are elected by the inhabitants. In 1847 the population of Alderney was about 950, it increased to upwards of 5,000 in 1858, in consequence of the Government works, and it is now about 3,000.

The ordinary garrison of the island consists of a strong body of royal artillery, and three companies of infantry of the line; besides the island militia, who are organized as artillery, and reported to be very efficient. The forts situated along the northern, eastern, and south-eastern shores of Alderney, now form quite a feature in the appearance of the island on those sides : of them Fort Albert is the most conspicuous, being situate on the crown of a remarkable conical hill, which rises from the comparatively low land at the north-east part of the island.

The HARBOUR of REFUGE in BRAYE BAY, on the north shore of Alderney and now nearly complete, encloses the old harbour of Braye as well as the anchorage in the road fronting it, also the new harbour of Craby; the latter built chiefly to shelter the vessels employed in laying the foundation for the N.W. breakwater, and otherwise about the Government works. The rocks at one time encumbering the harbour of refuge have been removed, and the anchorage is now quite clear, but on account of the rocky nature of the bottom, vessels using their own anchors should, in strong winds, always ride with a good scope of cable.

The harbour affords perfect shelter to the northward and westward, but easterly winds send in much sea.

The north-west breakwater of this harbour was commenced in 1847 and is now complete; it springs from the west point of Braye bay under Fort Grosnez and extends 1,609 yards to the eastward. Owing to repeated alterations and extensions of the original plan, the work has not been built in a straight line, but as follows : From Grosnez point straight for 1,000 yards N. 74 E., then a curve northwards for 173 yards in a radius of 500 yards, after which it runs straight to the end, N. 54 E., for the distance of 436 yards. The breakwater or pier is built on an artificial bank of rubble stone or *pierres perdues ;* the main part is 40 feet wide and 6 feet above high water at ordinary spring tides ; on the outer part of the breakwater there is built a promenade 10 feet in width and 21 feet above high water, and on the outer part of the promenade a parapet 4 feet wide and 25 feet above high water. The breakwater and pier is built over the Bouillonnaise and Malassise rocks, and the centre of it passes a cable's length to the southward of the Braye rocks. At the upper end of the pier there is a slipway for boats and small craft, with steps at the end descending to low water of spring tides ; there is also a flight of landing steps on the breakwater pier (within), at the distance of 930 yards from the shore. The inner part of the breakwater pier is now clear along its entire length, and the rubble bank on which it is built so steep that large ships may securely lay alongside at the distance of 50 feet. Mooring chains and bollards have been provided, and there are also iron ladders from low water to the quay level, at short intervals along its entire length.

Moorings.—Two sets of frigate's moorings and two for line-of-battle-ships have lately been laid down at a position near the inner part of the curve in the breakwater : the frigate's moorings are conveniently placed for warping to and from the breakwater, the line-of-battle-ships' moorings lie outside of them ; there is also another set of moorings near the head of the harbour.

Dangers inside the Breakwater have for the most part been removed by blasting the rocks ; of these the *Têtes Champignons*, lying N.W. by W., ¾ of a cable from Roselle point, have been reduced to 16 feet. Another group of rocks, lying W. by S. 2 cables from Roselle point, have now 12 feet over them ; and at the position of the late half tide rock there is 22 feet at low water.

The Aiguillons rocks may at present be considered to be the eastern boundary of the harbour of refuge ; they consist of a group of eight heads which dry at low tide, the easternmost rock, named the Great Aiguillon, lies N.N.E. ½ E., 1½ cables from Bibette head. A *beacon* has lately been placed on the small Aiguillon, which rock is the outer or northernmost of the group and lies due West, a cable's length from the Great Aiguillon. The beacon consists of a round tower of masonry, 19 feet high, and 9 feet in diameter at the base and 6 feet at the top, its summit being elevated 10 feet above high water at spring tides ; the beacon is painted black and white in horizontal bars, and may be seen under ordinary circumstances at a distance of two miles.

A dangerous reef of sunken rocks, with 10 to 6 feet over them, lies at the distance of three-quarters of a cable from the beacon, between the bearings of N. by E. and N.E. by E. ; they will be cleared to the westward by keeping the flagstaff in Fort Albert open to the westward of the beacon bearing S. by W., and the beacon in line with the outer Gross rock E. by N. will lead clear of the 16 feet rock in the harbour off Bibette head.

LIGHTS.—Two fixed *red* lights are exhibited at the head of the harbour of refuge to mark the fairway channel by night ; the lower light is exhibited through a long tube which screens it in every direction excepting on a line through the middle of the fairway ; this light is fixed on the parapet of the old pier at Braye and elevated 25 feet above high water at spring tides : it may be seen 5 miles in clear weather. The upper light is fixed at the north-east corner of Braye reading-room S.W. by W., 370 yards from the lower light ; it is elevated 55 feet above high water, and may be seen at the distance of 8 or 9 miles.

BRAYE OLD HARBOUR is formed by only one sheltering pier, built out in an easterly direction from the west side of Braye bay ; it dries at low water neaps, and was very insecure before the Admiralty breakwater was built; even now it is very inferior to the new harbour of Craby.

The best time to enter Braye old harbour is on a rising tide between half-flood and high water; at low water there is a depth of 8 feet between the iron beacons which are placed one on either side of the entrance on the two rocky clumps just without the pier head. The west beacon has a circular eye on its top, and the eastern one a cross. No leading mark is required, but the pier head should be rounded as close as possible.

CRABY HARBOUR was constructed by the Government in 1850, in the creek formerly called little Craby bay, between the old harbour of Braye and Grosnez point. In addition to the shelter of the breakwater, this harbour is itself protected by two small piers having an entrance between the pier heads, 40 feet wide, open to the north-east. This enclosed harbour is 100 yards long from west to east, and 90 yards wide, and affords 230 yards of quay room on its northern, western, and southern sides, or space sufficient to berth four colliers of about 150 tons burthen. The harbour dries out to the pier heads at low water of ordinary springs and 8 feet at ordinary neaps; at half-tide there is 9 feet between the pier heads. No special directions are necessary.

The approaches to Alderney on every side but N.E. are difficult and dangerous, from the numerous outlying rocks; and the dangers of the consequent intricate navigation are of course intensified by the great strength of the tidal stream: therefore, a stranger should not attempt to close with the island on any side but the N.E.; from which direction, however, a careful seaman may approach and enter the harbour of Refuge, by attending to the directions given hereafter at page 66.

ROCKS and DANGERS on N.W. and NORTH SIDES of ALDERNEY. —**Les Etacs**, the most remarkable of all the rocks near the west end of the island, form the southern boundary of the Swinge channel. They consist of a group of four; the highest is elevated 128 feet above high water; the centre of the group lies off the W.N.W. point of Alderney at the distance of 2 cables from the shore.

Les Boues des Etacs lie W.N.W. 1¾ cables from the outer Etac; the north-western head has only 1 foot on it at low water. The east end of the outer Noire Pute in line with the west end of the Coupé leads half a cable to the westward of them, and the north or lower part of Tourgis fort in line with south part of Clonque fort leads same distance to the northward of them.

The Clonques are three high rocks attached to the western shore of Alderney by a rocky ridge, which formerly uncovered at low water, but on which there has lately been built an elevated roadway to communicate with the Clonque fort. The Clonque fort has been built on the summits of the two rocks nearest the land. A wooden beacon stands in the rear of the fort, on the south-eastern head of the Clonque, and when this is brought in line with the white conical stone beacon on Tourgis hill, to the south of the fort, it points out the position of the Pierre au Vraic rock.

Plat Boue, Founiais and Ozard Rock, lie off the Clonques on a line bearing due west from the fort; the first close to the main reef; the Founiais (which dries 6 feet) at the distance of nearly 2 cables from the Fort, and Ozard rock (on which there is 4 feet at low water), nearly 3 cables from it. Ozard rock is very small: on the top of it the Great Noire Pute (the inner one) is seen just open (to the eastward) clear of the inner rock of Les Etacs S. $\frac{1}{2}$ E., and Tourgis beacon is in line with north tangent of Clonque fort, E. $\frac{1}{2}$ N. To clear the rocks use these marks as necessary.

Querouelles and Barsier Reefs, are two dangerous rocky clumps, situate to the northward of the Clonques. The middle of the former lies N.N.W. 2 cables from the fort, and the latter N. by W., 4 cables from it. The Querouelles dries 8 feet; the eastern heads of the Barsier 5 feet; and the western head is just awash at low water spring tides. The eastern head of Barsier (the highest) bears S.W. by W. $\frac{1}{2}$ W., 2 cables from Corbet rock; the western head of the reef lies on the same line of bearing at the distance of three-quarters of a cable from its eastern head. The eastern head of outer Noire Pute in line with the west end of Alderney S. $\frac{1}{2}$ W., clears the west side of Barsier by a half a cable, and Fort Albert flagstaff in line with the inner part of Grosnez fort E. by S. leads clear of its north side about the same distance.

Caution.—There is no safe passage inside Querouelles and Barsier, even for boats; and the first of the flood sets right on them; at this time, therefore, a wide berth should be given them in passing.

Corbet Rock lies half a mile N. by E. $\frac{1}{2}$ E. of Clonque fort, and N.W. by W. $\frac{1}{2}$ W. half a mile from Tourgis point, and is never wholly covered, though at very high spring it is awash. There is a small detached rock outside of Corbet that dries at low water; it lies at the distance of 20 fathoms on the line of Corbet and Tourgis fort. Corbet is attached at low water to Alderney by a dangerous ledge of rocks, and the ebb as well as the flood stream runs over this ledge with great rapidity. A large fort has lately been erected on Tourgis point.

The long western mark for the Corbet is the north-eastern lighthouse on the Casquets just seen open to the southward of the Ortac, W.N.W. westerly; and the southern extremity of the Casquets just shut in with the south end of the Ortac will lead to the northward of the Corbet and through the narrows of the Swinge. Between the Corbet and the east end of Burhou the streams rush with great velocity, and during a weather tide the sea breaks nearly across the Swinge; the smooth water then is mostly found near the Corbet.

The Grosse, a large prominent rock 14 feet above high-water springs, is steep-to and may be approached within half a cable's length. It lies E. by S. distant 4 cables from the Corbet, and North 2 cables from Tourgis point.

The Jumelles are two small ridges of rock, which uncover at half-tide, lying about E. ½ S. 8 cables from the Corbet, and 3 cables to the northward of Platte Saline bay. The end of the breakwater kept on a bearing of E. ½ S. will lead to the northward of all dangers on the south side of the Swinge, from the Barsier and Corbet upwards.

The Braye Rocks are a group of four heads, the outermost of which seldom covers, though awash at high-water springs; the three others, called the Follets, show at half-tide. The outer Braye lies N.E. ¾ E., 2¾ cables from the tower of the new fort on Grosnez point, and a cable from the breakwater. A rock, with only 3½ feet on it, lies E.N.E. a third of a cable from the outer Braye.

DANGERS on N.E. SIDE of ALDERNEY.—The dangers most to be feared on the north-eastern side of Alderney are the sunken rocks N.E. of the Aiguillons, the Grois, the Platte, the Ledge, and the Sauquet. The sunken rocks N.E. of Aiguillon are described at page 58.

Grois Ledge is an extensive dangerous reef, lying off L'Etoc point; it extends 2½ cables between the bearings of N. by E. and N.E. from the tower of the new fort on that point, which should not be approached on these bearings within half a mile. The peaked rock, called the outer Grois, the highest of the reef, is awash at high water ordinary springs, and bears N. by E., distant 1⅔ cables from the tower of the fort. Several of the heads show at half-tide, and many more at low water. The stream rushes over this reef with great velocity. The depth is 13½ feet at a cable's length to the W.N.W. of the outer Grois. Ortac and Noire Houmet in line and open of the end of the breakwater W. by N. leads half cable outside of the ledge.

Platte Rock lies S.S.E. 2¾ cables from the outer Grois, and uncovers 4 feet at low-water springs. From the rock, the tower of L'Etoc fort is in one with the Ortac, W. by N. ⅓ N., and the high rock, named Bon Ami, on the east side of Corbets harbour, in line with old Corblets barracks, S.W. The ground between the Platte and the outer extremity of the Grois reef is foul, and should not be approached by any vessel.

The Ledge, or Fosse de la Band, is a reef of considerable extent, with 13 feet over it at low water. It lies E. by S. five-sixths of a mile from the outer Grois rock, with the latter rock in one with the Ortac, W. by N. ¼ N., and the high conical shore rock named Honoré, at the west end of the Mannez quarries, in line with the small round tower of the new barracks on Essex hill, S.W. by W.

The long western mark to clear the dangers on the north-east shore of Alderney is, the Casquet lighthouses open to the northward of Burhou island, W. by N. ¼ N.

Sauquet Rock lies 2 cables to the southward of the Ledge, and 1½ cables to the north-east of the Homeaux Florains reef, on which a small fort has been constructed. The Sauquet uncovers 3 feet at low-water springs, and the western mark for it is, the tower of L'Etoc fort in line with the Ortac, W. by N. ⅓ N. Great Nannel in line with Grois rock, W.N.W. just clears it outside. The ebb stream running down for the Race of Alderney and for the Swinge, separates or forks off at the Sauquet, and its tendency is to throw vessels that are near this rock right on it. A berth should therefore be given it of 3 or 4 cables' lengths. The outer Grois and north-east point of Burhou island in line leads between the Ledge and the Sauquet.

DANGERS on EAST SIDE of ALDERNEY.—The principal dangers lying off the eastern side of the island are the rocky patches named the Brinchetaie, the Boufresses, and the Blanchard, with the rocky patches to the south-eastward of Port Longy.

The Brinchetaie are a dangerous group of semi-detached rocks forming a ledge off the eastern point of Alderney. The outer rock lies 3 cables from the shore and uncovers 5 or 6 feet; the inner rock uncovers 12 feet. Raz island flagstaff in one with south extreme of Essex castle or the high Noire Pute, inner Coquelihou and south side of L'Etac de la Quoire, in line bearing W. ¾ S., leads to the southward of the Brinchetaie ; and the *outer* part of Quenard fort in line with the *inner* part of Florains fort clears them to the eastward. Several shoals, awash at low-water great springs, extend to the south-east of these dangers, as far out as a third of a mile from the coast.

Boufresses Reef lies nearly 4 cables to the westward of the Brinchetaie, and its outer end is a quarter of a mile to the eastward of the new fort on Raz island or Houmet de Longy. The reef uncovers to a considerable extent at low water. Raz island flagstaff in line with middle of Essex castle leads to the southward.

Blanchard Bank is composed of rock, gravel, granite stones, and shells. At its western extremity, which lies 6 cables from the eastern end of Alderney, there is a mass of rock upon which there are only 2¾ fathoms water; from thence the bank extends E. by S. ½ S. for 3 cables, where there is another rock with only 12 feet on it; this is the "Blanchard Rock" which lies three quarters of a mile from Houmet Herbe on the outer or eastern edge of the bank; between its western end and the dangers off the east end of the island are from 9 to 12 fathoms water. The Blanchard is very dangerous, and particularly its eastern extremity, which rises precipitously from soundings of 20 and 25 fathoms, causing, during springs, eddies and a heavy sea on a weather tide.

DIRECTIONS.—To clear the Brinchetaie, Boufresses, and Blanchard, lying off the eastern end of Alderney, the Coquelihou rocks should be opened out their own apparent breadth to the southward of L'Etac de la Quoire, bearing W. ¼ N., but no more, as three unconnected rocky patches lie to the south-eastward of Longy, stretching off as it were from the tails of the Brinchetaie and Blanchard at the several distances of half a mile, three-quarters of a mile, and 1¼ miles from the latter. Upon the two outermost of them there are only 17 and 18 feet water, and 4½ fathoms upon the patch nearest the Blanchard. From the outermost rock, named the Raz or Race, the telegraph tower is 3 times its own length open to the southward of the L'Etac de la Quoire, and Doyle Column (Guernsey) is nearly in one with the Grande Amfroque. From the centre patch St. Anne mill appears twice its own length open to the southward of the Rousset; and from the northern patch St. Anne mill is in line with the southern angle of Essex fort. Doyle column just open to the northward of the northernmost bluff land on Herm W. by S. ¾ S., leads well to the southward of them all; and for the same purpose, do not bring the lighthouse on Cape de la Hague more easterly than E. ⅛ S., or keep the Casquet lights in sight to the southward of Alderney.

SOUTH COAST of ALDERNEY.—**Longy Bay**, formerly called Baie du Câtel, lies on the S.E. side of Alderney, and dries at low-water neaps; it affords but little shelter, excepting to small coasting vessels capable of taking the ground; and since the construction of Braye harbour of refuge has been but seldom used. The entrance to the bay lies between Raz island (formerly called Houmet du Câtel) and on which there is a fort, and the Queslingue rock. The distance between these points is less than 2 cables, and this small space is divided into two channels of equal width by a rock in the centre, which dries 2 feet at low-water springs; moreover both the ebb and flood tide set violently across the entrance of the bay. It will therefore be apparent that a stranger should never attempt to enter it except in a case of absolute necessity. In the event of such occurring, attention is called to the following :—

Directions.—The best time to enter Longy bay is with the wind between

N.W. and S.W., and between 2 and 5 hours ebb ; a vessel may then run aground, and on the succeeding tide she may be hauled up under Essex nunnery, on the sandy beach at the western side of the bay. The leading mark in with the above winds is the Nunnery just shut in to the westward of Queslingue rock, N. by E., easterly, and by borrowing within half a cable of the latter rocky point, the fairway sunken rock at the entrance will be avoided.

Anchorage.—Longy Road affords good shelter on northerly and northwesterly winds in from 10 to 14 fathoms water, sand, gravel, and shells. Anchor with the whole of Fort Albert just shut in with (and seen over) the west point of Longy bay, N. by W. ½ W. and the Grande Folie (rocky peak) just open to the eastward of Raz island fort, N.E. ½ N. This berth is in 9 fathoms, 1½ cables from the shore. A better berth than this and more out of the tide may be had off the middle of La Tchue bay, just to the westward of Rousset rock ; anchor here, at the distance of a cable and a half to the westward of Rousset rock, on the line of the west side of Raz fort, touching east side of Queslingue rock.

La Roque Pendante is a remarkable overhanging rock, on the apex of the bluff, within Rousset rock, and to the S.W. of fort Essex ; it may be seen from a distance of 9 or 10 miles on an easterly or westerly bearing, but on altering the bearing on either side it soon shuts in with the island, and is then invisible unless from a very short distance.

Queslingue and Rousset rocks are high and peaked, and lie within two cables east and west of each other.

L'Etac de la Quoire lies about the middle of the south coast of the island, at the distance of half a cable from the shore, with which it is connected at low water. It is a conical rock, about 30 fathoms in diameter, and 10 feet lower than the Great Coquelihou.

Bonit Rock lies nearly half a mile to the southward of the Etac de la Quoire. This dangerous rock is of small extent, and appears only at low-water springs, and has from 10 to 14 fathoms close to. The marks for it are the Grande Folie (to the eastward of Longy), between the Rousset and the Queslingue rocks ; and L'Etac de la Quoire rock in one with a beacon on the adjoining shore, bearing N.N.E. The Bonit may be avoided by not approaching Alderney nearer than a mile, or by keeping the Casquets in sight to the southward of the island.

Alderney South Bank extends from Bonit Rock to the southward and S.W. to the distance of more than 1½ miles ; the general depth on the main bank is 15 fathoms, gravel, from which as a base there rises 7 small banks of sand, some of them having as little as 6 fathoms on them. These small banks lie in an E.N.E. and W.S.W. direction, and have sharp ridgy apexes. The largest bank is less than a quarter of a mile long. The shallow spots commence at a distance of rather more than half a mile S.W. ½ S. from Bonit. A vessel may pass inside of them to the eastward, by keeping the Coupé rock open to the southward of outer Coquelihou, until Grand Folie comes open eastward of Queslingue rock, and outside by keeping Verte Tête open westward of outer Noire Pute N. by W. ½ W. until Grande Folie appears in line with Raz island fort, bearing N.E. ¼ N.

By night the Casquets lights bearing N.W. ¾ N. will lead one mile to the S.W. of Alderney bank, and half a mile on the same side of the Pierre au Vraic. Cape la Hague light kept on any bearing to the northward of E. ⅓ S. will lead to the southward of Alderney south bank.

Some of the heaviest overfalls in the race are caused by these banks, they must therefore be avoided in bad weather.

COQUELIHOU ROCKS lie nearly a mile to the westward of L'Etac de la Quoire, and about a quarter of a mile from the shore. They consist of a group of three, the middle or eastern one being much larger and higher than either of the others; this, called the Great Coquelihou, is elevated 116 feet above high water, and bears from Alderney telegraph tower S.S.E. ½ E., rather more than half a mile from it. A bank of sand extends from Great Coquelihou to the eastward, for the distance of a quarter of a mile, on which there is as little as 1½ fathoms. It makes a convenient anchorage for fishing boats and small craft in fine weather.

There is a 5 fathom channel inside the Coquelihous, close to the Alderney shore, but it is only a cable's length wide, and therefore not to be attempted by a stranger. Rocks awash at low water extend from the Coquelihous more than half way across to Alderney, and a continuous sunken chain unite them to the Joyeaux rocks, a scattered group lying about half a mile to the westward.

The NOIRES PUTES are a group of rocks, four in number; three of which are always uncovered; the two outer rocks are much larger and higher than the other; these lie east and west, rather more than a cable's length apart; the westernmost of these rocks is flattopped, and elevated 55 feet above high water. The eastern one has a peak elevated 70 feet; this is sometimes called the Great Noire Pute, it lies S.W. by S., nearly three-quarters of a mile from Alderney telegraph. The whole group are quite steep-to outside.

AIGUILLON, COUPÉ, and ORBOUÉE, are three rocks (elevated only a few feet above high water), lying between Noires Putes and Les Etacs, in a W.S.W. direction, distant half a mile from the S.W. extreme of Alderney, and forming the southern boundary of the anchorage called Fossé Malières, or west bay. The Coupé, the middle of three rocks, is sometimes called the Cocked hat, which it somewhat resembles in appearance ; it is one of the marks for the Pierre au Vraic. Orbouée rock, the outer of the group, is awash at high springs; it is connected with the Coupé under water ; is steep to the southward and to the west, but there is a rock with only 2 fathoms on it at low water, lying N.W. by N. 1 cable from it.

ORBOUÉE BANK extends S. by W. rather more than half a mile from Orbouée rock ; it consists of a bank of gravel, sand, and broken shells; the general depths on it are 8 and 9 fathoms, but near its outer end there is as little as 3¾ fathoms ; this part rises in a narrow ridge of fine sand from the main bank, and is very difficult to pick up ; it is thrown up, apparently, by the turning of the stream. On the shoalest spot the great Nannel is seen a little open westward of outer of Les Etacs, and L'Etac de la Quoire in line with the north part of outer Noire Pute. The bank will be cleared by keeping the Pierres de Bút open westward of Les Etacs N.N.E., until L'Etac de la Quoire comes open to the eastward of Noires Putes, E. by N.

ANCHORAGE.—The best anchorage at the west end of Alderney is at the Fossé Malières, or west bay ; anchor here in 10 fathoms gravel, with the great Nannel touching the outer end of western Etac N. by E. ½ E. and Great Coquilehou seen clear inside Aiguillons S.E. by E. ½ E. Here a vessel will lie out of the tide. There is anchorage also outside of Orbouée rock in 7 fathoms on a S.S.W. bearing from it at the distance of a quarter of a mile, but it is exposed to the full force of the flood stream, and therefore not safe.

DIRECTIONS FOR ALDERNEY, AND THE HARBOUR OF RE-FUGE.—From the N.E., in hazy weather, it will be prudent to obtain a bearing of Cape de la Hague, when a vessel may stand boldly for the N.E. end of the island ; but should the weather be so thick that it cannot be discerned at the distance of 2 miles, neither the Cape nor the island should be approached within that distance ; to avoid the outlying rocks.

When nearing the Cape or the island the tides must be carefully considered ; and it may be useful to note that, on nearing the east end of Alderney, the Great Coquelihou rock open eastward of the island will keep a vessel in the stream of the Race, and the Casquets lights open north of Burhou island will keep her in the Swinge or Channel stream.

In clear weather a vessel may stand direct for the island. The leading mark into the anchorage within the breakwater is the tower of St. Anne church in line with the pier-head of the old harbour of Braye, S.W. ½ W.; and in fine weather it can be seen 5 or 6 miles off.

By night, bring the harbour (red) lights in line, bearing S.W. by W., and run in on this line, making careful allowance for the set of the tide.

From the northward and westward, do not bring the Casquets lights to the northward of West until the harbour lights are in line bearing S.W. by W., then run in as before.

Caution.—On approaching the harbour be particular to have the harbour lights *exactly* in line before shutting in the Casquets lights with Burhou island. When near high or low water at spring tides, the stream sets *across* the entrance of the harbour with great velocity, and great caution is then necessary in entering ; the bearing of the upper light should never be altered more than a quarter of a point on either side, or the lower light lost sight of, to ensure avoiding the rocky patches outside the Aiguillons on one side and the toe of the breakwater on the other.

Anchorage.—If not desirous of using the Government moorings, anchor after clearing the inner Line of battle ships set ; with the high light open to the northward of the low one, in 5 fathoms.

From the Southward, through the Race.—To pass outside Alderney South bank, keep Ortac well open of the Noires Putes rocks until Grande Folie comes open eastward of Queslingue rock. To pass inside the banks use the directions given at page 65 : after passing Bonit rock bring the high Noire Pute in line with Great Coquelihou, which mark will lead midway between the inner Race rock and Blanchard rock ; when Fort Albert comes on with Grande Folie, the high Noire Pute may be brought in line with L'Etac de la Quoire, and run on until the end of the breakwater is seen open of Florains point, to clear the Blanchard, after which steer North until the Grois rock comes in line with the Great Nannel, N.W. by W. ¾ W., to clear Sauquet rock. Grois rock in line with the east point of Burhou island W. by N. ¾ N. will lead nearly midway between Sauquet rock and the ledge : and Ortac rock in line with Noire Houmet, and open of the end of the breakwater W. by N., will lead a cable's length outside the ledge, and nearly the same distance outside the Grois rocks.

By Night.—The Casquets lights N.W. ¾ N. will lead a mile to the south-westward of Alderney south bank, and Cape La Hague light E. ¼ S. will clear it on the south side by half a mile; therefore bring Cape La Hague light to bear East or E. ¼ S., and run for it until the east end of Alderney bears N.N.W. ½ W. to clear the Race rock, after which steer N.E. by N. through the Race; when Cape La Hague light bears S.E. by E., or the Casquet lights are seen to the eastward of Burhou, steer more northerly (according to circumstances) to bring the harbour lights of Braye in line ; after which proceed according to directions given above. The Casquet lights in line, or open and shut with the east end of Burhou, W. by N. ¼ N., leads just 2 cables outside the Grois and the Ledge.

From the Southward, through the Swinge: steer for the south-western end of Alderney : on approaching the Pierre au Vraic be careful to open Tourgis beacon to the northward of Clonque fort, to pass to the northward of it ; if it be desired to pass to the south of Pierre au Vraic, bring the Clonque fort in line with the west end of Les Etacs to clear all the rocks to the south-eastward of that rock : when within the Pierre au Vraic the Great Nannel will soon come on with the east side of Burhou N.N.E. ¼ E., which mark will lead between Les Etacs bank and the Boues des Etacs ; proceed with this leading mark until Fort Albert is seen clear to the northward of the *upper* part of Tourgis fort, after which open the Great Nannel well to the eastward of Burhou to clear South rock : when the high Noire Pute is seen clear of the inner rock of Les Etacs you will be to the eastward of south rock, and when fort Albert flagstaff comes over the middle of Grosnez fort you will be well clear of the Barsier reef, and may round the Corbet rock at the distance of a cable's length if desired. From Corbet a course may be shaped direct for the end of the breakwater ; the only dangers near this line are Jumelles rocks, described at page 61 : they will be passed at a safe distance by keeping the end of the breakwater on a line of bearing E. ½ S. or East.

By Night it will be useful to remember that the Casquets lights are eclipsed by Ortac on a W.N.W. bearing : the line of eclipse on the *south* side of Ortac passes nearly a cable's length North of the Corbet rock : the Casquets lights are seen again on the north side of Ortac at the distance of a cable and a quarter north of Corbet rock.

Large ships should pass to the westward of Pierre au Vraic and up through the middle of the Swinge : on the west side of the south rock bank and a cable and a half or two cables north of Corbet rock, on which track nothing less than 8 fathoms at low water will be met with. To clear the outlying rocks in passing see Dangers in the Swinge at page 54.

Caution.—The tidal stream must be carefully considered and allowed for in navigating the Swinge : the first of the eastern stream or flood sets *on* Alderney : after high water it turns off to the northward and north-west : therefore entering the Swinge from the south on the first of the flood, under ordinary circumstances, it would be advisable to pass to the westward of the Pierre au Vraic ; and to the eastward of it at the latter part of the tide ; *except* in thick foggy weather, when the Alderney shore should be closed with cautiously at all times and the vessels anchored on or near the Orbouée bank or in S.W. bay until clear enough to proceed. No vessel should attempt to pass through the Swinge either way, in foggy weather, *with the tide :* at springs the stream runs from 7 to 8 knots, and it will therefore be evident that, at such a time, should a vessel come suddenly into danger, her destruction would be inevitable.

When passing through the Swinge from the northward ; on the *first* of the ebb or south-western stream, proceed along the Alderney shore, past the Etacs, and eastward of Pierre au Vraic. After low water, keep Burhou island and Ortac aboard ; making due allowance for the set of the S.E. tide, which will be met with after clearing the Casquet banks.

In westerly gales it is particularly necessary to take the above prescribed routes to avoid the overfalls ; which shift their positions through a regular course according to the direction of the stream. At such times the Swinge is only navigable by steamers of large size and power, and at some risk.

Vessels from the northward and eastward, as well as those from Alderney, bound to Guernsey or Jersey during westerly gales, should endeavour to push through the Race or Swinge channels directly the eastern stream *begins* to slack : the sea being then comparatively smooth : for as the western stream makes against the gale so does the sea rise and become dangerous : and as during the strength of this stream both the Race and Swinge channels are covered with broken water and highly dangerous, it is recommended at such times that vessels anchor in Alderney harbour of refuge, and wait a tide or a lull in the gale.

TIDAL STREAM round **ALDERNEY** is subject to changes and variations similar to those round Guernsey and Jersey, but possessing local peculiarities different from those islands, arising principally from the more prominent position of Alderney out in the channel stream ; but also in a great degree from the different form of the island itself as compared with the others.

As described in the Guernsey pilot, the course of the tidal stream round that island, so at Alderney, the stream revolves from east round by north to west and south ; running from every point of the compass during one tide (an ebb and a flood). As at Guernsey also the stream attains its greatest strength about high and low water, but (as might be expected from the situation of Alderney) its direction at this time is different, coinciding more nearly with the channel stream ; thus the strength of the stream (flood and ebb) on the north side of Alderney and the Casquets, runs on a line of direction about E. $\frac{1}{2}$ N. and W. $\frac{1}{2}$ S., whilst at the same periods round the Guernsey group of islands its general direction is about E.N.E. and W.S.W.

This change in the direction of the tidal stream may be considered as taking place on a line running close to the northward of the Casquets, past the Nannels, northward of Alderney and Cape La Hague. A glance at the chart will best illustrate how the flood stream, after passing through the Race, Swinge, and Ortac channels, is turned in an easterly direction by the force of the channel stream; also on the ebb tide, the channel stream running in a westerly direction, past Cape La Hague, Alderney, and the Casquets, is forced through the channels between these places in a southerly direction; but this description of the stream only applies to the periods of high and low water; in its transition from one to the other, peculiarities occur requiring a particular description.

The flood or north-eastern stream begins to make through the Race and Swinge channels when the tide has risen 3 hours by the shore, and it attains its greatest strength (7 to 8 knots) about high water. An hour after high water by the shore, the stream in its revolving course is setting about N.E. by E. and begins to abate in strength; still veering in direction and slacking in strength, it sets faintly to the N.W. at 3 hours after high water, causing a short slack in the Swinge and also on the N.W. side of Burhou; after which the ebb tide comes down and rushes through these channels with a velocity nearly as great as the flood. After low water the tide begins to veer to the southward and abates in strength; an hour and a half after low water the stream is setting from the northward on Alderney and Burhou, causing extensive slacks or eddies to the southward of these islands, and at half flood the offing stream, now very weak, sets to the S.E., causing a dead slack for a short period in all the channels between Alderney and the Casquets.

Having thus described the general course of the main tidal stream round Alderney, it is necessary to describe some of the most important eddies caused by the peculiar turning of the tide and the obstructions of the islands and rocks.

Alderney, the Casquets, and intermediate rocks, all narrow in proportion to their length, and each lying on a line of direction nearly east and west, are in the line of tide when the stream is at its strength, on both ebb and flood; therefore at these times the resistance they offer to the free course of the stream is small and the eddies under them insignificant; but as the stream in its rotary course moves out of this line of direction, extensive eddies are formed under the lee of Alderney, alternately on its northern and southern shores; these eddies are called the inshore streams.

On the northern shore of the island the inshore stream commences at Sauket rock and extends to the westward as far as Corbet rock, and within it to the southward of the vortex of the Swinge; running 9 hours to the westward and only 3 to the eastward; the former commencing an hour before high water and the latter at 2 hours flood. Along the southern side of the island, between Orbouée rock and Raz island, there are 9 hours of eastern and but 3 hours of western stream; the former stream commences one hour before low water and runs along the land towards Longy during the whole flood and until 2 hours ebb again; in the neighbourhood of which, meeting with the south-western stream from the Race, it suddenly veers and unites with it; the latter stream commences at 2 hours ebb and sets towards the Orbouée for 3 hours or until 5 hours ebb, at which time it joins the south-western stream from the Swinge.

These two great eddies or inshore streams are exactly the reverse of each other; their general courses and action will be easily understood by reference to a chart of Alderney and a careful perusal of the above remarks; but as the northern eddy sets across the entrance of Braye harbour of refuge at times with great velocity and then constitutes the principal danger there, a particular description of its action will follow.

The direction of the flood stream, half an hour before high water (about which time it attains its greatest strength), is about East; this being the line of direction of Alderney it runs full on the west point of the island by which the stream is now fairly divided, one part rushing through the Race along the south side of the island with a velocity of between 7 and 8 knots, the other through the Swinge at about the same rate, leaving a small eddy (as noticed before) under the east end of the island, near the Sauket rock. At high water by the shore the turning of the offing stream from an easterly to a northerly direction relieves the pressure of the Swinge stream from the end of the breakwater; and at this time during a spring tide the Swinge stream is running to the eastward with a velocity of 3 knots at the distance of 60 fathoms from the end of the breakwater; the intermediate space being filled up by a stream setting round the breakwater to the westward at the rate of 3 knots: this latter is the inshore eddy or ebb stream: it commences in the eddy near Sauket rock and begins to set to the westward (as stated above) an hour before high water: at this period the western stream sets round the end of the breakwater in volume a mere thread, but it gradually increases in magnitude as the turning of the offing stream removes the pressure of the Swinge stream from the end of the breakwater.

The most dangerous period of this tide and eddy is about high water, at which time they set past each other, separated only a few feet, with the velocity stated above; great caution must therefore be used should it be necessary for a long screw vessel to enter the harbour during this period. The great length of the breakwater obstructing the course of the western stream being the cause of the danger, the current is of course strongest near the outer end of that structure, and therefore at such times it will be advisable to enter the harbour a little to the southward of the mid-channel course rather than risk a near approach to the end of the breakwater. An hour after high water the inner edge of the east-going Swinge stream is removed to the distance of 200 fathoms from the breakwater end, and both streams beginning to abate in strength, the danger gradually ceases.

At 2 hours ebb the Swinge stream, now slacking fast and veering to the westward, sets on the Nannels, the western stream running past the end of the breakwater at the rate of 3 knots, meeting the eastern stream in the Swinge a little outside Corbet rock, uniting with it and both setting towards the Nannels; within Corbet rock the western stream sets down to the west end of the island.

At half ebb by the shore the offing tide is setting faintly to the N.W., and there is slack water in the Swinge, but only for a few minutes, after which the westerly Swinge stream makes there, and immediately commences to run past the breakwater end with renewed strength until low water by the shore; gradually slacking as the offing stream veers from W. $\frac{1}{2}$ S. to the southward. Whilst the tide is veering through the latter section of its course there is slack water at the entrance of Braye harbour; after an interval of which, the stream sets across the end of the breakwater in an E.S.E. direction, 2 hours after low water.

The RACE of ALDERNEY is the name applied to the strait between that island and Cape La Hague. Here, as in the Swinge and Ortac channels, the stream sets to the south-westward at half ebb by the shore, and runs in that direction, with the variations given as under, for 6 hours, or until half-flood, and the contrary with respect to the north-eastern stream; for there is but little slack water there.

The greatest strength of the south-western stream (about $2\frac{1}{2}$ hours) begins 5 hours after high water at Alderney, and ends $4\frac{1}{2}$ hours before the following high water. The greatest strength of the north-eastern stream continues about 2 hours; that is, from one hour before high water at Alderney, until one hour after. In great springs, the velocity of the south-western stream or ebb is nearly 7 knots, and of the north-eastern stream nearly 8 knots, neaps $5\frac{1}{2}$ knots. The first $2\frac{3}{4}$ hours of the south-western stream in the Race, that is, from half-ebb till low water, sets W.S.W.; and the last 2 hours, that is, from low water till half-flood, sets S.W.; and the contrary for the first and last $3\frac{1}{4}$ hours of the north-eastern stream; which between half-flood and high water, sets very strongly round Cape La Hague. There is therefore $5\frac{1}{2}$ hours south-western, and $6\frac{1}{2}$ hours north-eastern stream, that is half an hour's difference between the Race tide and that in the Ortac and Swinge channels.

In boisterous weather, if the wind and stream are ever so obliquely opposed, the sea breaks in all parts of the Race, as if it were over small knolls or patches, which makes it difficult and often dangerous for small vessels to pass through; at such times there are heavy overfalls over all the sunken rocks and banks, which must of course be carefully avoided.

DANGERS in the RACE.—Both the outer and inner Race rock have been repeatedly examined and well sounded over without finding less water than 18 feet, reduced to low water of spring tides, and this is believed to be the true depth over each of them at that period ; and there is then 12 feet on the Blanchard rock.   There is a rocky bank lying W.N.W. 3½ miles from Cape La Hague light, which, although probably not dangerous, throws up a strong overfall, and should be avoided.   The fairway of the Race lies between this bank and the Race rock ; the distance between these points is 3¼ miles ; the soundings in this (the narrowest part of the Race) are regular, between 22 and 24 fathoms, but the bottom entirely rocky throughout.

Middle Rock, an isolated head with 7 fathoms over it at low water, lies S. by E. ¾ E. 4¼ miles from Alderney telegraph tower ; from it the Casquets bear N.W. ¼ N. 9¾ miles, and Cape La Hague E. ⅔ N. 8½ miles. When the tide is running strong, the position of this rock is marked by a breaker or overfall, and there is at all times a ripple over it ; it may be avoided by day or night by attending to the directions given at page 67 for passing through the Race.

CAUTION.—When running through the Race of Alderney, it is at all times best to take the fairway of the channel described above ; bearing in mind that the north-eastern stream (between half-flood and high water on the shore) sets very strongly round Cape La Hague, off which there project several sunken rocks.

The direct course from the Race to the Little Russel channel is W. by S. ½ S., and from the Casquets to that channel nearly S.W. ½ S. If bound therefore from the Race or Casquets to the Little Russel, between the periods of low water and half-flood, and of high water and half-ebb, allowance must be made for the stream, which obliquely crosses the courses during these periods, and great care must be taken to avoid the Middle rock and the Banc de la Schôle.

Bearings and Distances.

Casquets to Grunes d l'Ouest	S.W. by W. ¼ W.	16½	miles.
„	Hanois Lighthouse	S.W. by W. ⅙ W.	21½ „
„	Roustel Rock	S.W. ⅔ S.	14⅔ „
„	Blanchard Rock	S. by W.	18 „
Pierre au Vraic to Roustel Rock	S.W. ⅔ W.	14⅔ „
Race Rock to Platte Boue	W.S.W. (southerly)	15⅚ „
„	Roustel Rock	W.S.W.	19 „
„	Blanchard Rock	S.W. ¼ S.	18¼ „
„	E. side Paternosters	S.S.W. ¼ W.	25 „
„	Belle Hougue Point	S. by W. ½ W.	27⅕ „

BANC DE LA SCHOLE, lies nearly in the direct line between the Great Russel channel and the Race of Alderney ; like most other banks between the Channel Islands, it consists of a mixture of fine gravel, sand, and shell : it is very steep to the southward and westward, but shoals gradually on the N.E. side.

Taking the 5 fathoms line as the first contour of the bank it is 1½ miles long (in a N. by E. and S. by W. direction) and a quarter of a mile wide near the middle, tapering off to a mere ridge at the extremes. The 10 fathoms contour of the bank includes a space 2⅓ miles long (N.N.E. and S.S.W.) and ¾ of a mile wide : and the 20 fathoms contour will include a length of 5 miles by 1½ miles. The top of the bank is very narrow, and consists of small semicircular ridges of sand (convex to the S.W.), the general depth over which is 3 fathoms at the lowest spring tides ; near the middle of the bank, however, as little as 2 fathoms was found, having some spots near with 2½ fathoms.

The soundings taken on this bank at different periods tend to prove that its apex is continually varying in altitude, and it is probable, therefore, that it also shifts its position (within a particular and limited space) according to tide, weather, &c. : the position of the shoalest spot on the bank has not altered *perceptibly*, however, from 1861 to 1869 : the marks for it are Alderney telegraph tower N.N.E., ⅛ E., 7¾ miles. Casquet lights N. by W. 10½ miles, and Serk Windmill S.W. by W. 10 miles.

DIRECTIONS.—Between low water and half-flood it will be advisable to pass to the eastward of the Banc de la Schôle, but between half-ebb and low water to the westward, because in both these cases the tide will favour the attempt. Doyle column (Guernsey) in line with the Fauconnière rock, W. ¾ S., or the Etac de Serk open to the eastward of the Burons, or the lighthouse at Cape de la Hague, E.N.E., leads to the south-eastward and southward of the bank. Doyle column just open to the northward of the northernmost bluff land on Herm, W. by S. ¾ S., or the Gouliot pass kept open to the westward of the Bec du Nez (Serk) or the lighthouse at Cape de la Hague, E. ⅔ N., leads to the north-west-ward and northward ; St. Martin point, appearing mid-way between the Fauconnière and the south-western end of Herm island, points to its shoalest part ; and the whole of Burhou shut in behind the Etacs and Noires Putes, N. ½ W. will lead along the east side of the bank at the distance of more than a mile. In bad weather, if the wind and tide are ever so obliquely opposed to each other, the sea breaks very dangerously on all parts of the bank.

OYSTER-GROUND.—About 11 miles in a north-easterly direction from La Coupé point, the north-eastern extreme of Jersey, and nearly 14 miles in a south-eastern direction from the middle of Serk, lies an extensive oyster ground, the marks for which are as follows, viz., the island of Jethou in one with Bec du Nez (Serk), Rozel mill in line with the Burons de Drouilles, and the two high heads of the Pierres de Lecq in one with point Grosnez. There is, however, little or no difference to be observed with respect to the various depths of water in its neighbourhood.

CHAPTER III.

THE ISLAND OF JERSEY, WITH ITS APPROACHES AND ADJACENT DANGERS.

Variation 21° West in 1870.

JERSEY.—The form of this island is that of a parallelogram, its greatest length E.S.E. and W.N.W. being $9\frac{1}{4}$ miles, and its breadth $5\frac{3}{4}$ miles.

The middle of the island (in an E.S.E. and W.N.W. direction) presents an uniform level surface, elevated about 280 feet above mean tide ; its northern shore being from 100 to 150 feet higher. By a singular contrast with the island of Guernsey, the declivity of which lies towards the north-west, Jersey declines towards the south-east ; and to this circumstance may probably be attributed the pre-eminence which the latter enjoys in the richness of its productions, the luxuriant appearance of its surface, and the peculiar mildness of its climate.

Granite and syenitic rocks are the principal formations.

The interior of the island is well wooded, fertile, and intersected by deep beautiful valleys, running from south to north ; through which numerous streams find their way to the low land on the south coast ; several occasionally uniting before discharging themselves into the sea.

Jersey possesses several good bays or roadsteads besides its artificial harbours. The best among the former is Gorey roads, at Grouville bay, on the east side of the island ; and St. Aubin bay on its south coast ; in either of which a good and well found ship may ride out the heaviest gales from any quarter in safety. The principal artificial harbour is at the seaport of St. Helier, which is the chief town of the island, and is situated at the east side of St. Aubin bay. There are also harbours of inferior magnitude at St. Aubin (on the north side of the bay), at Gorey and Rozel, but they all dry at low water spring tides.

Jersey has its own legislature, *the States*, consisting of the Lieut.-Governor and the Bailiff of the Royal Court, appointed by the Crown ; twelve Jurats (Judges) of the Royal Court, elected for life by the ratepayers ; the Rectors of the twelve Parishes into which the island is divided, and the Constables of the same; also a Deputy for each Parish (St. Helier having three Deputies), elected in the same manner for three years. Appeals lie to the Queen in Council.

This island, like Guernsey and Alderney, is in the diocese of Winchester. Each parish has its own church, the spires of which serve as the principal landmarks.

The old Norman French is spoken by the natives, but the English language is rapidly coming into use.

The population of the island, according to the census of 1861, amounted to 55,613 ; it is now supposed to be slightly in excess of this number.

A considerable portion of the island is laid out in orchards; cider and apples being among its chief exports. Early potatoes are also raised in great quantity for the London market. The chief imports are grain, flour, cattle, and timber for ship-building ; the latter principally from Sweden, Norway, and North America ; the former from France.

Ship-building was formerly carried on with great success and some very fine and fast vessels have been built here of 500 to 1,200 tons burthen, but the trade is now in a state of decay.

There are now 446 vessels belonging to the island, and one steam tug, measuring 48,812 tons, and employing 4,014 seamen: sixty of these vessels, manned by about 600 seamen, are employed in or connected with the New-foundland cod fishery.

St. Helier, the chief, and, correctly speaking, only town of the island, is built on low land open to the south, but overlooked and sheltered on the north by a semicircular elevated plateau completely commanding it. The town is well built, and so extensive that in it are located about a half the population of the entire island, nearly 30,000 souls. It has a college and several churches ; the spires of which latter, together with the noble fortress of Fort Regent on the east side of the town, are the most remarkable objects from the sea.

Supplies.—St. Helier has a well supplied market, where fresh meat and poultry may be purchased at about the same prices as in London. Fish are scarce, vegetables and fruit abundant and cheap.

PILOTS.—The following is extracted from the Law on Pilotage issued by the States of the island of Jersey in January 1857 :

" The master of every vessel bound to this island, and arrived one mile West of the Corbière rock, shall lay his vessel to, as soon as a pilot boat is in sight, and take a pilot on board as soon as one presents himself, on pain of paying such pilot the highest rate of pilotage.

" Fishing boats and vessels admeasuring forty tons and less shall not be liable to take a pilot, but all other vessels employed in the coasting trade shall be liable so to do, paying half the pilotage dues, when it has been ascertained that they are employed in the coasting trade only, unless it be otherwise provided by the tariff.

" When the weather is so stormy as to prevent the pilot from boarding a vessel at sea, the master of such vessel and the pilot shall so steer that the pilot boat may take the lead, and serve as a guide, and such vessel shall be liable to the same pilotage dues as if the pilot had boarded her.

" Any pilot passing a vessel coming to the island shall be liable to a penalty of five pounds sterling, unless such vessel have already a pilot on board, or the weather is so stormy as to prevent the pilot from boarding her.

" Every pilot shall have a flag striped horizontally red and white, 6 feet long and 4 wide, which on boarding a vessel and taking charge, he shall direct the master thereof to hoist at the peak as a signal that a pilot is on board, under the penalty of five pounds sterling against the master refusing to do so.

" Any pilot undertaking to pilot a vessel shall, when required so to do, exhibit to the master or mate of such vessel his warrant, together with this law and the tariff annexed thereto, under the penalty of thirty shillings."

Like Guernsey and Alderney, Jersey is completely encompassed with dangers of every description, which are rendered doubly formidable by the great rise and fall, as well as rapidity, of the tides. The most remarkable are, the Pierres de Lecq (vulgarly called the Pater-Nosters) the Drouilles, and the Ecréhos, on the northern and north-eastern sides ; the Violet bank surrounding the south-eastern angle ; and the Minquiers ledge, with many other rocks, to the southward.

APPROACH TO JERSEY FROM THE NORTHWARD OUTLYING ROCKS AND DANGERS.

BANC DESORMES, lies $3\frac{1}{2}$ miles to the northward of Grosnez point and a like distance from the highest of the Pierres de Lecq, or Pater-noster rocks. It is a bank of rocky ground, a mile long N.N.W. and S.S.E., and a third of a mile broad; the depths on which are generally 12 to 15 fathoms, excepting near its extremes, where two large conical masses rise from the bottom ; the northern one to within 23 feet of the surface, and the southern to $7\frac{1}{2}$ fathoms at low water. The latter bears from the former S.S.E., distant three quarters of a mile.

On the 23 feet rock, La Moye signal post is only just shut in behind the outer part of Pinnacle S. $\frac{1}{2}$ W. ; and the south-western high rock of the Pierres de Lecq appears shut in with Belle Hougue point nearly as far as the outer part of its high bluff S.E. $\frac{1}{4}$ S.

These marks may be used as necessary to clear the rock in any direction, for it is very small and pointed and there is 9 to 12 fathoms close-to all round.

PIERRES DE LECQ, is a rocky group the western end of which lies N.E. by N., nearly 2¾ miles from Grosnez point, the north-west extreme of Jersey, and nearly abreast Grève de Lecq bay; from which the middle or highest rock bears N.N.E., distant 2½ miles. There are four large rocks, elevated from 20 to 30 feet above high water, lying near the middle of the S.E. side of the reef; from the highest of these, the reef dries to the N.W. for nearly a mile at low water : and within it (to the S.E.) for about the same distance there are banks of sunken rocks, the outermost of which have only 20 feet over them at low water. The most dangerous rock inside the main group is called the——

GRUNE DE LECQ, which dries 2 feet at low water, and lies S. b. E. ¼ E., nearly a half a mile from the aforesaid great central rock of the group.

DIRECTIONS.—The Pierres de Lecq may be cleared to the westward by keeping the Corbiere rock in line with Pinnacle point S. by W. ¾ W. A nearer mark may be had with St. Peters mill in line with Greve de Lecq flagstaff S. ¾ E. To pass inside of them, keep the Tour de Rozel shut in behind Belle Hougue point S.E., until the white tower in Greve de Lecq (a white sandy bay) comes in line with the eastern point of the bay S.W. ½ W., with which mark you may run to the north-eastward until Rozel mill appears over Belle Hougue point S.S.E. ¼ E., which clears the rocks to the north-eastward.

In absence of marks or at night, pass through the middle of the channel between Jersey and the Pierres de Lecq, Drouilles, Ecrehos, &c.

DROUILLES CHANNEL, lies between the dangerous rocky group of that name and the Pierres de Lecq : it is about 5 miles wide ; is quite safe for vessels of any size, and free of any outlying danger : having regular soundings in 13 fathoms throughout its entire extent.

For a description of the Drouilles and Ecrehos rocks, see pages 126, 130.

Appearance of Jersey from the Westward.—Vessels approaching Jersey from the westward will make the land about St. Ouen bay ; of which the high precipitous bluff of Grosnez, situate at its *north* extreme, will appear to be the most remarkable part. Special attention is called to this particular feature of Jersey, as in making the coast of Guernsey from the westward, the bluff land (at Pleinmont) would there appear as the *south* extreme of land, the northern part declining gradually to the sea level.

Note.—The soundings given in Chapter III. of this work have been reduced to a zero corresponding to a *range* of 37 feet tide; and the lowest tide registered in Jersey between 1864 and 1869 fell 22 inches below that level.

To the southward of Grosnez the high land runs nearly level. On the edge of the plateau overlooking St. Ouen bay stands St. Ouen mill, with the church (having a steeple) a little beyond it. Still farther in the background will be seen St. Peter's church, with its lofty spire ; and occasionally, glimpses will be had of the other churches and mills of the island, still more distant.

An extensive range of buildings known as St. Peter's barracks, is the most conspicuous object on the heights near the south part of St. Ouen bay ; the signal post of La Moye appearing to the southward of it, near the extreme of the land in that direction. Between these latter objects there is an extensive district covered with sand, called the Quenvais, part of which forms a very remarkable feature in the appearance of this part of the coast. On the extreme south of St. Ouen bay the huge rock called the Corbière will be seen (if not shut in with the high land of La Moye point) ; and to the northward of it, along the sandy shore of St. Ouen bay, will appear La Rocco fort and tower, and five other towers, besides the one at L'Etac point, near the north extreme of the bay. Between L'Etac and Grosnez points there is a very remarkable rock called Pinnacle.

ST. OUEN BAY, the appearance of which from the sea is described above, forms the western coast of Jersey between Grosnez point and the Corbière. It affords good shelter in easterly winds, but the greater part of the bay being rocky and foul, the anchorage is thereby limited to a space of ground about half a mile square, near the south part of the bay off La Rocco tower. This part is, however, very easy of access, and may be safely used by the largest ships without pilots. Of course no vessel should anchor in St. Ouen bay during westerly winds.

DANGERS in and off St. Ouen Bay.—An extensive reef, dry at low water, stretches off to the westward of La Rocco tower for about half a mile, and then runs along the shore to the southward in the direction of the Corbière, which it unites with Corbière point. The whole of this reef is covered before high water, except a small rocky clump near the middle of it. Between La Rocco tower and L'Etac there is a fine beach of white sand, but at low water it is fringed with rocks throughout its entire extent. Off L'Etac point to the westward this reef dries out to the distance of three-quarters of a mile from the shore at low water ; the greater part covers before half flood, and no part of it is visible at high water.

The Rigdon Bank lies at the outer edge of the sunken part of the L'Etac reef, nearly 2 miles to the westward of L'Etac point. It consists of ridges of rock, whose interstices are filled up with sand and gravel. It lies about E.N.E. and W.S.W., a mile long and a quarter of a mile wide. The general depth on the bank is 3 to 5 fathoms, but there are two rocks with only 11 feet over them at low water; one of these is situated near the middle of the bank, the other at its north-eastern extreme.   The bank is very steep-to on the outside; within (between it and L'Etac reef), there is a channel about a third of a mile wide called the Swatchway, in which the general depth is 6 fathoms, and which is frequently used by vessels of 200 and 300 tons burthen.

Plémont point open of Grosnez point, E. ½ S., clears Rigdon bank to the northward.   St. Peter church (spire) open southward of No. 2 martello tower (in St. Ouen bay), bearing S.E. ¾ E., leads to the south-westward of it, and St. Peter church (spire) open north-eastward of No. 1 martello tower, S.E. ½ S., clears it to the north-eastward.

The best leading mark through the Swatchway, between Rigdon bank and L'Etac reef, is to keep all the high heads of the Pierres des Lecq (or Paternoster rocks) about a half a point open of Grosnez bluff, bearing E.N.E.

WEST ROCK, known to some fishermen as Grey bank, lies 1½ miles outside, or to the westward, of Rigdon bank; it consists of a mass of rock, very steep on the outside, 1½ cables long N.E. and S.W. by a cable broad, on which the general depths are from 8 to 10 fathoms, excepting at its apex, near the middle, on which there is only 6 fathoms at low water. On this spot St. Peter's church spire appears a little open to the northward of a small square fort on the beach in St. Ouen's bay, and a little open to the southward of No. 2 tower. S.E. by E. ¼ E.   The highest of the Pierres de Lecq is open 8° of Grosnez bluff, and the same bluff and the Corbière rock subtends an angle of 72°.   The shoal part is well marked near low water by a strong ripple.

The channel between West rock and Rigdon bank is more than a mile wide and quite clear, with 12 to 15 fathoms in it.

The Great Bank extends from Corbière rock on a N.N.W. bearing to the distance of a mile and three-quarters, and is a third of a mile wide. It consists entirely of sand, and has a general depth of 8 to 9 fathoms over it, excepting at two spots, where narrow ridges of fine sand rise to within 5 fathoms of the surface at low water.   The outer of these ridges is situate at the north extreme of the bank, close to the deep water, and is about a quarter of a mile long in an E.S.E. direction; the inner ridge is similar to the outer one, but only about half its length.   The middle of the inner ridge lies N. by W. ½ W. half a mile from the Boiteaux rock. Between these ridges there is a good channel, rather more than half a mile wide, having regular soundings in it, from 8 to 9 fathoms, sand. St. Ouen mill open southward of No. 2 tower (about a third of the distance between it and the small square fort on the beach in St. Ouen bay) bearing E. ¾ N., touches the extreme end of the bank to the north-ward. Jument rock (a whitewashed rock eastward of the Corbière) open and shut of the inside part of Corbière rock, S.E. ¼ S., clears it outside to the westward; and Jument rock in line with the high-water rock, situate about midway between Corbière point and Corbiére rock, S.S.E., clears its inner extreme. St. Ouen mill a little open northward of Square fort, bearing E. by N. ⅔ N,, leads through the middle of the passage between the north and south ridges.

ANCHORAGE.—The only good anchorage in St. Ouen bay, where a vessel may be sheltered from the tide, is between the Great bank and La Rocco tower, with St. Ouen mill a little open northwards of the small square fort on the beach, between Nos. 2 and 3 towers, bearing E. by N. ⅔ N., and Corbière rock S.S.W., in 7 fathoms, sand.

La Frouquie Pass lies between La Frouquie and La Boue rocks. The former stands at the outer edge of the reef extending from La Rocco tower to the Corbière rock, bearing due North a half a mile from the latter. La Boue is situate near the inner part of the sunken reef within Les Boiteaux, N.W. ¾ N. a third of a mile from Corbière rock; it is elevated 1 foot above half tide. La Frouquie covers 6 feet at high-water springs. The clearing marks given above for the outer and inner parts of the Great bank are the best to enter this pass to the northward, for should La Boue and La Frouquie both be covered, you cannot go too near the former so long as you have Jument rock in sight inside the Corbière rock, nor can you touch La Frouquie without opening Jument rock to the eastward of the high rock between Corbière point and La Corbière rock. There is a small rock off La Frouquie with only 1 foot on it at low-water springs, which lies on the line of Jument rock and a beacon pole on the west side of the high rock between Corbière point and Corbière rock. With this exception there is a clear passage of more than a cable wide, having 2½ fathoms at low water.

From this description it will be seen that no vessel ought to attempt to run through when the tide is low; at half tide and above (that is when La Boue rock is nearly awash), it is quite safe for vessels under 15 feet draught.

At or about this period, therefore, enter the pass, about midway between La Frouquie and La Boue, with Jument rock midway between the Cor-bière rock and the large rock situate midway between it and Corbière point; and when St. Ouen church (spire) comes on with the high rocky clump outside, or to the south-westward of La Rocco tower, bearing N.E. by E., steer for the Corbière rock; which must be approached to the distance of three-quarters of a cable; circling round the Corbière rock at this distance from it, and running out to the southward when Pinnacle rock comes nearly in line with the outer part of the Corbière.

CORBIÈRE POINT, at the south-west end of Jersey, is a small low bluff with a flagstaff on the summit, and two small houses at its side. Just within the point the land rises at a steep slope, and soon unites with the high table land of La Moye.

CORBIÈRE ROCK, standing a quarter of a mile westward of the point, and connected with it by a reef of rocks which dry after last quarter ebb, is 70 feet above high water, and is very remarkable. It stands prominently out from the coast line of the island, and forms the principal landmark for vessels approaching from the westward; it may be seen in clear weather at the distance of 10 or 12 miles.

DANGERS OFF THE CORBIÈRE.—The principal dangers off the Corbière are the Green rock, Les Boiteaux, and Noirmontaise.

Green Rock, the outermost danger, has 11 feet on it at low water. It lies N.W. by W. nearly three-quarters of a mile from the Corbière, and 2 cables from the Boiteaux, on the same line of bearing. The marks for it are St. Ouen mill just within or to the eastward of No. 3 martello tower in St. Ouen bay (counting from the northward) bearing N.E. by E. $\frac{1}{2}$ E., and the whitewashed rock within the Corbière (called Jument) in line with La Moye point, S.E. $\frac{3}{4}$ E.

Another rock with only 8 feet on it, lies N.N.E. distant 1 cable from the Green rock. Both rocks will be cleared to the north-westward by keeping St. Ouen windmill open northward of the aforesaid martello tower; and to the southward by keeping La Moye signal-post open southward of Jument rock. La Moye signal-post in line with Jument rock leads 3 cables South of the Green rock, and half a cable clear (on the same side) of the Noirmontaise reef.

Les Boiteaux are two rocks only 30 fathoms apart, lying within the Green rock; they dry 9 feet at low water and bear about N.W. by W. $\frac{1}{2}$ W. distant nearly half a mile from the Corbière. From the southern Boiteaux, St. Ouen church is seen touching the southern side of the 4th martello tower N.E. by E. $\frac{1}{4}$ E., and La Moye signal-post is in line with the north side of the peak of the Corbière rock S.E. by E. $\frac{1}{2}$ E.

Noirmontaise Reef dries 4 feet at low water, and lies a quarter of a mile to the westward of the Corbière.

There is another reef lying a cable's length westward of the Corbière, having 4 feet over its shoalest part at low water: also a large rock bearing S. by E. distant a cable from the Corbière, and which uncovers after first quarter ebb. All these dangers may be cleared to the southward by the same mark used to clear the Boiteaux rocks.

There is a narrow deep-water channel between the Green rock and Les Boiteaux : also the narrow channel within the Noirmontaise and La Boue rocks, close to the Corbière leading to La Frouquie pass ; but the space included between Les Boiteaux and La Boue, and from the latter rock to within a cable's length of the Corbière, is so thickly studded with sunken rocks, as to be very dangerous, even for boats, at low water.

JUMENT ROCK, remarkable from having a large white patch painted on it, lies about a third of a mile within the Corbière to the south-east-ward, and an eighth of a mile from the high bluff next to the eastward of Corbière point ; with which bluff it is connected by a reef dry at low water. There is a dangerous rock which dries only at last quarter ebb, at half a cable outside the Jument ; it should not be approached therefore nearer than a quarter of a mile.

LA MOYE POINT, a high cliffy bluff, a mile to the eastward of the Corbière, is safe of approach from the westward, at a reasonable distance from the shore ; but at 1¼ cables off it, there is a sunken rock, having only 6 feet over it at low water ; and close to the eastward of this rock and probably connected with it, lie the dangerous rocky group called the Kaines, the highest of which only covers at last quarter flood. The outer sunken rock of the Kaines lies 2 cables from the shore.

All these dangers will be cleared by keeping the Corbière open a little to the westward of Jument, until Tabor chapel (a remarkable white building standing on the high land near the middle of and over-looking St. Brelade bay) opens out a little to the eastward of Grosse Tête.

ST. BRELADE BAY, near the south-west end of the island, between La Moye and Le Fret points, is much contracted by an extensive reef that fringes its eastern shore, and the anchorage in it is further cut up by the Fournier and Fourché rocks. It is therefore very inferior to St. Aubin bay, and more exposed to the sea in southerly gales ; neverthe-less, small vessels and even large open boats anchored off Port Bouilly, have been known to ride out fresh gales from this (the most exposed) quarter in safety.

Under all circumstances of wind and weather there is much less sea on the western than on the eastern side of the bay, and it seems to be quite certain, that if a breakwater were to be built out from Grosse Tête to the Fournier rock, the anchorage off Beau Port and Bouilly would be safe at all times.

On approaching St. Brelade bay from the westward the most remarkable objects seen are the high square rock (called Grosse Tête) under the high cliffy land of La Moye on the west side of the bay ; and Noirmont tower, standing prominently out at the end of the low point of that name to the eastward. On opening out the eastern side of the bay clear of Grosse Tête, the white sandy beach appears, and the two martello towers built to defend it; beyond are villa residences and scattered groups of houses; and overtopping all (on the high land near the middle of the bay) stands Tabor chapel (a plain white building with slate roof) forming the principal landmark in it.

DANGERS in and near ST. BRELADE BAY.—Near the middle of the bay are the Fournier and Fourché rocks, lying about W.N.W. and E.S.E. of each other, distant a quarter of a mile. The best anchorage is round the Fournier, distant from it rather more than a cable: the ground is quite clean up to the base of this rock, which is of very small extent. The Fournier dries 9 feet and the Fourché 10 feet at low water. The other but less important rocks of the bay are the Fournier du Hâvre, which dries 17 feet, at nearly a third of a mile within the Fournier, the Platte Houmet, drying 12 feet, in the bight of the bay near the shore, and the Rousse rock (60 feet high) on the east side of the bay.

Banc de St. Brelade is a reef of sunken rocks commencing at half a mile South of La Moye point, and extending eastward for nearly three-quarters of a mile: the least water found (29 feet) is near the middle of the bank.

Banc Le Fret, lying immediately off the point of that name, distant from it rather less than a quarter of a mile, is rather more than a quarter of a mile in length N.W. and S.E., and of an oval form. There are several rocks on its eastern side with 22 and 24 feet on them, and one on the west side with only 14 feet; the marks for the latter are Nicolle and Noirmont towers in line E. by S. ¼ S., and the western martello tower in St. Brelade bay in line with the Rousse Frouquie N.N.E. ½ E.

At 2 cables eastward of Banc Le Fret, in the direction of Noirmont tower, there is another rocky bank on which the least water is 20 feet. Both this bank and Le Fret, as well as Banc de St. Brelade, may be cleared inside (or to the north-eastward) by bringing the Corbière nearly on with La Moye point; and the two first named will be cleared outside by opening the peak of Corbière rock a little to the southward of Jument.

DIRECTIONS.—Vessels from the north-westward bound to St. Brelade or St. Aubin bay, on nearing the shore of Jersey should keep Plémont point open of Grosnez point E. ½ S., until the Corbière rock bears S. by E., or St. Ouen church and mill are in line S.E. by E., to clear the Rigdon shoal. With these marks they will be abreast the shoal, and from thence should steer so as to round the Corbière at the distance of about a mile: or keep St. Ouen windmill open northward of No. 3 martello tower in St. Ouen bay E.N.E., until La Moye signal-post is seen over the top of the Corbière, to avoid the Green rock. When La Moye signal-post opens southward of Jumet rock (white) bearing E. by S. $\frac{3}{4}$ S., or the outer part of the high table-land within Noirmont point is seen a little open of Le Fret point, a vessel will be clear of the Noirmontaise reef and all other dangers south-westward of the Corbière, and may run for La Moye point until La Motte islet is just shut in behind Noirmont point, and Noirmont tower bears S.E. by E. $\frac{1}{4}$ E., which is the leading mark for the fairway between the Kaines (off La Moye point) and Banc de St. Brelade. When Tabor chapel comes in line with or a little open of Battery point N.E. by E., take it as a leading mark through the western pass into the inner anchorage off St. Brelade. If desirous of approaching the inner anchorage through the eastern pass, open Tabor chapel a little to the eastward of a small dark-coloured house on the beach in St. Brelade bay N.E. $\frac{1}{2}$ N., and run in on that line.

Anchor within the Fournier rock, on the above given leading lines and between them, when La Moye bluff comes nearly in line (or a little open) of the outer part of Grosse Tête, about W. by N. $\frac{3}{4}$ N., in 5 fathoms, fine sand. Large vessels not wishing to anchor within the Fournier, may lie in 8$\frac{1}{2}$ fathoms gravel with the western pass leading mark on, and the Jumet rock just shut in with La Moye point. The ground in this bay is remarkable for holding.

PORTELET BAY, between Le Fret and Noirmont points, is small, and further contracted by rocks extending to the westward of the latter point as well as from the centre of the bay (westward of Janvrin tower), which together with the rapidity of the tidal stream across the entrance of the bay, render it dangerous of approach to vessels even of the smallest size.

The dangers are further increased by Portelet ledge, an isolated mass of rock lying S.W. by S., a quarter of a mile from Janvrin tower. The shoalest spot on this ledge is in 2 feet at low water ; from which La Moye signal-post is seen over a remarkable sharp-peaked rock, semi-detached from Le Fret point, N.W., and Noirmont tower is *within* the high part of Rocque Poisson, 2 cables from the latter. Noirmont tower in line with the high part of Rocque Poisson, or a little open *outside* it, just clears Portelet ledge to the southward.

Anchorage.—In case of necessity compelling a vessel to anchor in Portelet bay, the best spot is in 4$\frac{1}{2}$ fathoms, sand, with La Moye point just shut in with Le Fret point, and Janvrin tower N.E. Anchor *outside* Portelet ledge (only in the above case) a little to the eastward of it, in 6 fathoms; with Corbière rock nearly in line with La Moye point N.W. $\frac{1}{4}$ W., Janvrin tower N. by E. $\frac{1}{2}$ E., and Elizabeth castle just open southward of Noirmont tower, East.

ST. AUBIN BAY.—The whole of the anchorage in this fine bay, though surrounded on every side by rocks, is free from any ground capable of damaging a vessel's cable, and is sheltered from all winds but those from S.S.E. (round southerly) to W.N.W., and partially even from them. South-westerly gales send in a heavy rolling sea between half flood and high water, but in proportion as the water falls the sea subsides, the rocks in the offing greatly contributing to break its force and effect.

St. Helier, the principal town on the island, is on the north-eastern side of the bay, and the little town of St. Aubin with its castle (which gives its name to the bay) is on the western side, opposite St. Helier ; their distance from each other being about 2½ miles. Both these towns have stone pier harbours, wherein vessels lie aground at low water, upon a soft muddy sand ; the tide, at low water springs, receding half a mile from St. Aubin harbour, and half a cable outside the entrance of the new harbour of St. Helier. There is also a strong mole or breakwater projecting from the northern side of St. Aubin castle, sheltering a pier within, where vessels frequently refit and unload, grounding, however, at low water.

Elizabeth castle is built on a cragged rock on the eastern side of the bay fronting the harbours of St. Helier, and about three-quarters of a mile to the south-westward of the town : the top of its high central tower or keep, on which the colours are displayed, is 144 feet above the (low water) level of the sea. On the site of this castle was once an Augustine monastery, built in honour of St. Helier, a recluse, whose hermitage, built on the summit of a high rock, situate nearly a third of a mile to the southward of the castle, is still extant.

Elizabeth and St. Aubin castles are insulated every tide, and from their prominent positions afford shelter respectively to the two harbours, by breaking the swell which rolls into St. Aubin bay during south-westerly gales.

ST. HELIER HARBOURS are on the north-east side of St. Aubin bay. The old harbour has lately been completely enclosed by a new one, constructed from the designs of Mr. J. Walker, C.E., between the years 1840–50, at a cost of £170,000. Both harbours are alike in form, the new one being in fact a mere repetition of the old, on an extended scale ; excepting that from the inferior plan of the entrance to the new harbour, the south-westerly swell ranges freely into it in heavy gales, to the great injury of vessels compelled to remain there at such times. These harbours are nearly rectangular, narrow in proportion to their length, and have their entrances near their south-western corners.

The inner (or old) harbour is about 1,900 feet long by 300 feet broad, having a depth of 8 feet at its entrance at half tide, and 5 feet within it. The outer harbour is 2,600 feet long by 500 feet broad : it has 16 feet at its entrance at half tide, the ground rising gradually within the pier heads for a distance of about 300 feet, where there are 13 feet at that period: the bottom is fine sand and mud throughout.

There is a floating dock capable of accommodating vessels of 500 tons; there is also a steam tug always in attendance on the shipping.

A Lifeboat is stationed at St. Helier.

ST. AUBIN CASTLE, PIER, and HARBOUR.—Several rocks lie scattered to the southward and westward of St. Aubin castle, but most of them appear at low water. The two largest and most conspicuous rocks are called the Grosse and the Platte, which lie very close together, about a quarter of a mile from the castle, the former being the most elevated and showing about first quarter ebb. Both rocks are marked with beacon poles. There is also a group of rocks lying a quarter of a mile to the southward of the Grosse, the north-easternmost of which dries 7 feet at low water. All these rocks will be cleared to the eastward by keeping La Haule house open eastward of St. Aubin castle breakwater: to the eastward of this line the ground is all fine sand. At half-flood there is 8 feet water inside St. Aubin castle pier, at which period the water begins to flow into the entrance of St. Aubin inner harbour. The passage inside St. Aubin castle is not passable for boats until half flood.

LIGHTS.—The following *fixed* lights are exhibited all night for guidance of vessels bound into St. Helier's harbour.

A *white* light, from the lighthouse on the Victoria, or new south pier-head, 31 feet above high water, and visible about 6 miles.

Two *green* gas lights, one on the western angle of Albert pier; the other, within it, on the esplanade parapet wall, bearing from each other N.E. and S.W., distant 630 yards, and visible 2 or 3 miles.

These two green lights in line lead through the middle of the small road, between the Oyster and Dogs nest rocks, and between the Cloches rocks, clear of all danger. The lights in line may be used also (when they can be seen so far) to run between the Hinguette rock and Grune St. Michel; care being taken to open them a little one way or other in time to clear a rock having only 7 feet over it at low water lying in the fairway, 2½ cables outside or south-westward of the high head of the Hinguette.

In addition to the above, there is a *red* gas-light on the inside part of Albert pier-head, and another *red* gas-light in the upper pier road; the latter is elevated 46 feet above high water, and bears from Victoria pier-light E.N.E., distant 680 yards.

Note.—The *inner* green light will not be visible to vessels approaching the harbour from the eastward until it comes on a N.E. bearing.

Water of first rate quality may be procured at the inner quay of St. Helier old harbour, from pumps placed there for the purpose; it may be procured also in the same way at St. Aubin harbour.

DANGERS OFF ST. AUBIN BAY.—The principal dangers to be avoided in approaching St. Aubin bay (in addition to the St. Brelade and Le Fret banks, described at page 85), are the Vrachère ; the Hubaut, with its surrounding rocks ; the Grunes ; the Grunes Vaudin ; the Sillette rocks ; the Fours ; the Grunes aux Dards, and Danger rock on the western side ; the Rouaudière near the middle ; and the Grunes St. Michel, the Hinguette, Les Têtards, and Demie de Pas on the eastern side. The Diamond rock lies nearly on a line representing the chord of the bay, near the middle ; the Pignonet, Grunes de Port, and Les Junée lie along its western shore ; the Baleine and other sunken rocks to the eastward, off Elizabeth castle ; and Les Cloches off the entrance to the little road of St. Helier.

Some of the passages between these rocks are extremely narrow, and all are dangerous from the rapidity of the tides, and from the general discoloured state of the sea preventing the rocks being seen when close to them. Strangers should therefore never attempt to navigate these channels without a competent pilot.

Les Vrachères is a rocky bank of small extent forming the outer or south-western danger off St. Aubin bay. Its highest head, called Frouquie, with only 5 feet on it at low water, lies at the eastern extreme of the bank, with Princes tower touching the western corner of Fort Regent E. by N., and the western tower in St. Brelade bay in line with the western head of Rousse Frouquie N.N.E. $\frac{1}{2}$ E.

Hubaut, Grande and Petite Grune, are all grouped together between Les Vrachères and Point Le Fret. The narrow channels separating these rocky banks should never be attempted by vessels. From the Hubaut, which dries 2 feet at low water, the western tower of St. Brelade bay is in line with the west side of Rousse rock N.N.E. $\frac{1}{4}$ E., and the east end of Almorah Terrace is touching the inside part of Noirmont tower E. by N. $\frac{1}{4}$ N.

From the Grand Grune (which dries 6 feet at low water) Princes tower is in line with Elizabeth castle hospital (a small red-tiled building standing between the highest part of the castle and its north-eastern angle) bearing E. $\frac{3}{4}$ N., and the western tower in St. Brelade bay is a little open of the high-water extreme of Le Fret point N. by E. $\frac{3}{4}$ E.

The Petite Grune has 10 feet on its shoalest part, from which St. Mark church spire is just shut in with Noirmont point E. $\frac{3}{4}$ N., and the western tower in St. Brelade bay is midway between Rousse rock and Le Fret point N. by E. $\frac{3}{4}$ E.

When approaching the western passage from the south-west, keep Seymour tower open outside La Frouquie rock until the Corbière bears North, or the eastern tower in St. Brelade bay comes open of La Cotte point. The Dogs-nest rock in line with the *white patch* on the sea wall at Grève d'Azette (heretofore used as the leading mark for the western channel) leads *very close* inside all these dangers, and their eastern boundary is marked by Tabor chapel seen in line with the high-water extreme of Le Fret point.

Les Grunes Vaudin are an extensive bank of rocks lying off Noirmont point and a mile to the eastward of the Vrachères. The two highest rocks (each dry 5 feet at low water) lie near the middle of the bank, about N.E. ½ E. and S.W. ½ W. of each other, and nearly 2 cables apart. The north-eastern rock is called the Grande Vaudin, and the other the S.W. rock : from the latter the gateway of St. Brelade church is just in sight to the eastward of Rousse rock N. ½ W., and St. Mark church spire is a little open to the eastward of the south-east part of Elizabeth castle E.N.E. From the S.W. rock a chain of dangerous sunken rocks extend in a W.N.W. direction for a quarter of a mile, and also to the north-eastward for half a mile ; the eastern part of the latter is semi-detached from the Vaudin bank, and sometimes called Les-Poches-à-suie ; there is as little as 4 feet on it at low water.

La Sillette lies immediately within the Grunes Vaudin, distant from them only a quarter of a mile, but separated from them by a 7-fathom channel. La Sillette is a small reef, less than 2 cables in diameter, but the rocks generally are higher than any others in the neighbourhood ; its highest head, which lies close to the eastern side of the reef, dries 12 feet at low water, and is marked by a swinging beacon (pole) 23 feet high ; from which the spire of St. Mark church is seen touching the south-east angle of Elizabeth castle E.N.E., and Icho tower is in line with the north side of La Frouquie rock S.E. by E. ¾ E.

Grand and Petit Four.—The Grand Four uncovers 3 feet at low water. From it the New mill at Millbrook is in one with the rocks off Noirmont point N.E. and Nicolle tower is its apparent breadth open southward of the white patch on the Dogs Nest rock (a rock with white patch on it surmounted by a small iron beacon) bearing E. ¾ S. The inner head of the Grand Four lies about N. by W., distant a cable from the highest rock (just described), and has 6 feet over it at low water.

The Petit Four consists of a bank of sunken rocks extending a quarter of a mile east and west, lying to the eastward of the Grand Four, and distant from it only 1½ cables. The highest rock is near the middle of the bank to the south-westward, and dries only one foot at low water. There is another rock close to the south-east side of this one-foot rock, that dries only 6 inches at low water ; and a third lying E. by N., distant 1½ cables from it, that is just awash at that period: the latter is close to the east side of the reef ; and from it Fort Regent flagstaff is seen on the north side of False Hermitage rock bearing E. by N., and Mont Plaisir house is touching Point de Bût N. by E. ¼ E.

Grunes aux Dards is a rocky bank about a cable's length in diameter, lying about a quarter of a mile to the eastward of the Sillette. From its highest head, (which lies near the north part of the bank and dries 5 feet at low water,) St. Mark church is seen midway between the Hermitage and the Close rocks N.E. by E. ¾ E., and Janvrin tower is in line with the south-western high-water extreme of Ile Percée N.N.W.

There is another rock close to this, on a N.N.E. bearing, which dries 4 feet ; and a third which dries 3 feet, distant half a cable S.S.W. from it. A rock awash at low water bearing S.S.E., distant a cable, marks the limit of the bank in that direction ; and to the eastward of the highest rock, and distant 1½ cables from it, lies the Frouquie ; a sunken rock entirely detached, on which there are 5-feet at low water.

Danger Rock has 5 feet over it at low water. It lies on the east side of a sunken reef lying to the southward of the Grunes aux Dards. and from it the east end of Almorah terrace appears just touching the north side of the Hermitage N.E. by E,, and Janvrin tower is just open of the south-west high-water extreme of Ile Percée N.N.W.

Rouaudière Rock dries 4 feet at low water. It is small and steep-to, except on its S.E. side, from whence a ridge of sunken reef extends to the distance of about ½ a cable. From the rock La Haule house is seen just open on the west side of St. Aubin castle N. ½ W., St. Saviour church is in line with the north-west side of False Hermitage E.N.E., and Icho tower is touching the south side of Tas de Pois (or White rock), S.E. by E. A *red* buoy, carrying a *staff* and *black ball*, has lately been moored at 50 yards to the westward of this rock, in 5 fathoms at low water.

Grunes St. Michel consist of two small banks of sunken rocks lying nearly north and south of each other, little more than half a cable apart ; the longest diameter of the southern group is about a cable, in an east and west direction, having the least water (3 feet) to the westward. The highest head of the northern group dries 5 feet at low water, and from it La Moye signal-post is seen over and about half way down the slope of Le Fret point N.W. ¼ W., and St. Mark church spire is in line with the northern white patch on Albert pier N.E. ¾ E.

Hinguette Reef, lying a quarter of a mile south-eastward of the Grunes St. Michel, is a quarter of a mile long N.E. by N. and S.W. by S., and most of the rocks on it dry at low-water springs : the highest, lying near the north-west end, dries 11 feet, and another, lying three-quarters of a cable within the south-west end, 5 feet at low water.

The highest rock (which dries 11 feet) lies with the west end of Victoria college in line with Dogs Nest rock N.E. by E., and La Moye signal-post *just* open south-westward of Noirmont tower N.W. ¼ W. From this rock the reef extends to the eastward rather more than half a cable, and for 2 cables to the S.S.W.

Les Têtards has only 2 feet over its outer head at low water ; from which Seymour tower is seen touching the inside part of La Frouquie E. by S. ¼ S., and the west end of Almorah terrace is a little open eastward of Dogs-nest rock N.E. by N.

Nine-Feet Rock lies nearly midway between Les Têtards and Tas de Pois, and from it Icho tower appears the apparent breadth of La Frouquie open inside of it S.E. by E. ¾ E. ; Fort Regent signal-post is in line with the east side of Crabière rock N.N.E. ¾ E. ; and No. 2 tower in St. Aubin bay is seen just within or on the east side of Gros du Château rock N. ⅓ W.

DANGERS in St. AUBIN BAY. — The Rouaudière rock (described at page 91) lies right in the fairway off the middle of St. Aubin bay, S. by W. ¼ W. distant nearly half a mile from the Diamond rock. The main channel to the little road of St. Helier from the westward is between the Rouaudière and Grunes St. Michel : it is half a mile wide at this part, and has an even bottom, with a depth of 6 fathoms at low water.

Diamond Rock lies near the middle of St. Aubin bay, and has 8 feet over it at low water. From it Fort Regent flagstaff is seen touching the north side of Close rock E. ⅓ N., and La Haule House appears midway between St. Aubin castle tower and the end of the breakwater extending from it, N. by W.

Pignonet, Grunes du Port, and Les Junée are the most important dangers off the western shore of St. Aubin bay.

The Pignonet uncovers 10 feet at low water on the line of Le Fret and Noirmont points, distant from the latter a quarter of a mile. It is marked by a beacon (pole and ball), from which La Haule house is seen touching St. Aubin harbour pier head N. by E. ¼ E., and St. Saviour church is just open to the north-west of the spire of St. Mark church E. by N.

There are many rocks between the Pignonet and Noirmont point : the most dangerous one, which is outside the line between these two places, is the same height as Pignonet, and lies with the outer apex of Le Fret bluff in line with Noirmont tower, distant 1¼ cables from the latter.

Les Grunes du Port is a rocky group nearly a cable long, north and south. The southern rock has 3 feet over it at low water, and the northern head dries 6 feet at that period ; on this latter rock Upper Blanc Pignon house is just touching the end of the high wall extending from the north-west side of St. Aubin castle N. ⅞ E., and Fort Regent flagstaff is in line with Elizabeth castle flagstaff, East.

Les Junée are a sunken rocky group lying 2 cables N.N.E. from Les Grunes du port. From the southern rock (which is covered 2 feet at low water) the lower Blanc Pignon is just shut in with the semi-detached bastion eastward of St. Aubin castle N. ¾ E., and the Fort Regent signal-post is seen over and shut in with the north-eastern extreme of Elizabeth castle E. ¼ S.

The Baleine Rock, the most important danger within the bay on its eastern side, lies between Gros du Chateau and the Diamond rock, and has 2 feet over it at low water. From it the lighthouse on Victoria pier is seen just touching the north side of Close rock E. by S. ¼ S., and the east end of Almorah terrace is on the north side of the high rock next to the north-eastward of Gros du Chateau N.E. by E. ¾ E.

Outer Rock, off Hermitage reef, has 7 feet on it at low water, and lies with the outer extreme of La Motte in line with Oyster rock beacon S.E. ¾ E., and the east end of Victoria terrace over the north extreme of Elizabeth castle N.E. by E. ½ E.

Les Cloches are two sunken rocks immediately off the entrance to the Little road of St. Helier. The western rock has 8 feet over it at low water, and lies with Nicolle tower a little open to the southward of Dogs Nest rock beacon E. ¾ S., and the Oyster rock beacon in line with the north-eastern extreme of Elizabeth castle N.N.E. ¼ E. The eastern rock of Les Cloches (with only 2 feet over it at low water) bears from the western rock E.S.E. 1¾ cables; another rock with 8 feet over it bears N.N.W., distant 1½ cables; and a third with 7 feet over it at the same period bears N.E. by N., distant 1½ cables. This last rock lies with Elizabeth castle flagstaff in line with the Oyster rock beacon, distant from the latter exactly one cable. A chain of sunken rocks connects this last rock with the Oyster rock group, but close to outside of it (or to the southward) there are 3 fathoms with clean ground.

Oyster Rocks and Grune Moulet occupy positions one on either side of the entrance to the Little road of St. Helier. They lie S.E. ¼ E. and N.W. ¼ W. of each other, a quarter of a mile apart, and are each marked with a swinging beacon, consisting of a pole bearing a ball. The marks for the Oyster rock are, the new windmill (on the beach at Millbrook) in line with the eastern apex of Gros du Chateau bearing North, and the north-western angle of St. Saviour touching the south-east angle of St. Helier church.

The Oyster rocks uncover 13 feet at low water. The beacon pole is marked in 23 divisions of a foot each. When the rocks are awash there are 10 feet water between Victoria and Albert piers; and by deducting the number of divisions seen above water from 33 it will give the depth between the piers.

The Grune Moulet dries 11 feet at low water. Its beacon is marked in 10 divisions of 2 feet each.

Platte Rock lies within the entrance to the Little road of St. Helier E. ¾ N., exactly a cable's length from the Oyster rock beacon. It dries one foot at low water; and from it the S.E. rock (off the Hermitage) is seen just open clear of the east side of Elizabeth castle. There is no safe channel between the Oyster rock and the Platte.

Sharp Rock dries 3 feet at low water, lies S.E. by E. ½ E., 1¼ cables from the Platte. The channel into the Little road lies between Platte and Sharp rocks; and in it there are 22 feet water at the lowest equinoctial spring tides. In passing between these rocks (constituting the narrowest part of the channel) the former (the Platte) will be cleared to the eastward by keeping the spire of St. Mark church on the east side (a little open) of the northern white patch on Albert pier; and the latter will be cleared to the westward by bringing the east end of Almorah terrace a little open on the west side of Albert pier.

ANCHORAGE.—There is plenty of room for eight or ten vessels to lie at single anchor in St. Aubin bay; but in mooring there the hawse should be open to the south-west from September to March; the prevailing winds during this period being from that quarter.

The best position is within the Diamond rock; with St. Saviour church (tower) just open northward of St. Mark church (spire) and in line with the high rock between Gros du Chateau and La Vrachére E. by N., or Fort Regent signal-post seen over Elizabeth castle and in line with Gros du Chateau bearing East, and La Haule house in line with the outer or north-east extreme of St. Aubin castle breakwater N. by W. ¼ W., in 21 feet at the lowest spring tides. This spot is N.N.E. nearly 2 cables within the Diamond rock.

A large ship wishing to lie as near as possible to St. Helier, may anchor in 5 fathoms at low water, with La Haule house in the same line of bearing, but St. Mark church (spire) touching the south-east side of Hermitage rock N.E. by E. ½ E. The Oyster rock beacon will here be in line with De Pas tower.

This last position should only be used by vessels under the above circumstances in fine or moderate weather, but at or near the first described anchorage within the Diamond rock, vessels whose draught is not over 18 feet might ride out a heavy southerly gale in safety, as they would there be sheltered from the force of the tidal stream; and further, because from below half tide the ocean swell is broken by outlying rocks. During neap tides vessels of 22 feet draught might safely anchor inside the Diamond rock, but for heavier ships there is no safe anchorage on any part of the south coast in very bad weather.

The anchorage in the best part of the Little road lies to the northward of Grande Mangeuse rock, in 10 feet water, with Fort Regent signal-post over the middle of the entrance to the harbour E.N.E., and Noirmont signal-post touching the south-west side of Close rock N.W. by W.: or farther out in 16 feet, with Fort Regent signal-post a sail's breath open to the south-east of Victoria pier lighthouse, and Elizabeth castle flagstaff in line with a remarkable pointed rock eastward of the Hermitage N. by W. ¾ W, Vessels intending to remain in the Little road should always moor, for the anchorage space is only 1½ cables wide N.W. and S.E., although nearly a quarter of a mile long, N.E. and S.W., and it is surrounded by dangerous sunken rocks.

PASSAGES INTO ST. AUBIN BAY.—There are nine passages leading into St. Aubin bay, viz.: The North-west, the Western, the South-west, the Sillette, the Danger rock, the Middle, the Hinguette, the South, and the Eastern.

In westerly gales the best time to pass through any of these rocky channels is between first quarter flood and high water. The first of the ebb throws up a very dangerous overfall off Noirmont point, and when the westerly tide has fairly made, overfalls extend right across all the channels, which continue with more or less intensity, according to the height of the ocean swell and strength of the wind, until the ebb tide slacks.

The **NORTH-WEST PASSAGE,** although only 1¾ cables wide at the narrowest part (between Point Le Fret and the rocky bank of that name off it), is perfectly safe for the largest vessels, and has not less than 7 fathoms at low water in any part of it. It is indeed more frequently used than the other channels, being the steam-packet route between Southampton, Guernsey, and St. Helier.

DIRECTIONS.—Having rounded the Corbière, as directed at page 85, and passed between La Moye point and Banc de St. Brelade, by shutting in La Motte with Noirmont point, and having Noirmont tower on the line of bearing S.E. by E. ¼ E.; run direct for the tower until the peak of Corbière rock is seen touching La Moye point, bearing N.W. ¼ W.; with this mark the vessel will pass through the middle of the narrowest part of the channel off Le Fret point, in 8 fathoms at low water. Continue on the same line until the white patch on the sea-wall at Greve d'Azette comes on with Dogs Nest rock (it has a white patch on it surmounted by a small iron beacon) bearing E. by S. ¼ S.; this mark leads through near the middle of the channel between Noirmont point and the rocky reefs off it, called the Fours; it also leads a safe distance inside the Rouaudière rock (nearly 1¼ cables), and exactly midway between Les Cloches and the 7-feet rock lying a cable's length outside the Oyster rock beacon.

After passing the Oyster rock beacon, St. Mark church (spire) will soon come in line with the white patch at the south end of Albert pier (which is the mark to *enter* the Little road with); but after passing inside the

Platte rock bring the church spire in line with the *northern* white patch on Albert pier, to clear the Mangeuse rocks.

A description of the dangers off and within the Little road (as well as anchoring marks) will be found at pages 93 and 94; and a description of the Little road, together with directions for entering by day and night, will follow at pages 100 and 102.

The **WESTERN PASSAGE** is between the Hubaut reefs and the Banc de St. Brelade. It is rather more than a quarter of a mile across at its most contracted part, which is between the Petite Grune and the Banc le Fret; and there is here 9 fathoms water in it. It is the most direct route to St. Aubin bay and St. Helier harbour from the westward, one leading mark only being required (the white patch on the sea wall at Grève d'Azette in line with the white patch and iron beacon on the Dogs Nest rock), but as these marks are not easily made out in misty weather, and might then be mistaken, the North-west passage is probably the best for a stranger to take.

DIRECTIONS.—The line of the white patch on the sea wall at Grève d'Azette and the Dogs Nest rock bearing E. by S. ¼ S., passes very little more than half a cable to the northward of the Petite Grune, and almost touches the north side of a sunken rock with only 14 feet over it at low water, lying half a mile outside or to the westward of the Petit Grune; therefore in entering the channel from the westward, keep the Corbiére rock well open outside Jument (white), until the white patch in the sea wall at Grève d'Azette is seen clearly open to the northward of Dogs Nest rock. Run in on this mark (keeping them open), until Tabor chapel comes in line with Le Fret point, to clear the Petite Grune, after which they may be brought in line and used as the leading mark up to the entrance of the Little road, as directed above, on passing through inside the North-west passage.

Should the white patch at Grève d'Azette be obscured, De Pas tower in line with Noirmont tower will do equally as well, provided the Hermitage rock is opened out clear of Noirmont point before shutting in Tabor chapel with Le Fret point, to clear the 20-feet rock lying eastward of Banc Le Fret: and if all objects to the eastward and near the town are invisible and the land about Noirmont and Le Moye be tolerably clear, (which is often the case in very fine weather,) Noirmont point may be approached to the distance of a cable's length; but in passing to the eastward of it do not shut in Le Moye signal-post with Le Fret point until St. Aubin castle is seen open, clear of the land of Noirmont, to clear a dangerous rock lying between and without the line of Noirmont tower and Pignonet beacon. After passing Pignonet beacon bring Noirmont tower a little open to the north-eastward or inside of it, and when about a quarter of a mile to the eastward of the beacon anchor until the weather clears.

The **SOUTH-WEST PASSAGE** is between the Banc Les Vrachére and the Grunes Vaudin; to the eastward of the Grande Grune and westward of the Grande Four. The narrowest part of the channel is between the 6-feet sunken rock at the north-west side of the Grande Four, and another sunken rock with 20 feet over it : these rocks bear from each other W.N.W. and E.S.E. distant 2 cables.

DIRECTIONS.—Captain Saumarez's house (it is called the Firs, is coloured yellow, and stands about half way up the slope of the hill a little eastward of St. Matthew church,) in line with Noirmont tower bearing N.E. $\frac{1}{2}$ E., leads midway between the Frouquie of the Vrachère and the westernmost of the Grunes Vaudin : enter the channel therefore on this line and run on it until the white patch in the sea wall at Gréve d'Azette come in line with the white patch on the Dogs Nest rock E. by S. $\frac{1}{4}$ S., with which as a leading mark proceed to the eastward as before.

As the leading mark through this channel leads dangerously close to the west side of the Grande Four, it is recommended (when the flood tide is running) that vessels should only run in on it so far as to bring Tabor chapel open and shut over the upper part of the slope of Le Fret bluff, and run on this line until the eastern leading mark comes on as before.

Tabor chapel, standing on the high land overlooking St. Brelade bay, is here given as the most conspicuous mark for a stranger to recognize, but this leading line approaches the Grande Grune rather nearer than is desirable : for the *middle* of the channel, Tabor chapel should be shut in altogether, and the Pic-nic hotel (white gable), situate in the bay on the low land to the westward of it, brought in line with the extreme of point Le Fret.

As there are overfalls and strong eddies from the rocks in this channel on both ebb and flood, it should never be taken from choice except in very fine weather.

The **SILLETTE PASSAGE** is between the Sillette rocks and the Grunes aux Dards, (which is the narrowest part of it), the channel here being 2 cables wide, with an average depth of 6 fathoms ; but a large sunken rock occupies the middle of the fairway, and as it has only 26 feet over it at low water, not more than this can be counted on.

DIRECTIONS.—The Sillette passage should never be attempted in a sailing vessel without a fair commanding wind, as the tidal stream both ebb and flood sets right across it. The leading mark is the western martello towers (white) in St. Aubin bay in line with the east side of Grosse rock (on which there is a beacon) bearing N.N.E. This line leads barely $1\frac{1}{2}$ cables eastward of the sunken rocks at the entrance of the channel called Les Poches à Suie (on which there are only 4 feet at low water); midway between the Sillette and Grunes aux Dards, nearly $1\frac{1}{4}$ cables eastward of the Petit Four; $1\frac{1}{2}$ cables eastward of the Pignonet; half a cable westward or (inside) the Grunes du Port, and very close inside the western head of Junée.

The **MIDDLE PASSAGE** is between Danger rock and the Grunes aux Dards to the westward, and Les Têtards, the Hinguette reef and the Grunes St. Michel to the eastward. The apparent narrowest part of the passage is more than half a mile across, this being the distance between Danger rock and the Grunes St. Michel; but there are two sunken rocks with only 14 and 15 feet over them at low water, lying outside (or to the southward of) the Grune St. Michel, distant from it nearly half a mile. thus breaking up the channel into two parts. The westernmost rock of the two (15 feet on it) occupies a position near the middle of the channel at its entrance, and bears from Danger rock E.S.E. nearly half a mile. The best part of the middle passage lies between Danger rock and this 15-feet rock; the ground here is clean and the soundings regular in 7 fathoms; the eastern side of the Middle passage is rocky, and the depths irregular.

DIRECTIONS. — Mont Plasir house touching the western side of St. Aubin castle tower bearing North, is the leading mark through the Middle passage. This line leads nearly $1\frac{1}{2}$ cables westward of the 15-feet sunken rock; a quarter of a mile east of Danger rock, and rather less from the Frouquie of the Grune aux Dards (on which there are 5 feet at low water); nearly 2 cables westward of the Rouaudière; $1\frac{1}{2}$ cables eastward of the Grunes du Port; and outside but very close to Les Junée (sunken rocks).

If desirous of proceeding to the anchorage in St. Aubin bay, haul to the eastward when the east end of Almorah terrace comes in line with La Vrachère (the innermost high rock northward of Elizabeth castle) to clear the Diamond rock, and anchor as convenient when La Haule house is seen on the east side of St. Aubin castle tower.

DANGER ROCK PASSAGE lies between the Grunes aux Dards and Danger rock, and at this part is a third of a mile wide, having a depth of $5\frac{1}{2}$ fathoms near the middle, but there are sunken rocks close to the southward, one of which has only $2\frac{3}{4}$ fathoms over it. This passage, like the Sillette, is dangerous at times for sailing vessels, and should never be taken without a pilot. To steamers, however, whose captains are acquainted with the pilotage, it has attractions, as being the only *direct* passage to the Little Road of St. Helier from the south-west.

DIRECTIONS. — Bring St. Mark church (spire) in line with S.E. rock (off the Hermitage) bearing N.E. by E. $\frac{1}{4}$ E., and steering for it, the vessel will pass nearly $1\frac{1}{2}$ cables southward (or outside) the southernmost rock (awash at low water) of the Grunes aux Dards, and rather a greater distance *inside* Danger rock. The same line passes rather more than $1\frac{1}{2}$ cables southward of the Rouaudière rock, and close to the eastward of an 8-feet sunken rock off the Oyster rocks ; between this 8-feet rock and the Bieuse rock (marked by a beacon pole), and as far to the eastward as the Oyster rocks, the ground is quite clear of rocks.

HINGUETTE PASSAGE, lying between the Hinguette reef and Les Têtards, is nearly half a mile wide, has 7 and 8 fathoms in it, and is a good and safe passage at slack water, but requires care in making proper allowance for the tide, which sets right across it.

DIRECTIONS.—Enter this passage with St. Mark church (spire) in line with Dogs Nest rock N.E. $\frac{1}{4}$ N., and run through between the Hinguette reef and Les Têtards. After passing inside the Hinguette, St. Matthew church will soon come in line with the Gros de Chateau rock N. $\frac{1}{4}$ E., with which mark run between Les Cloches rocks up to the entrance of the Little road of St. Helier.

The SOUTH PASSAGE is between Les Têtards (having only 2 feet on them at low water) and a sunken reef to the eastward, the shoalest spot on which is 14 feet at low water. This channel is barely a quarter of a mile wide, and has 8 fathoms in it, but is not so safe for a vessel to take as the Hinguette passage or the Eastern passage.

DIRECTIONS.—St. Matthew church (tower), a dull white-coloured building, in line with Gros de Chateau rock N. $\frac{1}{4}$ E., leads through about mid-channel, and, as before stated, between Les Cloches and up to the entrance of St. Helier Little road; but should it be desired to proceed to the anchorage in St. Aubin bay—when St. Peter church (spire) comes in line with the lower Blanc Pignon N. by W. $\frac{1}{4}$ W., take it for the leading mark up to the anchorage.

When near low water St. Peter church spire may be lost sight of before arriving at the anchorage in St. Aubin bay, in which case care must be taken to refer the line of its direction to some other object.

The EASTERN PASSAGE.—The narrowest part of the passage is between Demie de Pas (on which there is a beacon pole) and a sunken rock with 11 feet on it at low water. The latter rock lies W.N.W. nearly a third of a mile from Demie de Pas, and from it the 9-feet rock (see page 92) bears N. $\frac{1}{2}$ W. distant nearly a cable. The ground outside Demie de Pas is clean up to the foot of the rock, which is not more than 40 yards from the beacon.

DIRECTIONS.—The new mill on the beach at Millbrook, just in sight or open and shut of the high rocks on west side of the Hermitage bearing

N. ¼ W., leads 1¾ cables westward of Demie de Pas, and barely a cable eastward of the sunken rocks above described. A vessel may therefore enter the channel on this line, and run on it until Nicolle tower comes in line with Tas de Pois rock (white), after which, St. Matthew church must be brought in line with Gros de Chateau rock, as for the South channel, to run up to the entrance of the Little road ; or St. Peter church spire in line with Lower Blanc Pignon to approach the anchorage in St. Aubin bay.

ST. HELIER LITTLE ROAD lies to the eastward of the Hermitage rocks, and is frequented only by vessels intending to enter the harbour at tide time, or during the neaps, in fine weather, with off-shore winds. The depth in it is from 16 to 6 feet at low-water springs, but the anchorage is so much contracted by rocks that vessels over 8 feet draught would be compelled to moor. At low-water springs the Little road is completely sheltered on the east by a rocky barrier entirely dry, extending from Point de Pas to the Dogs Nest rock ; there is also a chain of sunken rocks on the west side of the Little road, extending from the Hermitage to the Oyster rocks and beyond to the distance of 600 feet outside the beacon : there are narrow gaps of deep water through this rocky barrier, but they are too tortuous to be available as ship channels, therefore no vessel of greater draught than 5 feet should attempt to pass this barrier at low water.

The principal dangers in the Little road are described at page 94.

DIRECTIONS.—When bound from St. Aubin bay into the Little road of St. Helier harbour, it is best to weigh and proceed about half flood ; at which period there will be 16 feet water between the pier heads of Victoria harbour and 8 feet between the pier heads of the Old harbour : at the highest springs there are 36 feet at the entrance of Victoria harbour, and 27 feet between the pier heads of the Old harbour.

From the anchorage in St. Aubin bay into the Little road, inside (or to the northward) of the Oyster rock—steer towards the middle of the passage between the Oyster rock and the Hermitage ; being careful not to open Almorah terrace to the eastward of the latter until the iron pole beacon on the Grande Mangeuse rock is in line with the outer or southern high chimney of the Engineers' barrack (a long brick building on Point de Pas adjoining the north side of the tower) bearing E. ¼ S.; with this mark on a vessel may run through a gap in the barrier reef, in not less than 8 feet at low water. When S.E. rock (lying off the east side of Hermitage) is shut in with Elizabeth castle she will be within the limits of the anchorage in the Little road, and may anchor as convenient or proceed into the harbour : in the latter case St. Mark church spire in line with the northernmost white patch on the Albert breakwater is the leading mark up to the entrance.

The width of this gap in the barrier reef is only 60 yards; it is bounded to the northward by a small rock that dries 1 foot at low water, and to the southward by a sunken rock with 2 feet over it at that period.

Outside the Oyster Rocks from the Westward.—The channel between the westernmost of Les Cloches (which rock has 8 feet on it at low water) and the outer sunken rock off the Oyster (which has 7 feet over it) is 1½ cables wide and has 5 fathoms in it at the lowest spring tides. The white patch on the sea wall at Grêve d'Azette and the Dogs Nest rock beacon in line leads through the middle of it; run on this line therefore until St. Mark church spire comes in line with the white patch at the end of Albert pier N.E. by E., with which mark enter the Little road; but after arriving inside the Platte rock, edge away to the northward until St. Mark church spire is in line with the northernmost white patch on the same pier; which, as already stated, will lead to the anchorage in the Little road or up to the entrance of the harbour.

From the Southward.—Pass between Les Cloches with St. Mark church spire in line with Victoria pier lighthouse N.E. by E.; when inside the Oyster rocks St. Mark church spire should be brought in line with the white patch at the end of Albert pier; and after passing the Platte St. Mark church spire should be brought in line with the northern white patch on Albert pier as before.

From St. Aubin Bay over the Bridge to the Little road or St. Helier harbour—Steer so as to pass half a cable northward of La Vrachère rock (having a small beacon pole on it), or bring St. Mark church spire on with the north side of the hospital, and run with this mark on until De Pas tower opens a little to the northward of the northernmost white patch on the Albert pier, with which run over the bridge (this part has one foot water at half tide) and enter the harbour, or haul out into the Little road.

By Night.—Bring the Victoria pier light (*white*) to bear N.E. b. E. ½ E. and steer for it. When the pier road light (*red*) is seen keep it a little open northward of Victoria pier light and pass between Grune aux Dards and Grune St. Michel, about a cable's length to the southward of the Rouaudière rock; within which steer to the south-eastward to bring the two green lights on Albert pier in line N.E.; which is the mark to lead up to the anchorage in the small road or to enter the harbour.

The two new green lights on Albert pier in line, bearing N.E., is by far the best mark to run in for St. Helier by night, care being taken to proceed as directed at page 134.

CAUTION.—In entering the harbour allowance must be made for the tide, which at or near springs runs in and out of it with considerable strength. The most dangerous period for vessels entering is about half flood ; at such times they are frequently forced over against the sandbank fronting the south pier of the old harbour before they have time to turn their heads up the harbour.

GENERAL DIRECTIONS.—Small vessels when working up towards the narrows of the western channels, may (when to the eastward of the Kaines) stand into St. Brelade bay until Jument rock (white) is open and shut of La Moye point; and to the southward until Elizabeth castle is seen (just seen) in line with Noirmont point E. ½ S. When in the narrows of the western channel, backing and filling is recommended (with a beating wind) : if with the flood, with the vessel's head off shore, and if with the ebb, with her head in shore ; unless one half the flood at least has run, for at this period (half tide) there are 13 feet over all the rocks in the offing of St. Aubin bay, with the exception of the Pignonet, Hinguette, and Sillette, on which there are only 9, 8, and 7 feet respectively.

If bound into the Little road or St. Helier harbour, in order to avoid the Rouaudière, it may be useful to remember that St. Mark church spire touching the south side of Close rock leads 60 yards to the northward of it ; and the same spire in line with the False Hermitage leads to the southward.

A vessel from the north-westward running for shelter in St. Aubin bay during a gale from that quarter, should keep at the distance of 1½ miles from the Corbière to avoid the breaking sea near it (this is especially necessary from half ebb till low water), and when the land of Noirmont is well open steer for its point, until Grosnez point comes in line with the Corbière, after which haul up for La Moye and bring the marks on for the north-west channel (page 95), where much less sea will be found than in the others.

In heavy westerly gales the whole space included between the outlying rocks off Noirmont point is a confused mass of foaming breakers ; clouds of driving spray create an impenetrable mist that obscures all marks near the horizon, and beacons marking the rocks are all out of sight under water : but even under such circumstances the North-west passage could be safely taken by a person well acquainted with it, as both Le Fret and Noirmont points are safe of approach for large vessels to the distance of a cable's length.

On arriving abreast of Noirmont point attend to the directions given at pages 95 and 134, or do not shut in La Moye signal-post with Le Fret point, until the white tower in St. Aubin bay is seen open eastward of St. Aubin castle to clear the Pignonet rocks (the first of the flood sets right on these rocks into St. Aubin bay). It may be useful to remember that when La Haule house comes on with the inside part of the wall extending to the westward of St. Aubin castle the vessel will be midway between the Grunes du Port and the Diamond rock ; and that St. Saviour church tower just open northward of St. Mark church spire and in line with La Vrachère rock will lead up to the anchorage in St. Aubin bay, well clear of the Diamond rock.

THE COAST eastward of St. Helier is all low and sandy to La Roque point, also to the northward of La Roque point as far as Mount Orgueil bluff; the whole of which part is inaccessible to shipping, from the extensive rocky reefs with which it is fringed, and which dry at low water of spring tides to the distance of nearly 2 miles from the shore.

The outer edge of this reef to the southward is generally steep, and fortunately well marked by a number of large rocks, which although sometimes nearly awash at high water, are never entirely covered. There are also two stone towers on this reef, each about 45 feet above high water level; one lying about 3 miles S.E. of the Little road of St. Helier, called *Icho* tower ; the other called *Seymour* tower, situate nearly 2 miles farther to the eastward, near the middle of the Violet bank, off La Roque point.

The Violet Bank, above referred to, is the name applied to the eastern part of the great reef lying eastward of St. Helier. It stretches out rather more than 2 miles from La Roque point, at the S.E. extreme of Jersey, and consists of gravel, shingle, and sand, interspersed with numerous ledges of sharp-pointed rocks ; the whole of which dries at low water of spring tides. The greater part of this bank covers at half flood; there is then 1 foot water on the ridge of sand and shingle extending from La Roque point to Seymour tower ; this spot is near La Roque point, where the Ridge is lowest, and most favourable for the passage of boats. At high water the bank is entirely covered, and is then only marked by La Conchière rock at its south extreme ; Seymour tower near the middle ; Karamé rock (at this time awash) on the S.E. ; and Little Seymour rock (also awash, but marked by a pole and basket beacon) near its eastern side.

From half flood to half ebb the stream runs with great velocity over the Violet bank, attaining the rate of 6 knots at springs, in a N.E. and S.W. direction.

As before remarked, the reef eastward of St. Helier, as well as the southern edge of the Violet bank, is well marked by conspicuous rocks ; which rocks, together with the dangers along this line, will now be described.

Dogs West Rock, as already stated at page 100, is situate near the outer

extreme of a rocky ridge stretching out from Point de Pas, and forming
the eastern boundary of the Little road of St. Helier: it is nearly awash
at high water, and its apex is marked with three white spots, and surmounted by an iron pole beacon.

Tas de Pois, or White rock, bears from the Dogs Nest rock S. b. E. ¼ E.,
distant three-quarters of a mile. Although only elevated 5 feet above
high water at spring tides, it is very remarkable, from its upper part
being well whitewashed all round, and from there being another rock
situate 2 cables to the eastward of it, which is rather larger and of black
colour.

White rock is fronted to the westward for 1½ cables by dangerous rocks
that never show; and to the N.W., distant a quarter of a mile, lies a rocky
group that uncovers about half tide. A chain of rather high rocks extend
from White rock to the shore.

La Frouquie lies three-quarters of a mile from White rock to the
S.S.E. It is 4 feet lower than White rock, and therefore awash at high
water springs. A chain of high rocks extend from La Frouquie to the
Le Croc point; the inner and highest of which is called *La Motte*. This
line of rocks marks the limit of the first bay eastward of St. Helier, which
is called *La Grève d'Azette*. The coast included between La Motte and
La Roque point is called St. Clements bay. A dangerous reef extends
from La Frouquie to the S.W. for the distance of a quarter of a mile.

Demie de Pas is the outermost of a long string of rocks extending
W.N.W. half a mile from La Frouquie, and for nearly the same distance
in a southerly direction from White rock. It dries 20 feet at low water,
is steep-to outside, and is marked by a pole beacon.

La Moye signal-post in line with Le Fret point bearing N.W., leads a
cable and a half outside all the rocks off Demie de Pas and La Frouquie.

Between La Frouquie and Icho tower there are no rocks visible at high
water to mark the outer edge of the reef, but at half tide and under it is
well marked by *Rouget* rock, which stands close to the edge of deep
water, and which bears S.E. ¼ S., distant five-eighths of a mile from La
Frouquie. Also by *Jinquet* rock, which dries 25 feet, and bears E.S.E.,
distant half a mile from Rouget rock. A third of a mile to the eastward
of Jinquet rock lies the *Grande Frouquie*, which is always 7 or 8 feet
above water at the highest tides, and which lies about half a mile to the
westward of Icho tower.

ICHO TOWER is surrounded by high rocks, being in this respect
different from Seymour tower, which at and above half-tide appears to be
completely isolated, and rises at once from the sea.

L'Echiquelez Rock is one of the principal sea marks near Icho tower,
from which it bears South, distant nearly half a mile. It is elevated

5 feet above the highest spring tides ; is steep-to on the outside to the westward ; but to the southward at the distance of $1\frac{1}{2}$ cables there is a half-tide rock ; and to the N.W. there are several dangerous rocks, the farthest of which dries 5 feet at low water, and lies at the distance of 2 cables S.S.W. from the Grande Frouquie.

Between Echiquelez rock and La Conchière the edge of the reef makes a line convex outward for the distance of nearly a quarter of a mile.

ICHO BANK, a dangerous bank of sunken rocks forming an irregular ridge in a N.N.W. and S.S.E. direction, about $4\frac{1}{2}$ cables long, and $1\frac{1}{2}$ cables broad, lies S.W. $2\frac{1}{4}$ miles from Icho tower.

The least water, $2\frac{1}{2}$ fathoms at low water springs, will be found on the north extreme of the bank, and from this shoal spot La Platte Roque tower is just seen on the west side of Icho tower N.E. $\frac{1}{2}$ E. easterly ; and St. Peter's church spire in line with Lower Blanc Pignon house, N. by W. $\frac{1}{4}$ W. On other parts of the bank there are from 3 to 5 fathoms at low water springs.

The channel between this bank and the rocks fronting Icho tower is 2 miles wide and clear of danger.

LA CONCHIÈRE ROCK lies on the line of Orgueil castle and Seymour tower, distant 2 miles from La Roque point at the south extreme of the Violet bank : it dries 41 feet at low water of spring tides, and is therefore never covered, although sometimes awash. A reef extends from it to the southward for the distance of about a cable ; Conchière rock should not therefore be approached nearer than a quarter of a mile.

Clearing Marks, for the line of reef just described, between La Frouquie and La Conchière rocks.—Keep the peak of Corbière rock just in sight touching La Moye point, until the Grand Anquette beacon comes open outside of La Conchière rock.

The VIOLET CHANNEL.—A sunken reef commences at La Conchière rock, and extends to the eastward on the line of L'Echiquelez and Conchière rocks to the distance of $1\frac{1}{2}$ miles. Within this line, and to the northward of it for the distance of rather more than a mile, the entire space is shoal water, and rocks innumerable ; so that at low water it would be difficult for a stranger to pick his way through them even in a boat. From La Conchière rock to the eastward the outer or southern edge of this reef is well marked, at the last quarter ebb, by a long string of rocks called *La Route en Ville ;* its eastern extreme is bounded by a sunken rock called the *Petit Four ;* and it may be said to extend to the northward as far as Le Cochon, La Noire, and the Grande Haisse rocks.

The navigable part of the Violet channel lies between the sunken part of the Violet reef just described, within, and the rocky banks without (or to the southward) called the Plateau de la Fourquie (on which are La

Goubinière and Platte Rousse rocks), and the Anquette rocks to the eastward. The narrowest part of this channel lies between the Petit Four and
the sunken rocks inside the Petite Anquette rock, where it is about
half a mile wide.

The Anquette Channel leads from the middle of the Violet channel
out between the Grande and Petite Anquette rocks to the eastward. The
water is deeper here than in the Violet channel, but, from the absence of
good leading marks, the passage is more difficult. The general depth in
it is 6 to 7 fathoms, and there are 5 to 6 fathoms in the Violet channel at
low water; but in the latter on the line of Princes tower and Little
Seymour beacon, and with the Grande Anquette beacon bearing E. $\frac{1}{2}$ S.,
I found a rock with 23 feet on it at low water, and another near it with 25
feet at that period : both these rocks were repeatedly examined by me; but
it is possible nevertheless that there may be 3 or 4 feet less water than is
here given. **Caution** is therefore necessary in passing this part of the
channel at low water, in large ships. In vessels above 15 feet draught it
will be prudent to wait until the flood tide has fairly made, and with any
swell on, such vessels should not pass until first quarter flood.

ROCKS and DANGERS in the VIOLET CHANNEL and its Approaches.
—La Conchière rock, described at page 105, is the principal mark at the
western entrance of the Violet channel.

Taxé lies to the eastward of La Conchière, distant from it rather more
than half a mile, and exactly on the line of La Conchière and Echiquelez
rocks; it dries 10 feet at low water.

A quarter of a mile eastward of Taxé rock ; with Echiquelez rock a
little open southward of La Conchière, lies the highest of the western
rocks of the Route en Ville, which dries 11 feet ; and there is another
rock a cable's length to the eastward of it, which dries 10 feet at low
water.

From these rocks to the eastward, for about half a mile, lying close to
the deep water, the Route en Ville chain extends on a line convex outward. Most of the rocks are nearly awash at low water.

St. Martin's church (spire) in line with Gorey tower N. by W. passes over
a rock with only 2 feet over it at low water, lying half a cable within or
westward of its eastern end. They will be cleared to the S.W. by keeping
Icho tower open a little outside of Conchière rock, until Princes tower
comes in line with Seymour tower ; after which keep Echiquelez rock
open South of Conchière until Princes tower comes in line with No. 5
tower.

The Petit Four, having 2 feet on it at low water, marks the eastern
extreme of the Violet reef: it lies with Karamé rock just shut in with the
outer part of the high table-land above Noirmont point, N.W. by W. $\frac{1}{4}$ W.

The sentry box of Coupe guard-house (a stone turret on the apex of Coupe bluff) over the end of the bluff just within the breakwater house at Verclut point, N. ¼ W. ; and the Grand Anquette beacon on the north side of Petite Anquette rock S.E. by E. ¼ E.

La Goubinière Rock dries 20 feet at low water ; it lies at the western end of the Plateau de la Frouquie, a very little to the eastward of the line of Orgueil castle, Seymour tower, and Conchière rock ; distant from the latter nearly a mile and a quarter. On the rock, La Moye signal-post is seen over the outer part of Le Fret point N.W.

There are several rocks to the northward of La Goubinière, the outer of which (named Conger rock) dries 16 feet at low water, and lies at the distance of a cable from it.

Orgueil castle a little open to the westward of Seymour tower and Conchière rock clears the Goubinère and all dangers on the west side of the Plateau de Frouquie.

Frouquie Aubert Rock lies on the south-western edge of the Plateau de la Frouquie, 1¼ miles south-eastward of the Goubinière ; it uncovers 26 feet at low water, and does not cover at neaps. On it St. Peter's church spire is in line with the white patch on South hill N.N.W. ¼ W., and St. Martin's church spire is a good sail's breadth open north-eastward of Seymour tower N. ¾ W.

La Rousse Platte Rock marks the east side of the Plateau de la Frouquie, and lies E. ¾ S. rather more than a mile from La Goubinière : it is a large flat rock, about half a cable in diameter, and dries 14 feet at low water. Between this rock and La Goubinière are several rocks, one of which dries 15 feet at low water ; another, which dries only 4 feet, is however the most dangerous, from standing more prominently out in the channel.

Pierre de Enfans Rock lies a quarter of a mile to the southward of Rousse Platte, and being 6 feet higher than it, makes a very useful mark when Rousse Platte is covered by the tide.

Les ANQUETTE ROCKS lie at the distance of 2½ and 3 miles to the eastward of Conchière rock, and form the eastern boundary of the Violet channel. *The Petite Anquette* uncovers 20 feet at low water. On it La Bergerie (a remarkable insulated house on the heights above Noirmont point), is in line with the north side of La Motte rock, N.W. by W.; and Archirondel tower appears its apparent breadth open north-eastward of Rozel manor-house, N. by W. ¼ W.

An extensive reef lies off the Petite Anquette to the northward, one of the most dangerous clumps on which are called *the Seals*. The westernmost Seal dries 4 feet, and lies about N.N.W. a third of a mile from the Petite Anquette. There is a sunken rock with only 12 feet at low water, lying an eighth of a mile to the westward of the western Seal. Also a dangerous clump called *Marin Reef*, which lies N.N.E. nearly three-quarters of a mile from Petite Anquette, having only 3 feet on it at low water. All these rocks are probably connected with the Petite Anquette.

Grune Le Feuvre lies N.E. ¼ N., 1⅓ miles from Petite Anquette, and has only 6 feet on it at low water.

The Grande Anquette Rock lies S. E.½ E., 3⅝ miles from Seymour tower: it formerly covered at about 8 feet above half tide, but is now marked by a stone pillar beacon* (painted in horizontal bands of *red and white* alternately), 20 feet above high water, and surmounted by staff and ball. From the beacon Petite Anquette rock bears N.W. by W. ¼ W., distant three-quarters of a mile; Rousse Platte rock W. ⅔ S., 2¼ miles; Grande Arconée (which dries 9 feet) S.S.E. ¼ E., 1 mile ; and Porpoise rock S.W. by W. ¼ W., seven-eighths of a mile.

Anquette Patches, a small rocky bank with 2 fathoms on its east end, lying N.E. by N. nearly a mile from the Grande Anquette. Seymour tower is in one with La Motte rock, N.W. by W. ½ W. ; and Rozel mill is in line with St. Catherine tower, N.N.W. ½ W. Another bank of rock and gravel lies W.N.W. ¼ W., 2 miles from the Grande Anquette. Its shoalest part, 3 fathoms, lies with Rozel windmill a little open eastward of St. Catherine's tower N.W. by N., and Grande Anquette and La Conchée rocks in line W.N.W. ¼ W.

The Sunken Reef South of the Grande Anquette.—There are some dangerous sunken rocks lying at the distance of a quarter of a mile S.E. of the Anquette beacon ; and the space to the southward of it for the distance of 1½ miles is occupied by a vast reef, called by the French *Plateau de la Arconée ;* some of the rocks on which begin to uncover soon after the last quarter ebb of a spring tide, others are only awash at low water, and by far the largest part of them never appear at all.

The Grande Arconée rock (which dries 9 feet at low water) stands on the east side of this plateau ; *the Porpoise rock* (drying 4 feet), marks its western boundary ; the *Grand Four rock* (drying 7 feet) lies just within its south-west extreme ; with *La Hauch rock* (drying 6 feet) lying at the distance of a mile to the south-eastward of the latter.

The channel between Plateau de la Frouquie and Plateau de la Arconée has 5½ fathoms at low water, but its free navigation is impeded by a string of rocks extending across, between Pierre des Enfans and the Grand Four, about a cable apart ; some of which are awash, and others have 5 feet over them at low water springs.

The great strength of the stream at this part of the channel, and the

---

* This beacon has been washed away by the sea, but is to be replaced.

absence of good marks, render its navigation extremely perilous near low water; no vessel should attempt to pass through, therefore, until after first quarter flood.

Coupe guard-house turret perceptibly open outside the breakwater house of Verclut point (same mark as for northern entrance of the Violet channel), will lead through the best part of the channel, but even this line leads *over* one of the rocks, which must be avoided, and after passing it, haul out gradually round Frouquie Aubert.

ANQUETTE GRAVEL BANKS commence near the south-west extreme of the Plateau des Arconies and extend to the south-eastward in an almost continuous line, for a distance of 5 miles. They consist of a number of narrow ridgy banks of fine gravel, having generally a depth of 3 and 4 fathoms over them at low water: excepting on one detached bank near the end, where there are only 2 fathoms. The marks for this spot are, La Moye signal post just inside (or to the northward) of Frouquie Aubert N.W., westerly: and the Grande Anquette a little within Verclut point N. by W. $\frac{1}{2}$ W.

Note.—There are good 7-fathom channels on either side of this bank.

DIRECTIONS from St. Helier to the eastward, and through the Violet channel.—Having cleared the dangers outside the Little road, according to directions already given for entering, proceed with La Moye signal-post in line with Le Fret point, bearing N.W., until the peak of Corbière rock is seen just open of La Moye point, bearing N.W. $\frac{1}{2}$ W., which now becomes the leading mark until Orgueil castle comes on with Icho tower; at which position (distant from the outer edge of the reef about half a mile) the Grande Anquette beacon will be seen a little open of Conchière rock bearing E. by S. $\frac{1}{2}$ S.

From hence steer S.E. by E. $\frac{1}{4}$ E., parallel to the outer edge of the reef. The depth along this line will be 5 to 7 fathoms at low water. Conchière rock will be passed at the distance of about one-third of a mile; and when to the eastward of it, bring the Echiquelez rock in line with Noirmont tower, N.W. $\frac{2}{3}$ W., for a leading mark, until Princes tower comes in line with Seymour tower: near the intersection of these lines the Platte Rousse will bear S.W., distant a third of a mile, and the Grande Anquette beacon East. Steer now N.E. to pass through the deepest part of the channel, or East (for the Grande Anquette beacon) to pass through the middle of it, until the stone turret of Coupe guard-house comes in line with (or a little open to the eastward of) the house on the breakwater under Verclut bluff, N. $\frac{1}{2}$ W., with which mark run up to abreast the Petit Four.

As the narrowest part of the channel lies between the Petit Four and Petite Anquette, it may be useful to know that the stone turret on Coupe point, and the breakwater house at Verclut point, exactly in line N. $\frac{1}{2}$ W., leads a cable's length outside the Petit Four : at this position Rozel wind-mill is seen touching the north side of Mont Orgueil castle, N. by W. $\frac{1}{2}$ W., and St. Catherine's tower (white) is in line with Archirondel tower (red). When abreast Petit Four, Karamé rock will be seen just shut in with the high land above Noirmont point, N.W. by W. $\frac{1}{4}$ W., and the Grande Anquette beacon on the north side of Petite Anquette, S.E. by E. $\frac{1}{4}$ E.

From this position the same leading mark (Coupe turret a little open eastward of breakwater house, N. $\frac{1}{2}$ W.) will carry you up inside the Banc du Chateau, past the Giffard rock, to the anchorage in Gorey road. After passing Giffard rock these objects should be brought exactly in line to pass through the centre of the channel.

If it be desired to haul out to the eastward of the Chateau bank, a small vessel may do so when Echiquelez rock comes open north of Karamé rock, but a large vessel should not attempt it until Icho and Seymour towers are in line, to avoid some stony banks lying to the northward of Grune le Feuvre, on which there is only 25 feet at low water.

GROUVILLE BAY, which derives its name from a hamlet near St. Clement Church, is situate on the east side of Jersey, between La Roque point and Mont Orgueil. Its outer boundary to the southward commences on the N.E. side of the Violet bank, and is very rocky; there are numerous clumps of rocks scattered along the low-water line of the bay to the northward (which dries out to the distance of a mile from the shore); there are also many rocks within this line as well as without; nevertheless the beach of Grouville bay, at low water, presents a coast scene of great beauty ; consisting of a vast expanse of fine white sand, rising with a gentle slope towards the shore, bounded on the south in the distance by the rugged rocks of the Violet bank and Seymour tower, and on the north by the stately Mont Orgueil, crowned by its venerable castle.

GOREY HARBOUR lies immediately under Mont Orgueil castle to the south-west. It is formed by a stone pier built out from the S.W. part of Orgueil head. The accommodation for vessels is very limited ; the outer pier berth having only a depth of 9 feet alongside of it at half tide, and at low water springs the sand dries for the distance of a cable outside the pier-head ; nevertheless vessels of 300 tons may occasionally be seen here ; and as it is the head quarters of the oyster fishery, there are a large number of sloops (from 30 to 50 tons burthen) belonging to the place. Immediately off the outer end of the pier, and at the distance of 400 feet from it, there is a space of ground paved with flat stones for depositing the oysters. This place is marked by a rough pole beacon near its north-eastern end, at the distance of 60 feet from its outer edge. With this exception the bottom of Gorey harbour is good for grounding vessels, consisting of mud and sand. At night a faint light is shown from the end of the pier.

Caution.—At spring tides and after half flood the stream sets with great force round the pier-head to the northward, for which due allowance must be made. Sharp vessels not provided with legs should always get a pier berth, and list in, assisted by their mast-head tackles on shore, to prevent their falling over at low water. During the severe gales in winter a vessel will strain less in taking the ground, be much better sheltered, and will experience far less scend in this harbour than in any other in the Channel islands.

ROCKS and DANGERS in GROUVILLE BAY.—Among the most prominent—

The Equerrière is the largest and most conspicuous rock off Gorey harbour, from which it is distant a third of a mile : it dries 35 feet, and is marked by a pole and fish-tail beacon.

The Ecureuil, lying a quarter of a mile S.W. of the Equerrière, dries 14 feet, and is marked by a pole and basket beacon.

The Horn Rock lies a mile to the southward of the Ecureuil ; it is the outer rock of Frouquies de la Grève, dries 16 feet, and is marked by a staff and horizontal cross beacon.

Amongst other rocks of less importance are : *Little Seymour* rock (awash at high water, and marked by a pole and basket beacon), from which a long string of rocks extend out to the eastward, and which may be said to form the southern boundary of Grouville bay at low water. Along this line of rocks are *The Grande Haisse* (which dries 22 feet), and *La Noire* (dries 14 feet), the latter lying nearly a mile outside Little Seymour beacon.

The Giffard is the outer danger of the long string of rocks above mentioned. There is 1 foot on it at low water. From Little Seymour beacon it lies E. by N. $\frac{1}{2}$ N. nearly $1\frac{1}{4}$ miles, and W. by S. $\frac{1}{2}$ S., nearly half a mile from the middle of the *South Ridge* sand at the south end of the Banc du Chateau (on which there is only 12 feet at low water). On the Giffard rock Rozel mill is in line with La Crête guard-house, N. by W. $\frac{1}{2}$ W. ; and Little Seymour beacon is a little open northward of Gros Etac, W. by S. $\frac{1}{2}$ S.

The other rocks in Grouville bay, off Gorey harbour, of inferior magnitude, although probably not less dangerous, are—*Azicot rock,* which lies a quarter of a mile outside the end of Gorey pier : it dries 5 feet at low water, and is marked by a spar buoy. *Les Guillimots,* a group of rocks lying S.S.W., distant a quarter of a mile from Azicot ; the outer rock of the group dries 6 feet, and is marked with a spar buoy. *Les Burons,* a rocky group lying S.S.E. a quarter of a mile from Les Guillimots, the highest rock of which lies to the N.E., and is marked with a spar buoy.

La Grune du Port, having 5 feet over it at low water, lies outside the Burons, on a line with the end of Gorey pier and Horn Rock beacon ; a third of a mile within the latter.

The Road Rock has 9 feet on it at low water, and lies an eighth of a mile outside La Grune du Port, on a line of direction opposite to No. 2 tower. St. Catherine tower (white) is *just* shut in with Le Crête point N. ¾ W., and No. 5 tower is in line with the extreme end of the high table-land southward of Grouville mill W. ¼ S.

There is a small rock with 26 feet on it at low water, lying at the distance of a quarter of a mile from the Road rock, in the direction of Verclut point; within which lies the *Inner Road rock*; having 16 feet over it at low water. On this rock St. Catherine tower is just shut in with Le Crête point N. ¾ W., and Gorey tower is in line with the Ecureuil beacon, the latter being rather less than a quarter of a mile distant.

The TRES GRUNES lie outside, to the eastward of Equerrière rock, distant from it nearly a quarter of a mile. They are awash at low water. Little Seymour beacon in line with Seymour tower clears them outside to the eastward by three-quarters of a cable, but passes *over* another rock with 26 feet on it at low water ; which rock may be considered to be the extreme end of the ledge, for the water is deep close to the outside of it. Therefore when passing the Tres Grunes in a large ship, open Little Seymour beacon perceptibly to the westward of Seymour tower.

North of the Tres Grunes, and distant from them about an eighth of a mile, lies the *Pacquet rock*, having 2 feet on it at low water, within which to the N.W., and about the same distance, are the *Arches rocks*, a small group which dry 15 feet at low water ; the south-eastern of which is marked with a *spar* buoy.

BANC DU CHATEAU lies off Grouville bay to the eastward, nearly parallel to the low water line of the shore, and distant from it rather more than a mile. Taking the 5-fathom contour line, it is rather more than 2 miles long, by a third of a mile wide. The main body of the bank has a general depth of 3 fathoms at low water, over a gravelly bottom ; but on this base are numerous narrow sandy ridges, running across the bank, in an E.S.E. and W.N.W. direction. Near the middle of the bank, for the space of about a mile, these sand ridges lie so close together that they may be considered as one continuous bank ; accordingly they have been named the *Middle bank*. At the lowest spring tides this part occasionally dries.

The North Sand Ridge lies rather more than a quarter of a mile within the north end of the Banc du Chateau, and has 10 feet at low water ; just to the southward of this, however, there is a smaller ridge with only 5 feet at that period.

The South Sand Ridge has 12 feet on it at low water, and lies along the south-western and southern edge of the bank, close to the deep water. There can be no doubt that the Banc du Chateau has been formed entirely by the action of the tidal stream, and that the upper part of it is continually shifting (within a particular and limited space). During westerly winds the ridgy apexes of the sand-banks on it are so sharp that, when they are awash, a boat may easily knock them down in passing over. At such times the banks are about 4 feet higher than with easterly winds.

This bank is of course a great protection to the anchorage in Gorey roads.

Clearing Marks.—Grouville mill in line with the outer end of Gorey pier W. by S. ¾ S., just clears the 5-fathom contour line at the north extreme of the bank. Icho tower and Little Seymour beacon in line, W. ¾ S., leads clear close to its southern end. Coupe guard-house turret in line with the breakwater house close under Verclut bluff, bearing N. ½ W., clears the N.W. corner, and leads down its west side, nearly in mid channel; and the same Coupe guard-house turret in line with St. Catherine breakwater lighthouse, bearing N.N.W., will clear the bank to the eastward, as well as a rocky 5-fathom patch outside of it.

Tongue Banks are two small shoal spots, lying due east from South ridge sand; distant from it nearly 1 and 2 miles respectively, but separated from Banc du Chateau, and from each other, by good sound channels of deep water. They are of the same character as Chateau bank, having sharp ridgy apexes of fine sand. The least water on the eastern bank is 36 feet, and on the western 23 feet at low water.

On the 23 feet ridge Coupe turret appears a little open of St. Catherine's breakwater lighthouse, N.N.W., and Icho tower is open a little northward of Little Seymour beacon W. by S.

ANCHORAGE.—Between the west side of Banc du Chateau and the 5-fathom contour line fronting Grouville bay lies the Great road, which is a safe anchorage, and sufficiently capacious to accommodate 10 or 12 sail of the line, it being a mile long N. and S., by nearly half a mile broad. The eastern limit of this anchorage is marked by Coupe guard-house turret being in line with the breakwater house at Verclut bluff, N. ½ W. At its western limit St. Catherine tower (white) and Archirondel tower (red) are in line. At its north extreme Gorey tower is in line with the end of the pier; and to the southward No. 4 tower and the Horn rock beacon in line marks the boundary. Within the space included by these lines will be found 6 to 8 fathoms at the lowest spring tides, over an even bottom of gravel and shells.

The Inner road lies within the 5-fathom contour line, between the Outer and Inner road rocks, and between the Ecuriel beacon and the Burons rocks. Near the centre of this space are the Government moorings, marked by a large buoy in 18 feet at low water. The ground chain of these moorings lies north and south; there are 38 fathoms of chain on each arm, and anchors of 24 and 30 cwt. A cable's length within this buoy there are 2 fathoms, and 4½ fathoms at the same distance outside. The best line to anchor on in the outer road is Grouville church spire in line with Fort Henry, and in the inner road, Princes tower open to the northward of Fort William its apparent breadth. Princes tower will at the same time be in line with the buoy of the Government moorings. The buoy lies nearly on the leading line for Gorey harbour, viz., Gorey church in line with the end of the pier.

The anchorage in Gorey roads deserves to be better known than it is, for without any doubt it is the only place in the Channel Islands (including also the entire coast of the gulf in which they are situated) to which a squadron of heavy ships might run for shelter in a westerly gale with the certainty of finding it; and the approach is so easy that, with a proper chart and sailing directions, any seaman of ordinary ability should be able to take his ship in without a pilot.

DIRECTIONS for GROUVILLE BAY.—When running for Grouville bay from the northward, and having cleared the Pierres de Lecq and the Drouilles, as well as the dangers lying near the north end of Jersey according to directions hereafter given, be careful to give Nez du Guet and La Coupe points a berth of at least a quarter of a mile when rounding them, in order to avoid the foul ground which projects from each. By keeping the land at Belle Hougue in sight to the northward of Tour de Rozel, bearing N.W. ¼ W., it will lead to the northward of the Pillon rock and dangers off Coupe point; and La Roque tower in one with Equerrière rock S.W. ¼ S. will lead to the eastward of them.

The North Channel into Gorey road lies between Fara ledge and the north end of Banc du Chateau, and is only a quarter of a mile wide at its narrowest part, with a depth of 6 fathoms at the lowest tides; but it is a half a mile wide with 4 fathoms, and therefore perfectly safe with ordinary care, even for the largest ships. .

Enter this channel with Grouville mill touching the upper part of Orgueil bluff bearing W. by S. ¾ S.; and when Little Seymour beacon comes in line with Seymour tower S.S.W. ¼ W., or the Equerrière rock beacon in line with No. 2 tower bearing S.W. ¼ W., you will be inside the Banc du Chateau, and must haul round to the southward, to bring the stone turret above Coupe guard-house (a ruin) in line with the break-water house under Verclut bluff, at the inner part of St. Catherine breakwater, bearing N. ½ W., which is the fairway leading mark inside Banc du Chateau ; it is also the eastern limit of the anchorage in the Outer road.

Should it be desired to anchor as near the shore as possible, Coupe guard-house turret may be shut in a little over Verclut point ; but Little Seymour beacon should be kept perceptibly open westward of Seymour tower until Gorey tower comes open of the pier end, or until the best anchoring lines (given above) are approached.   Anchor as convenient according to directions already given.

The South Channel lies between the south end of the Banc du Chateau and the reefs lying north of Petite Anquette without, and between the former and the Giffard rock within ; the latter of which is its narrowest part, being here barely a half a mile wide.   The water is deep throughout, having not less than 8 fathoms at the lowest tides.

Approaching this channel from the northward, keep Coupe guard-house turret outside St. Catherine breakwater lighthouse, N.N.W., until Princes tower comes in line with Gorey pier end, to clear a rocky bank outside the Banc du Chateau ; after which the Coupe may be brought inside the breakwater lighthouse as far as the outer arches ; and when Icho tower is seen a little open to the southward of Little Seymour beacon, haul in round the south end of the bank.

Rozel windmill over La Crête bluff clears the inside part of South ridge sand, but the mid-channel leading mark is Gorey church spire in line with the end of the pier (marked by a white patch) N.W. by N., until Coupe comes in line with the breakwater house under Verclut bluff, N. ½ W., with which run up to the anchorage in the outer road ; anchoring as convenient, after passing the line of Horn rock and No. 4 tower, according to directions already given.   Working a large ship into the Great road through the South channel, do not open Icho tower to the southward of Seymour tower until the Coupe comes to the westward of the middle of St. Catherine breakwater, to clear the stony banks, north of Petite Anquette, on which there is 25 feet at low water.

To enter Gorey Harbonr.—Keep Grouville church (spire) on the north side of Fort Henry, W. ¾ N., until Gorey church (spire) comes open a little southward of the end of Gorey pier N.W. by N. ; with which mark run up to the entrance of the harbour.

There are two small warping buoys off the entrance ; one situate nearly on the line of the inner part of the pier, distant nearly a cable's length from the end ; the other within this line, distant only a third of a cable from the pier end.   Pass between this inner buoy and the end of the pier, being careful not to approach the latter too close, as the flood tide sets round it to the eastward with great strength.   When the Horn rock (of the Frouquies de Grève) is awash there will be 10 feet water just off the end of Gorey pier, and 5 feet at the outer berth within it.

Grouville Bay to the South-eastward.—Bring Gorey church (spire) in line with the white patch at the end of Gorey pier, N.W. by N., as before, and run out until Icho tower comes midway between Seymour tower and Little Seymour beacon W. ¼ S.; haul out to the eastward on this mark until the Coupe is seen a little open eastward of St. Catherine's breakwater lighthouse, N.N.W. ¼ W.; which marks will clear all danger off the Anquettes.

Grouville Bay to the Southward through Le Beuf Channel.—After clearing the Anquette N.E. patch, as above, steer to the southward, and bring Coupe turret in line with St. Catherine's breakwater lighthouse, N.N.W.; with which mark pass westward of the east Anquette patch, and to the southward. As the line of Icho and Noirmont towers is approached, Coupe turret may be brought a little inside the lighthouse; and when to the southward of this line, and clear of the Grande Arconée, Coupe turret should be brought (within or) to the westward of the lighthouse at least one third the distance to Verclut point, to clear the west side of the *Basse Occid des Bœufs*; from whence a S.S.W. course will lead down to the channels through the Anquette gravel banks (described at page 109) which may always be seen by the tide rippling over them, and easily avoided. When La Moye signal-post appears open of Le Fret point, N.W., the gravel banks will be cleared, and a vessel may haul out to the westward.

In passing through this channel it will be useful to remember that Coupe turret touching the outer part of St. Catherine's lighthouse, N.N.W., leads *over* the Anquette N.E. patch, and also *over* the *Basse Occid des Bœufs*, the cross mark for the latter being Bergerie house in line with Rousse rock, N.W. ¾ W.

A small vessel, bound from Gorey to the southward, may, on the flood tide, pass inside Grune *L Feuvre* and the Anquette N.E. patch, by bringing St. Martin church spire open northward of the white patch on the north side of Mont Orgueil castle (about the breadth of the patch at least), N.N.W. ½ W.

A small vessel may also (at or above half-flood) pass between Fronquie Aubert and the Arconée by keeping the Coupe turret in line with the breakwater house at Verclut point, N. ½ W., until La Moye signal-post appears a little open of Le Fret point N.W., when she may haul out to the westward.

If on approaching Le Beuf channel from the southward the marks on Jersey are indistinct, bring Mount Huchon, on the French coast, in line with the sandy point of Blainville river, E.S.E., or Coutances cathedral in line with the south end of Blainville village, S.E. by E., which may lead up until they can be made out.

It being generally difficult to distinguish the marks for this channel, owing to their great distance, no vessel of heavy draught should attempt to pass through, except in charge of an experienced pilot, and at the upper stages of the tide; nor should square rigged vessels generally attempt to work through, excepting under such conditions.

Grouville Bay through the Violet Channel. — When leaving the anchorage in Gorey road, bring Gorey church (spire) in line with the white patch on the pier head N.W. by N., and run out until the Gros Etac comes on with the south side of Little Seymour beacon W. by S. $\frac{1}{2}$ S. This position will be abreast of the Giffard rock, where Coupe guard-house turret will be seen a little open eastward of the breakwater house under Verclut bluff, which is the leading mark to enter the Violet channel with. When approaching the Violet channel be particular that Coupe guard-house turret is *only just open* eastward of the house at Verclut point. As a check, it will be useful to remember that so long as you can see any part of the white tower in St. Catherine bay open to the eastward of Archirondel tower, you will be quite far enough to the eastward. Another good mark for the middle of the channel when abreast the Petit Four is, Rozel mill touching the north side of Mont Orgueil castle N. by W. $\frac{1}{2}$ W.

When abreast the Petit Four, Karamé rock will appear just shut in with the high land above Noirmont point N.W. by W. $\frac{1}{2}$ W., and Grande Anquette beacon in line with the north side of Petite Anquette rock S.E. by E. $\frac{1}{4}$ E. From this position steer so as to bring Coupe guard-house turret in line with Verclut point house, and use it for a leading mark still; or you may bring Rousse Platte rock on a S.W. bearing, and steer direct for it until Grande Anquette beacon bears East. In either case proceed due west from Anquette beacon until Icho tower comes in line with Conchière rock, when you will be clear of the Route en Ville, and may steer so as to pass about a third of a mile to the southward of Conchière rock; or using the sailing marks given at page 109 in an inverse order to proceed to the westward with.

Anne Port Bay, between Grouville and St. Catherine, is small, and the approach to it dangerous, from outlying rocks; there is, however, good anchorage off it, which is used occasionally by fishing boats and other small craft, in fine weather. The principal dangers off it are :—

The Seven Grunes, a long straggling reef, extending out from and to the eastward of the Gross Moie for the distance of about a third of a mile. The highest of these rocks (near the middle of the reef) uncovers 7 feet at low water, and the outer Grune has 5 feet over it at that period.

Les Cloches, lying at the distance of a third of a mile from La Crête point, are the southern rocks of the Fara or St. Catherine bank. They dry 5 feet at low water. Between these rocks and the Seven Grunes lies the anchorage off Anne Port above referred to, which, although only a quarter of a mile in extent north and south, has an even depth of 5 fathoms over it, and is sheltered from the tide.

ST. CATHERINE BAY, on the eastern shore of Jersey to the northward of Mont Orgueil castle, though much contracted by rocks, affords excellent anchorage for small craft in 2 and 3 fathoms water, over a bottom of muddy sand, with very long grass and seaweed; it cannot, however, be entered or left by a sailing vessel but with a leading wind. The bay is completely sheltered from northerly, westerly, and south-westerly winds. South-easterly and easterly winds, however, blow right in, and at such times, near high water, there is a short, turbulent, chopping sea; in proportion as the tide falls, however, the sea subsides.

A harbour of refuge was begun in this bay in the year 1847. The northern breakwater has been carried out 826 yards in a south-easterly direction from Verclut point, the northern extremity of the bay, and over the rocky bed named the Pierre Mouillée, and has a depth of 5 fathoms at its outer end at low water. It was completed in 1855, and forms an admirable pier, with a lofty parapet, alongside of which a steamer might coal, water, land or embark troops with ease, in any wind from N.N.E. round westerly to S.W.

The southern breakwater was designed to extend in an E. $\frac{1}{2}$ N. direction from the point near Archirondel tower, and to be carried out over the Basse de Fara. Of this about 200 yards, as far as the tower, has been built; the remaining 1,400 yards are not yet begun.

This harbour when completed may at no distant period be very useful in bringing Jersey into closer commercial communication with France; but from the great strength of the tides across its entrance, and the dangerous rocks near, it is difficult of access to sailing vessels in bad weather, and therefore fit only for ordinary use of steamers.

Light.—A light tower (an octagonal structure of iron, painted white, and 30 feet high from base to vane,) stands on the outer extremity of the parapet wall of Verclut pier or breakwater. It exhibits a fixed white light, dioptric and of the fifth order, at 60 feet above the mean level of the sea, and visible from 10 to 12 miles off.

DANGERS off and in ST. CATHERINE BAY.—The approach to St. Catherine bay from the south-east is completely barred by a large bank of rocks about half a mile square, called St. Catherine bank, the outer part of which extends to the eastward of Archirondel tower for the distance of three-quarters of a mile. These rocks begin to uncover about the last quarter ebb, many show at low water, but by far the greater number never appear at all.

This bank is bounded on the south by Les Cloches, already described; on the east and north by the Grande Fara, or Le Fara, and the Grune du Nord, and within to the north-west by the Basses de Fara. Of these rocks Le Fara is the largest and most conspicuous; it is about half a cable in diameter, and dries 9 feet.

Fara Ledge lies south-eastward of the Grande Fara, distant from it about a third of a mile; it is a rocky bank about a cable in diameter, and (about the same distance) detached from the outer part of St. Catherine bank. The least depth we found was 21 feet at low water, but there may be a foot or two less. No. 2 tower and Equerrière beacon in line, S.W. ¼ W., just clears its S.E. side; and Little Seymour beacon in line with Seymour tower, S.S.W. ¼ W., just touches its western extreme. This latter mark also touches the outer eastern extreme of St. Catherine bank in 28 feet; which same part will be cleared to the north-eastward by bringing Coupe guard-house in line with, or a little open to the eastward of, the breakwater lighthouse, bearing N.N.W.

Eureka Rock, having 12 feet on it at low water, lies off the end of the breakwater, distant a quarter of a mile from the lighthouse. On the rock the north side of the breakwater is a very little open, and No. 4 tower is just shut in with Orgueil point.

The Pillon Rock has only 4 feet at low water, and lies due north from Eureka rock, distant from it a cable and a quarter, and exactly 2 cables from the end of the breakwater. On the rock St. Martin church (spire) is just shut in with the breakwater lighthouse, and No. 3 tower is in line with Orgueil point.

Within St. Catherine Bay, on a line between the breakwater lighthouse and Achirondel tower, and distant nearly 2 cables from the lighthouse, there is a rock with only 8 feet on it at low water; and another rock with only 7 feet over it at that period, lying a little to the northward of a line drawn through the breakwater lighthouse and St. Catherine tower, and with Coupe guard-house just showing over Verclut point.

Caution.—During spring tides the stream sets over St. Catherine bank into the bay, also round the end of the breakwater, with great velocity, due allowance for which must be made.

ANCHORAGE.—There is barely room for one large vessel to anchor in St. Catherine bay. The best position is off the middle of the breakwater, distant from it about a cable or a cable and a quarter, in 5 fathoms at low water.

Small vessels may lay farther in towards the depth of the bay, with St. Martin church spire in line with the south extreme of the bluff north-

ward of St. Catherine tower, W. by N. ½ N., and Seymour tower in line
with Grosse Moie, S. by W. ½ W. The depth here is 2 fathoms at low
water springs; at the distance of a cable within this position there is
only 1 fathom, and at the same distance off shore, 3¼ fathoms. The bottom
is a mixture of fine sand and mud throughout.

DIRECTIONS.—From Grouville to St. Catherine bay, run out of the
Inner road off Gorey, with Princes tower in line with the north side of,
or a little open of, Fort William, until Little Seymour beacon is seen
just open west of Seymour tower, S.S.W. ½ W., to clear the Tres Grunes
and foul ground outside of them; to the northward of which, bring Little
Seymour beacon and Seymour tower exactly in line, to pass inside Fara
ledge, in 23 feet at low water; or No. 2 tower a little open south-eastward
of Equerrière beacon, S.W. ¼ W., to pass outside Fara ledge.

When Coupe guard-house is open a little eastward of St. Catherine
breakwater lighthouse, you will be clear of all the rocks of St. Catherine
bank, and may steer for the lighthouse, hauling into the harbour when at
the distance of a cable from it, and anchoring as convenient, according to
the marks already given.

At the distance of a cable south of the breakwater lighthouse, St.
Martin church spire will appear, nearly shut in over the bluff to the northward of St. Catherine tower, which is the best mark to run into the bay
with.

There is another passage into this bay, lying to the southward, and
within Les Cloches, between them and Le Crête point, which, although
much encumbered with rocks nearly awash at low water, may occasionally
be useful to small craft with pilots. A very useful mark for this small
channel during the lower part of the tide is, to bring St. Catherine tower
on the east side of Petite Fara rock, to clear the outer rock of the Seven
Grunes, and to open the tower a little inside Petite Fara before passing
La Crête point, to clear the sunken rocks lying along the inside part of
St. Catherine bank. You may pass inside Petite Fara (close to it) in 9 feet
at low water.

Coupe Point is a bluff about 180 feet high, connected with the neighbouring land by a narrow neck of little more than half that height, from
which the name is derived. On the apex of the bluff there is a ruined
guard-house, surmounted by a stone sentry-box or turret; the latter thus
making a conspicuous and very useful mark. An extensive range of farm
buildings stands near the edge of the plateau within and overlooking
the Coupe; and it may be further known by two high rocks, lying at the
distance of half a cable outside the bluff, from which a dangerous reef
extends out to the eastward for nearly 2 cables.

FLIQUET BAY is between Verclut and La Coupe points, and since the completion of the north arm of the breakwater affords good shelter with south-westerly winds, but it is quite exposed to those between south, round easterly to W.N.W. As Gorey road affords no shelter with southerly winds, trading vessels bound to Gorey harbour, during strong winds from that quarter, and not able to save their tide in, may anchor under the break-water until two hours flood, when they would still carry sufficient southerly tide to enable them to reach the road by the time they would have water into the harbour. No vessel, however, should remain at anchor in this bay longer than a tide, for fear of a sudden shift of wind to the S.E. or N.E., which would place her in a precarious position. The bottom is composed of hard sand, and quite free from any foul ground, with the exception of the Brayes, a small group of rocks extending a cable's length from La Coupe point, and the Coupe rock, with 10 feet on it, which lies E.S.E. 4 cables from Coupe guard-house turret, and N. by E. nearly half a mile from the outer part of St. Catherine breakwater.

Anchorage.—Coming from the northward, Seymour house in line with or a little open to the eastward of the breakwater house under Verclut point, S.S.W. ½ W., will lead between the Brayes and Coupe rock ; and coming from the eastward, Rozel windmill in line with Fliquet tower, N.W. by W. ¾ W., will lead between the Pillon rock and the bank. The best anchorage in Fliquet bay, with southerly or south-westerly winds, is in 6 fathoms water midway between the breakwater and the Coupe bank, with Nez du Guet and La Coupe points in one, N.W. by W., and the martello tower on the hill to the northward of Mont Orgueil castle in line with the centre of the breakwater, S.W. by S. With westerly winds, anchor nearer La Coupe point, about the centre of the bay.

Telegraph Cable, between Jersey and France, lies in a N.W. by W. ¼ W. and S.E. by E. ¼ E. direction between Fliquet bay, Jersey, and Piron, France. The shore end landing in Jersey is marked by a white martello tower, on which is painted in black letters the word *Telegraph,* sur-mounted by a green disc.

To prevent damage to the cable by anchors, grapnels, oyster dredges, &c. used by fishermen, the following directions are given :—The course of the cable is distinctly indicated by the two towers, which, during the day, are a sufficient guide for clearing it. Fishing vessels on the coast of Jersey having no compass can avoid the cable to the south by keeping Coupe point in one with Tour de Rozel, and to the north by keeping the guard-house in Bouley bay in one with Tour de Rozel.

ROZEL BAY lies between La Coupe and Nez du Guet points, and being exposed to all winds between S. by W., round easterly, and N.W. by N., vessels never remain at anchor in it longer than to await water into the harbour. In addition to the foul ground off the points of the bay, there is a rocky group called the Hiaux, which uncovers 3 feet at the lowest tides, and lies a cable's length from the western shore and $1\frac{1}{4}$ cables from the pier head, with Rozel hotel in line with the white patch on the pier-head, W.S.W. There is also a sunken rock with 5 feet over it at low water on the eastern side of the entrance to the harbour, a cable's length from the shore.

HAVRE du ROZEL.—This small but useful harbour, situated at the bottom of Rozel bay, has a stone pier capable of affording shelter to 20 small cutters, such as are employed in the oyster fishery. A great quantity of cider is shipped here during the summer months, and the harbour will afford berthing places to six vessels of from 40 to 50 tons burthen. North-westerly winds cause a great range, so much so that vessels carry away the large hawsers they use to moor alongside the pier. Gorey harbour is far preferable in every respect.

The navigation of this harbour is much obstructed by a large flat half-tide rock, lying on the south side of the entrance, not leaving a greater space between it and the pier-head than to allow two small cutters to enter abreast. If this rock were removed, or three or four buoys, similar to those at Gorey, were laid down, it would save much time, and greatly facilitate entering this harbour, as vessels arriving or leaving with a foul wind are obliged to kedge in or out.

DIRECTIONS.—Approaching Rozel bay from the northward, and intending to enter the harbour, keep St. Catherine's breakwater lighthouse in sight outside Coupe point, until the Royal hotel at Rozel comes in sight to the southward of the white patch on the pier-head, W. by S. $\frac{1}{2}$ S., which mark will lead to the southward of the Hiaux, and to the entrance of the harbour. Give the pier-head a close shave, to avoid the half-tide rock. If the tide should not serve to enter the harbour, the best anchorage will be found in the north-west side of the bay, with the Royal hotel in line with the white patch on the pier-head, W.S.W., and the lower and the upper part of the wall of Nez du Guet fort in one, or the two chimneys of the guard-house in the fort in one. To keep outside the Hiaux, do not shut the Tour de Rozel in with Nez du Guet.

Tour de Rozel, is a conical mass of rock, 155 feet high, and semi-detached from the point within it; lying about a third of a mile to the westward of Rozel harbour. The top of this rock is generally kept whitewashed, and then forms a most useful mark. There is a half-tide rock lying immediately off it, at the distance of three quarters of a cable; with this exception the approach is quite safe.

BOULEY BAY, on the northern side of Jersey, between Tour de Rozel and Belle Hogue point, affords good shelter from any wind between W. by N., round southerly, and S.S.E. The only dangers in and near this bay are the rocky patches called the Oyster rocks, the Troupeurs, the Sambues, and a small rock called the Grune de Vicard.

The Oyster rocks lie within the Troupeurs, distant 1½ cables from Meulet point, and dry 13 feet at low water.

The Troupeurs rocks lie near the middle of the bay, outside the Oyster rocks. They may be described as a small rocky bank, having two heads, lying from each other about N.E. and S.W., distant a third of a cable. The outer head has 10 feet over it, and the inner only 7 feet, at low water springs. On the outer head the inner high rock of the Pierres de Lecq appears a little open of Belle Hogue point N.W., and west side of Meulet point is in line with west side of the high cliff immediately above it, S.S.W. These rocks may be cleared outside by keeping the whole of the Pierres de Lecq well open of Belle Hogue point; and inside by shutting the largest rock of the group (near the middle) in behind Belle Hogue point.

The Sambues lie off and to the eastward of Belle Hogue point, distant nearly a quarter of a mile from the shore, and appear soon after half ebb. La Coupe Guardhouse turret just open outside, or to the north-eastward, of Nez du Guet, and Tour de Rozel S.E. by S., leads clear outside of both the Sambues and Troupeurs.

The Grune de Vicard lies at the distance of nearly a cable from the shore, between the two guardhouses, and has two feet over it at low water springs.

Anchorage.—Outside the Troupeurs, keep the whole of the Pierres de Lecq at least a point open of Belle Hogue point to the westward, or Coupe open of Tour de Rozel to the eastward; and the white tower of Castle house (situated on the high land overlooking the bay) in line with Bouley pier, S.W., in 8 to 10 fathoms, gravel. Or further in, with the white tower of Castle House open of the pier, bearing S.W. by W.; and Belle Hogue point a little open of Vicard point, N.W. by N.; in five fathoms, fine sand.

This is a safe anchorage in southerly winds, but open to those from the northward. Vessels anchored in this bay during S.W. gales should therefore be prepared to weigh directly the wind begins to veer to the N.W., and proceed either to St. Catherine's bay or Gorey road.

BELLE HOGUE POINT, lying about a mile to the westward of Bouley bay, is the highest and (excepting Grosnez) most remarkable bluff on the north coast of Jersey. A reef of sunken rocks extends from it to the distance of 2 cables off shore. This reef is cleared on its N.E. side by keeping Coupe turret a little open of Tour de Rozel, and to the northward by keeping Plemont point in sight outside Ronez point.

Giffard and Bonne Nuit Bays lie close to the westward of Belle Hogue point, between it and Fremont point; (which latter is also a high bluff.) La Crête point divides these points from each other.

Giffard bay is small, but the ground is clean.

Bonne Nuit bay, lying westward of Giffard bay, may be easily recognized on nearing it by St. John's barracks, a long range of low buildings near the middle of it; also by Mont Mado mill, which stands on the high land above them. Near the middle of the bay, about 2 cables from the shore, there is a large black rock (which only covers at great spring tides), named Cheval Guillaume. There are several sunken rocks lying at the distance of half a cable outside Cheval Guillaume; and a mass of partly sunken reef extends from Fremont point out to the northward for a quarter of a mile; the outer extreme of which is marked by a rock drying 16 feet at low water, named *Demie Jeffrey*.

Anchorage.—The best berth lies about a quarter of a mile northward of La Crete point, in 7 to 9 fathoms, sand. A vessel will be here very well sheltered from southerly and westerly winds, but she must be prepared to slip in case of a sudden shift to the northward.

Shamrock bank, lies North from Fremont point, distant nearly three-quarters of a mile: it is a sunken reef, 2 cables in diameter. The least water found (9 feet at low-water springs) lies on the inner part of the bank, and there are 7 and 8 fathoms close to all round it. On the 9-feet rock, Plemont hotel is seen just within the outer part of Ronez point, W. by N. ½ N., the western house of St. John's barrack is a little open of Fremont point, S. ½ E., and Tour de Rozel over the outer extreme of Belle Hogue point; these marks may be used for passing either side of the bank.

St. John's Bay, situated between Fremont and Ronez points, is but a slight indentation of the coast, and can scarcely be called a bay; its shore is, moreover, so fringed with reef as to be almost inaccessible; there are also outlying rocks extending nearly 2 cables from the shore; between which and the Shamrock bank, however, is a passage nearly half a mile wide.

Strangers are advised not to attempt passing through this channel without a pilot, nor to approach the coast here about nearer than a mile.

This part of the coast is remarkable from the extensive granite quarries which add to its naturally barren and wild appearance.

RONEZ, SOREL AND PLEMONT POINTS, unlike Bell Hogue and Grosnez points, are all low at their outer extremes, but rise within at rather steep inclines, uniting with the high level plateau, which distinguishes the north coast of the island, at distances but little more than a quarter of a mile.

Ronez and Sorel points are steep to; but between them, at the distance of half a cable outside the chord of the bay, there is a sunken rock with only 3 feet over it at low water, called—

GRUNE DE VICQ, which may be cleared outside by keeping Lipendi point open of Ronez point, until La Plaine point comes open of Sorel point.

LA PLAINE POINT has a reef extending from it to the distance of half a cable at low water; outside of which, however, it is steep to.

From La Plaine Point to Grave de Lecq the coast is cliffy, precipitous, and dangerous of approach, having outlying reefs and sunken rocks extending more than a quarter of a mile from the shore.

GREVE DE LECQ BAY lies in the depth of the bight between Sorel and Plemont points: its position may be recognized at a distance by a whitewashed martello tower, standing near the middle of a high sandy beach.

ANCHORAGE, off Greve de Lecq, is good and safe in all winds, excepting those from the northward: the best position is in 9 to 6 fathoms sand with Greve de Lecq tower from S. by W. to S.S.W. ½ W., distant from it half to a third of a mile: at the latter position Plemont point will be a little open of the Grand Becquet. The dangers in and near Greve de Lecq are—

LES DEMIES, the highest of which dries 16 feet, lie off the eastern bluff of the bay, a quarter of a mile from the shore, and N.E. by N. 4 cables from the white martello tower.

GRUNE DE BECQUET, having 21 feet over it at low water, lies N.E. ½ E., nearly ¾ of a mile from Grand Becquet head. On the rock Grosnez bluff appears a little within the low point of Plemont W. by N., and Greve de Lecq tower S. by W. ¼ W.

GRUNE DE DOUET, with 12 feet over it, lies a third of a mile within Grune de Becquet, and E. ½ N., distant a quarter of a mile from Becquet head.

GREVE AU LANCON (situate between Plemont and Grosnez points) is a small but remarkable bay, from its fine level white sandy beach; which, however, (unlike Greve de Lecq,) is all covered by the tide long before high water: at which period the sea rolls into the numerous caverns of the cliffs bounding the bay, cutting off all communication with the high land above, and imparting a wild aspect to the coast.

The dangers here are, a rock on the west side of the bay, lying a cable from the shore, and which dries 14 feet at low water, and the reef which dries at low water, extending a cable's length from Plemont point.

ANCHORAGE.—The best position is off the middle of the bay, with Grosnez bluff bearing about west, in 9 to 6 fathoms sand.

Small vessels bound round Grosnez point to the southward, between the periods of half flood and half ebb, and unable, in light winds, to stem the northern tide, may advantageously anchor in this bay till half ebb, when the southern tide will have made and favour their proceeding through the swatch-way; or, if they are bound to the eastward, between the Pierres de Lecq and the island, and having anchored on the ebb, can weigh at low water, and carry a fair tide as far as La Coupe.

CAUTION.—The holding ground is not good, and a sailing vessel approaching or leaving the bay must be prepared for unsteady flaws of wind from the high land, and varying eddies of tide.

Of course no sailing vessel would anchor in any of the bays along the north shore of Jersey in northerly winds, but should any be so caught at anchor by an unexpected shift of wind, it *may* be advisable not to weigh before the weather tide makes, to ensure getting out.

THE ECREHOS ROCKS lie about midway between the north-eastern coast of Jersey and Cape Carteret. They are separated from another rocky group to the westward, called the Drouilles, and from the Ecreviere banks to the eastward, by only very narrow and shallow channels.

The whole of these reefs and banks together occupy an elevated plateau of shoal water, 9 miles long in a N.W. by W. and S.E. by E. direction, and 2 miles wide. This line of reefs and banks afford considerable protection to the north coast of Jersey, as well as to the fine broad and deep channel lying between, named *Le Ruau.*

The main group of the Ecrehos rocks occupy a space near the centre of the reef, about $\frac{3}{4}$ of a mile N. and S., and $\frac{1}{2}$ mile wide; the whole of which space dries before low water. Maitre isle, the largest of the group, marks the southern extreme of this reef to the eastward; and along its steep eastern side to the northward lie the rocky islets called *Marmotier, Blanc isles, Tas de Pez,* and *La Vielle;* the two latter being conical shaped rocks 50 and 54 feet high respectively.

The western side of the reef is marked to the southward by the high rocks called *Les Cotes* and *Colombier;* and to the northward by *Grosse Tête* and *Petite Tête;* the latter of which is the only one that covers with the tide.

Maitre isle, Marmotier, and Blanc isles are the largest of the Ecrehos group, and each have huts erected on them, for the use of fishermen, on their occasional visits. The former only is large enough to preserve its soil from being swept away by stormy winds and the sea, and is therefore the only islet having any vegetation on it, which consists of coarse grass and a few stunted shrubs. Large rats are found here in great numbers. There is neither fresh water nor fuel on any of these islets.

The natives of Jersey resort here during the summer season, for the purpose of fishing and cutting vraic.

Maitre isle being one of the principal stations for the survey of Jersey, the exact position of the instrument has been marked by a pole, surmounted by a barrel, and having a large pile of stones at its base : it stands on the highest part of the island near the middle, and makes a conspicuous and useful beacon.

Along the eastern side of the main reef of the Ecrehos above described, but separated from it by a narrow channel, lies a tangled mass of reef ; narrow at its northern end near La Vielle, but enlarging and increasing its distance from the main reef as it runs southerly on a convex line, to abreast (eastward of) Maitre isle, from which its outer edge is a mile distant. Here the rocks suddenly terminate, and a bank of gravel and sand commences ; and extends to the southward.

Of the above described rocky group we need only specially notice those used for sailing marks, viz., Bigorne, Sabloniere, and Grand Galere.

BIGORNE is a very remarkable horned rock, whose apex is 20 feet above high water : it lies nearly half a mile to the eastward of Maitre isle. Sabloniere and Grand Galere, lying a little to the north-east of Bigorne, are less elevated than it, although never covered by the tide. Bigorne, midway between Sabloniere and Grand Galere, leads through the middle of the western channel into the Maitre isle anchorage.

ECREVIÈRE ROCK, the south-easternmost of the Ecrehos group covers 8 feet at high water springs, and lies E. by S. ¾ of a mile from Maitre isle. From this rock to the southward extends the—

BANC DE L'ECREVIÈRE, the south extreme of which (taking the 5 fathoms contour line as a boundary) lies S. by E., a mile and five eighths from the rock. Its greatest breadth, near the north end, is half a mile ; tapering off to less than a quarter of a mile at its south extreme.

The bank is very steep along its western side ; its apex consists of a number of semi-detached fine gravel and sandy ridges, convex to the south-westward, lying nearly parallel to each other, drying from 3 to 5 feet at low water, and separated only by small narrow channels of 3 to 8 feet in depth.

The streams setting over this bank cause a confused sea in bad weather.

Bigorne rock and Tas de Pez in line marks the direction of the south extreme of the bank, and by opening these objects of each other a point either way the end of the bank may be rounded as necessary.

Grouville mill *in line* with Orgueil bluff passes *over* the bank, a quarter of a mile within its south extreme, awash at low water. Therefore, to clear the south end of the bank open Grouville mill a little, to the southward of Orgueil bluff, bearing W. by S. Or bring Rozell mill in line (or a little open southward) of Coupe turret W. ¾ N.

RONDE SELLIERE, the southernmost of the Ecrehos rocks, uncovers 7 feet at low water ; on it Marmotier islet appears on the right high (or eastern) extreme of Maitre isle ; and St. Martin's church (spire) is a little open north of Fliquet tower W. ¾ S.

There is another rock of similar character and appearance (but drying 8 feet at low water), lying a sixth of a mile to the N.W. of this ; and a third (named Petite Noire), drying 12 feet at low water, which lies to the northward about the same distance : the three rocks thus forming an equilateral triangle.

There is also a reef awash, at low water, lying a cable's length to the eastward of Ronde Selliere.

These rocks may be cleared outside to the S.W. by just shutting Plemont point in behind Ronez point. St. Martin's church spire in line with Fliquet tower W. ½ S. clears them to the southward. Tas de Pois on the east side of Marmotier N. ¾ W., leads between Ronde Selliere and Ecreviere bank. To keep clear outside of Grande Noir rocks, the whole of Petite Rousse rocks must be well open of the high rocks off Maitre isle. Bigorne rock midway between Sabloniere and Grande Galere, N.E., clears Ronde Selliere rocks inside, to the westward.

ANCHORAGE, south of Maitre isle and within Ronde Selliere (for small vesels only). The best position is with Marmotier, houses, just open on the east side of Maitre isle, North ; and Bignorne midway between Grand Galere and Sabloniere N.E., in 5 fathoms gravel at low water.

Large vessels wishing to anchor here should keep outside the line of Ronde Selliere rocks and Ecreviere bank ; anchoring on the leading line already given (Tas de Pois on the east extreme of Marmotier) in 8 fathoms gravel.

Nipple Rock may be said to form the outer or western corner of the western entrance to the inner anchorage off Maitre isle : the nipple rock near its centre dries 16 feet at low water ; at this spot the Grande Galere is open of the south extreme of Maitre isle N.E. by E. ½ E., and Grosse Tête a little open West of Colombier N. ¼ E.

Les Demies are two rocks scarcely a cable's length apart, whose apexes are exactly at half tide level ; they lie a half a mile north from Nipple rock, and about the same distance westward of the Ecrehos main reef.

On the outer Demie, Marmotier appears just open southward of Les Cotes rocks E.N.E. ; La Vielle a little open west of Colombier N.E. ¼ N., and St. Martin's church spire over the Coupe W. by S. ¾ S.

The Rouquet Reef consists of several detached clumps of sunken rocks lying on the north side of the Ecrehos, but separated therefrom by narrow channels of deep water. The highest rock of the eastern clump is awash at low water, and lies with St. Catherine's lighthouse midway between the tower north of Mont Orgueil and the end of the plateau above Gorey S.W. ¼ S., and Maitre isle beacon midway between Gross Tête and La Vielle S.S.E. ¼ E.

Petite Rousse Rock has 3 heads, elevated 12 to 14 feet above high water, and lies on the N.W. side of the Ecrehos reef, distant from it ¾ of a mile : the whole of which space (excepting a narrow and tortuous channel) is filled up with rocks ; a great number of these uncover every tide. There is also a clump of dangerous rocks awash at low water, lying S.S.W., distant half a mile from Petite Rousse.

Grande Rousse Rock is elevated 22 feet above high water, and lies rather more than half a mile N.W. from Petite Rousse. Like the latter it is surrounded by dangerous reefs. There is a channel of deep water between Grande and Petite Rousse rocks, but it is very narrow and tortuous.

THE DROUILLES.—This rocky group lies about 3 miles westward of the Ecrehos, and nearly 4 miles to the northward of La Coupe point. It is about 1½ miles in diameter, and consists of broken detached masses of reef, the whole of which covers with the tide, excepting only 3 small rocks near the S.W. side, the two largest of which,—

The Burons, are of conical form, about the same height (7 feet above high water), lying only a few fathoms apart. Although so small, they are most useful marks to vessels navigating Le Ruau channel, and should therefore be made more conspicuous by building a beacon on the outer or largest rock of the two. Outside the Burons there is another large rock (called *Frouquie*), which is 8 feet lower than them, being just awash at high water.

Joli is a small pinnacle rock, drying 6 feet at low water, and lying W.S.W., distant nearly ¾ of a mile from the great Buron. On the rock Maitre isle beacon is on the middle of Les Cotes rock S.E. by E. ¾ E., and Rozel mill is open southward of La Tour S.S.W.

La Hau is a sunken rock with 12 feet over it at low water, lying outside, or to the southward of Joli ; from which it bears S.W. by S., rather more than a third of a mile. This rock forms the northern boundary of Le Ruau channel, at its narrowest part.

Platte rock is one of the largest of the Drouilles group, and marks their southern boundary to the eastward, as well as the western side of the entrance to L'Etoc channel, to the southward. It dries 33 feet, and is therefore covered before high water of spring tides.

On the rock Rozel mill is in line with the fort on Nez du Guet, S.W. ¼ S., and the Great Buron N.W. ¼ W., ¾ of a mile.

Among the less important rocks of the Drouilles group are *La Grese* which lies North nearly ½ a mile from the Platte, and uncovers 29 feet at low water: *Noire Roque,* lies N.E. by E., ¼ of a mile from great Buron, and dries 35 feet: *Clump rock,* marking the northern visible extreme of the group, dries 15 feet. *The Grunes* are an extensive bed of rocks, visible only near low water, lying ½ a mile westward of Clump rock.

La Kosem is the northernmost sunken rock of the group, and has 12 feet over it at low water.

DIRECTIONS.—Verclut point shut in by La Coupe clears the Drouilles to the westward; but a better mark for this is Rozel mill open westward of the Tour, bearing S. by W. Maitre isle beacon open a little to the N.E. of Grosse Tête S.E. ¼ S. clears their north extreme. Seymour house and Verclut point in line S.S.W. ½ W. clears their eastern side, and leads through the Passe de L'Etoc and La Vielle; and Grande Rousse rocks in line E. ¾ S. will clear them to the southward.

LE RUAU CHANNEL, between the Drouilles rocks and Jersey, is at its narrowest part 2½ miles wide, very deep, and entirely free from danger at all times of the tide, although the confused sea occasionally thrown up by a strong weather tide running over the rocky uneven bottom is so violent as to resemble breakers.

The northern entrance to Le Ruau, between the Drouilles and Pierres de Lecq, is 5 miles wide, and free from danger; the approach to Le Ruau from the westward, between Pierres de Lecq and Jersey, is also roomy and quite safe; and any seaman of ordinary ability, having a good chart, should be able to sail his vessel into the outer Road off Gorey without a pilot.

Passe de L'Etoc is formed between the east side of the Drouilles group to the westward and the Grande Rousse, L'Etoc, and Fierco rocks, besides Grune du N.W., Grune du S.W., and many others to the eastward. The narrowest part of the channel lies between the Platte rock and Grune du S.W., where it is but little over a quarter of a mile wide.

Grune du S.W. lies on the east side of the southern entrance of the Passe de L'Etoc; S. by E., half a mile from the Platte rock. It has 5 feet over it at low water. On the rock Seymour house appears a little open of the breakwater house under Verclut point S.S.W. ½ W., and Maitre isle beacon in line with the south side of Les Cotes rock S.E. by E. ¾ E.

L'Etoc. This rock is in the form of a saddle, and uncovers 16 feet at low water. It lies on the eastern side of Passe de L'Etoc; E. ½ N. nearly a mile from the Platte rock, and N.E. by E., a mile from Grune du S.W. The marks for it are, the highest heads of Pierres de Lecq in line with the northern head of the Burons W. by N. ½ N., and the martello tower northward of Mont Orgueil on with the middle of St. Catherine's breakwater S.S.W. ¾ W.

Le Fierco stands near the middle of a reef of rocks (most of which never uncover) a quarter of a mile in extent N. and S.: it lies E.N.E., 3 cables lengths from L'Etoc, and uncovers 7 feet at low water.

Grune du N.W., having 7 feet over it at low water, is the shoalest rock of the northernmost reef on the east side of the Passe de L'Etoc. It lies N.E. ½ E., 1¼ miles from the Platte rock, and N. by E., nearly ¾ of a mile from L'Etoc; with Rozel mill its length open eastward of the Fort on Nez du Guet point S.W., and Grosse Tête rock touching the south end of Maitre isle S.E. ¾ S.

Directions, the best mark to run through the Passe de L'Etoc is Seymour house in line with Verclut point S.S.W. ½ W.; but when passing abreast of Grune du S.W. (marks for which are given above) should the tide be low, Seymour house may be brought a little within or to the westward of Verclut point; provided the leading line be regained immediately afterwards, to avoid passing too near the Platte. The same may be done also to give a good berth to a sunken rock with 7 feet on it at low water, which lies on a line with Tas de Pas and L'Etoc rock.

The Passe de L'Etoc has a general depth of 8 fathoms in it, and the bottom, although very rocky, is tolerably regular; the tides, however, both ebb and flood, set across it for a considerable period; no stranger should therefore attempt to pass through without a pilot.

There is a 5-fathom channel between the Grande and Petite Rousse rocks; it is, however, in some places but little more than a cable wide, tortuous and studded with rocks.

Above half tide, a vessel under 12 feet draught could, with a leading wind, safely pass through by bringing the tower on the hill northward of Orgueil castle in line with the lighthouse at the end of St. Catherine's breakwater S.W. ⅓ S.; but below half tide the channel is dangerous to navigate, even for boats.

Bearings and Distances.

			Miles.
Corbiere to Roches Douvres lighthouse	W. by N.		22½
,,	Hanois lighthouse	N.N.W. ½ W.	23½
,,	St. Martin's Point	N. by W. ½ W.	18¼
,,	Western rock of Rigdon bank	N. ¾ W.	3¾
,,	L'Etac d'Serk	N. ⅕ E.	14⅓
,,	N.W. Danger rock, Minquiers (Brisant du Nord Ouest.)	S.W. by S.	11½
,,	Outer Danger south of Hubaut rock.	S.S.E.	2⅞
,,	Icho Bank	S.E. ½ S.	7⅔
,,	Frouquie Aubert	S.E. ¼ E.	11¾

GENERAL DIRECTIONS.—It cannot be too deeply impressed on the mind of the mariner, when approaching the channel islands at night in thick hazy weather, or when navigating amongst them under such circumstances, the necessity for taking regular and careful soundings; for although the islands and the rocky reefs generally are steep to, so that the lead *may* give little or no warning of their near neigbourhood, yet it is possible for a vessel to be set inside the boundaries of the sunken part of some of these dangers without seeing them; where a knowledge of the depth afforded by the lead might enable her to anchor, and thus save her from wreck.

Moreover, there are extensive banks of gravel and sand amongst the islands, as well as other occasional irregularities in the bottom, which the careful pilot would know how to turn to account in estimating his position. Again, there is the French coast within the islands; where the soundings are generally so regular that the lead may be taken as a safe guide in estimating distances from the shore.

Whenever the lead is hove it may be assumed there is *some* degree of uncertainty about the position of the vessel. On such occasions, therefore, the lead should be kept on the ground for a minute or two, and the setting and drift of the stream noted. For as the tidal stream varies considerably in strength and direction according to position, and diagrams containing precise information on this subject are engraved on the chart, a comparison of the two might occasionally be found very useful.

When the stream runs strong, tide ripples and overfalls always make their appearance over sunken rocks, or banks lying out in the channels, or other exposed places; in foggy weather, therefore, *they* may be turned to good account by the pilot. An anchor should always be in readiness, when navigating any of the channels between the islands, in thick weather; but before letting go always turn the vessel head against the tide, if possible; otherwise, the chances would be very much in favour of snapping the cable.

JERSEY, APPROACH BY NIGHT, From the northward.—Having made Cape La Hague light, enter the Race of Alderney as near mid-channel as possible, and from thence steer S. by W. or S.W. by S., according to the tide. Should the weather be clear, the position of the ship may be ascertained, and the course regulated by the coast lights with absolute accuracy. If the lights are obscured, Serk should be sighted, or the ship should be anchored, as convenient; remembering that a moderate depth and good anchorage may be secured by hauling in a little towards the coast.*

---

* In easterly winds there is good anchorage in Vauville Bay, to the southward of Cape La Hague, and along the coast nearly to abreast of Cape Carteret, at the distance of 3 to 4 miles from the land in 12 to 14 fathoms.

Should there be too much swell to anchor, any position desired may be maintained by means of the lights ; or in hazy weather, by a near approach to Serk, which is very steep-to and safe of approach, excepting on a south-easterly bearing (the direction of the *Blanchard* rock). At the upper stage of the tide bring the middle of Serk to bear S.W., and on its lower stage, N.N.E.; *in calm weather* the drift will then be *away* from the island.

From the middle of the Race *towards the east coast of Jersey, through the Drouilles channel,* steer on the above-mentioned courses until Cape Carteret light bears E. by S. St. Catherine's light will now be seen, and if it be kept *open and shut* with Coupe point, bearing S. by E. ¾ E., you will pass nearly midway between the Drouilles and Belle Hogue point. When inside the Drouilles, open the light of Coupe point, and do not approach Jersey nearer than a mile ; after passing the light bring it to bear N.N.W. ½ W., distant a mile or a mile and a half, and anchor in 9 fathoms until daylight.

Should St. Catherine light not be seen when Cape Carteret light bears E. by S., proceed with caution ; remember that from the northernmost of the Pierres de Lecq, Cape Carteret light bears E. ½ S., and that a line drawn from one to the other of those objects clears the north extreme of the Drouilles reef by a mile. The Drouilles are all so low that they would hardly be seen at night till you were amongst them ; but as they are faced to the northward by a fringe of sunken reef or bank, the lead *might* possibly give warning of their neighbourhood.

The Pierres de Lecq are steep-to on the east side, and some part of the rocks always visible ; they are therefore much safer to approach at night than the Drouilles. Of course none of these or any other dangers should be approached under circumstances of difficulty *with the tide.* Grosnez bluff bearing W. by S. just clears the inner or south extreme of the Pierres de Lecq reef.

Through the Deroute channel, round the west coast of Jersey for St. Helier.—From the middle of the Race steer S. by W. or S.W. by S. as before, until Cape Carteret light bears S.E. by E. ½ E., or E.S.E., to clear the *Blanchard* rock off Serk ; after which haul out more to the westward into the Deroute channel clear of the Pierres de Lecq. When the east extreme of Serk bears North, or Grosnez point South, steer S.W. by S. or S.S.W., along the west coast of Jersey, until abreast the Corbière rock ; to the westward of which, at the distance of 2 or 3 miles, a vessel may heave to, and wait for daylight, or for a pilot.

In thick weather do not approach the Corbière nearer than 17 or 18 fathoms, and lay the vessel's head N.W. by N., during the whole of the flood ; as the stream sets very strongly down towards the Minquiers reef and many vessels have been wrecked there through neglecting this precaution.

Should there not be too much swell a vessel could anchor for a time on the great bank, in 5 to 8 fathoms, N.W. by W., distant 1½ miles from Corbière rock ; or between this position and No. 4 tower in St. Ouen's bay, where the water would be smoother and the tide not so strong.

From the north-west.—From St. Peter Port, Guernsey, steer direct for the Corbière rock (allowing for the tide) until within 5 miles of it, or Grosnez point bears E. by S., when if it be desired to pass outside of *West rock* (on which there are 6 fathoms), steer S.W. by S. until past that danger, after which proceed as before directed until daylight. A steamer of light draught, in charge of an experienced pilot, might in a fine clear night, and during the upper stage of the tide, safely proceed on into St. Heliers harbour. In which case she should approach the Corbière on the above direct course until within 2½ or 2 miles of it, then endeavour to *make good* a S.S.W. course, until the rock bears east, after which steer direct for Noirmont point, which should be approached to within a quarter of a mile ; from this position steer out a little to ensure clearing the Pignonet rock, then E. by S. for the entrance of the small road ; look out for the two green lights on Albert pier, and when they come in line run on them up to the entrance of the harbour.

From the westward.—Endeavour to make either the Hanois light at Guernsey or that on Roches Douvres, and fix the position of the ship accurately by bearings, before shaping a course for the Corbière rock or Grosnez point ; according as desired to proceed to the southern or northern coasts of the island. Should a vessel pass inside the line of the above lights without seeing them during foggy weather, the lead ought to be frequently hove until the position be ascertained beyond doubt. On the meridian of the Hanois, 34 fathoms will be obtained, shoaling to 32 and 30 fathoms along the Deroute channel as far as Serk, whilst to the southward of a line drawn from Roches Douvres to Grosnez point the depths will vary between 26 and 23 fathoms.

From the south-west.—Do not approach the reefs fronting St. Aubin bay into a less depth than 10 or 12 fathoms, and should this depth be obtained, anchor if practicable, and wait for daylight.

LIGHT.—On the Plateau des Roches Douvres is an iron white lighthouse, which exhibits at 180 feet above the sea, a white light showing a *flash* every *five seconds*, and visible from a distance of 14 miles. During foggy weather a bell is sounded at intervals of three seconds.

TIDES.—It is high water, full and change, all round Jersey at 6h. 29m.: ordinary springs rise 33 feet, ordinary neaps 23 feet ; great springs range 39 feet, neaps 14 feet. Along the northern and southern shores of the island, between Grosnez point and Belle Hogue point and between Seymour tower and Corbière rock, the whole of the flood runs to the eastward and the ebb to the westward, each 6 hours, and according to the trend of the land, the velocity of the springs being about 4 knots, and of neaps about 2 knots.

In Grouville and St. Catherine bays, the stream, between half flood and half ebb, runs to the northward ; and to the southward, between half ebb and half flood ; and the same in St. Ouen bay, with a velocity in each at the springs, of $4\frac{1}{2}$ knots, and at the neaps of $2\frac{1}{2}$ knots ; the streams will consequently meet at the four principal extremes of the island, viz. La Coupe point, Grosnez point, La Corbière point, and the Conchière rock.

The rotary motion of the tidal stream round Jersey being the governing cause of the various sets close to its shores, some description of its action is necessary. Commencing therefore at the period of high water, and in a position about 4 miles S.W. of St. Helier, the stream which has been setting S.E. and East. quickly alters its direction to N.E. ; which a glance at the chart will show is *full* on to the south coast of the island, making the space included between the above position and the land what pilots call the *crown* of the tide, causing slack water as the shore is approached.

The north side of the island lying in the lee or eddy, there is slack tide there also, but along the east and west coast of the island the tide is setting to the northward at its full strength : at half ebb the offing stream has veered round from north to N.W. and S.W. ; the crown of the tide is now on the east side of Jersey, and the west side is on the lee or eddy, making slack water therefore at this period in Grouville and St. Ouen bays ; the stream running at its full strength along the north and south coasts of the island. At low water the tidal stream is setting from a northerly direction on to the north shore of Jersey, making the crown of the tide on that side, and the lee to the southward of the island ; at half flood the crown of the tide being on the west coast of the island with precisely similar results.

A careful consideration of this revolving motion of the tidal stream will serve to explain all the peculiar sets of the tides met with in the bays round the island. Thus at Noirmont point near half flood, when the east going stream attains its full strength, there is an outset from St. Aubin bay, which runs with considerable strength between Point de Bût and the Pignonet rocks, and which is sensibly felt within the bay as far as St. Aubin castle ; this is at first a mere eddy of the flood stream, originating under Noirmont point ; but as, after half flood, the stream shifts from east to the north-eastward, and sets right on the Hermitage rocks and Elizabeth castle, the very gentle incline of the sandy shore here and the great space to be covered causes the level of the sea at this part of the bay to be considerably elevated above that of the western side of the bay, and the water of course runs off in the direction of the lower level.

On referring to the chart, it will be seen that the peculiar configuration of the bay tends materially to turn off the stream from the north-east to a northerly direction; it will not therefore be difficult to understand that the small eddy under Noirmont point being united with the westerly flow round the head of the bay, causes the continuous outset from Noirmont point above mentioned; this outset runs for 9 hours, viz., from half flood to high water and during the whole of the ebb; it attains its greatest strength about an hour after high water, and at this period during a westerly gale and spring tides throws up a dangerous breaking sea or race off Noirmont point.

From causes similar to those explained above, (viz., the offing stream shifting and impinging on the land,) the tide sets across the harbour's mouth at St. Helier to the northward as well as into the harbour, during the whole of the flood, and out or to the southward on the ebb; except near the bridge inside Elizabeth castle, where the tide sets north-westerly from last quarter flood until the bridge is awash (at one foot under half tide).

Out in the offing to the south-westward, clear of the island, the strength of the tidal stream (ebb and flood) is found to run in a N.W. and S.E. direction, remaining longer near those points than any other; and it has been already shown, that at near high water it quickly changes its course to east and north-east (at this latter point running full on the island and making high water there); it does not stay any time on this point, however, but it continues to veer round by the north until it attains a north-westerly direction, where its shifting movement is much slower; the strength of this north-westerly stream is felt at half ebb on the south coast of Jersey. To arrive at a right understanding of the force and effect of the ocean swell along the south coast of Jersey in westerly gales it will be necessary to follow this changing direction of the offing stream.

An hour before high water, on the slacking of the south-easterly stream in the offing, the westerly stream sets round Noirmont point, and to the westward of it; checking the advancing westerly swell (during gales from that quarter), and causing it to break heavily. As this *natural break-water* forms at Noirmont point and its outlying reefs, the water within and to leeward (both in St. Aubin bay and the road of St. Helier) become smoother, and as the westerly (or ebb stream) increases in strength so does the swell continue to decrease within; after the tide has fallen below half ebb, the outlying reefs gradually uncovering with the tide, assist materially in blocking the swell out; but after low water the offing stream changes; the westerly swell rolls in again with the southerly stream, increasing in force with the rising flood, until again checked as before by the slacking of the offing stream and the making of the westerly stream inshore.

INDEX.

	Page
Aiguillons - - - -	65
———— rocks - -	58
Albert breakwater - -	101
——— fort - - -	44
——— pier and light -	88
Alderney - - -	55
——————— south bank -	64
——————— telegraph tower -	47
Almorah terrace - -	89
Amfroque rocks - -	25
Ancresse bay - -	20
Anfré beacon - -	10
——— rock - -	17
Anne port bay - -	117
Anne, St. - - -	56
——————— church - -	47
Anons bank - -	31
Anquette channel - -	106
——————— rocks and beacon -	107
——————— rock, Grand -	108
——————— gravel banks -	109
Approaches to the Channel islands -	6
Arches rock and buoy -	112
Archirondel tower -	107
Arconée, Grande, rock -	108
Aubin, St., bay - -	87
——————— anchorage -	94
——————— dangers in -	92
——————— dangers off -	89
——————— directions -	102
——————— over the bridge	100
——————— passages into	95
——————— castle - -	88
——————— breakwater -	94
——————— harbour and pier	88
——————— town - -	88
Auquière rock - -	44
Aurigny - - -	55
Autelêts rocks - -	38

	Page
Baie du Câtel - -	63
Baleine bay - -	36
——— rock, Jersey -	93
——————— Serk -	35
Balliene rock - -	18
Balmée rock - -	36
Banquette bay - -	38
———, Petite -	39
———, point -	35
Barbes - - -	25
Barsier reefs - -	60
——— rock - -	53
Basse occid. des Bœufs -	116
Battery point - -	86
Battue, Grand - -	24
Baveuse - - -	40
Beau port - -	84
Bec du Nez - -	36
Becquet, Grand -	125
Belle Hougue land and point	78, 123
Belvedere house - -	30
Bergerie house - -	107
Bibette head - -	58
Bieuse rock - -	99
Bigorne rock - -	127
Bisé bank - -	24
Blainville river - -	116
——————— village -	117
Blanc isles - -	126
——— Pignon house, lower -	100
———————————upper -	92
Blanchard bank - -	62
——————— rock - -	35
Blanche - - -	27
Boin - - -	15
Boiteaux rock - -	83
Bonit rock - -	64
Bonne Nuit bay - -	123
Boue rocks - -	82
——— Agenor - -	29
——— Auber - -	22

	Page
Boue Baker - - -	16
—— Blondel - - -	11
—— Corneille - - -	21
—— de Baie - - -	40
—— de Vazon - - -	22
Boues des Etacs - -	59
—— des Kaines - -	55
—— Genitales - -	29
Boufresse - - -	28
Bouillonnaise rock - -	57
Bouilly port - -	84
Bouley bay - - -	122
Boulliones rocks, Grands -	31
Braye bay - - -	57
—— du Valle - -	1
—— new town - -	56
—— old harbour - -	58
——, Petite - -	21
—— rocks - -	61
—— Grande -	13
Brayes rocks - -	121
Brecqhou - - -	33
Bréhat island - -	43
Brehon tower - -	13
Brelade, St., bay - -	84
—— anchorage -	84
—— dangers in and near	85
—— directions -	85
—— church -	90
Bretagne - - -	41
Brinchetaie - -	62
Burhou island - -	51
——, Little - -	51
—— reef - -	46
Burons near Jersey -	111, 129
—— near Serk - -	35
Bût point - - -	91
Cacquerau house - -	24
Cancale - - -	3
Canteen house, Vale -	26
Canupé rocks - -	28
Caquorobert rock - -	31
Carteret, Cape - -	132
Casquets - - -	43
—— anchorage -	44, 49
—— Little rock -	43
—— Middle bank -	49
—— S.W., S.S.W., and S.S.E. banks - -	48

	Page
Castle house - - -	123
Câtel church - - -	2
Catherine, St., bay - -	118
—— anchorage -	119
—— dangers off -	118
—— directions -	120
—— breakwater and light -	113
—— Fara bank -	119
—— tower -	110
Cavale rock - -	29
Chapelle - - -	38
Chateau bank - -	112
—— point - -	34
Cherbourg - - -	56
Cheval-Guillaume rock -	124
Chevichon - - -	25
Clements, St. - -	1
—— bay - -	104
—— church -	110
Cloches rocks - -	89–118
Clonques rocks - -	59
Clonque fort - -	48
Close rock - -	91
Clump rock - -	130
Coal hole - -	29
Cobo bay - -	11
Cocked hat - -	65
Colombelle - -	22
Colombiere - -	126
Colotte rock - -	43
Conchée rock - -	35
Conchière rock - -	105
Cochon rock - -	105
Cone rock - -	51
Conger rock - -	107
Convache - - -	36
Coquelihou rocks - -	65
Corbée du Nez - -	36
Corbet rock - -	60
Corbette rock - -	27
Corbière point - -	1, 83
—— rock - -	2, 83
Corblets - - -	56
Cordonnier - - -	53
Corner rock - -	16
Cornet castle - -	8
—— breakwater light -	10
Cotes rocks - -	126
Cotte point - -	89
Coupée, La - -	33

	Page
Coupe bank - - -	11
——— guard-house - -	107
——— point - - -	120
——— turret - - -	120
Coupé rock - - -	65
Coutances cathedral - -	3, 116
Crabière rock, Guernsey -	20
——— Jersey -	92
Craby harbour - -	59
——— village - -	56
Crête guard-house - -	111
——— point - -	112
Creux harbour - -	34
——— rock - -	28
Crevelt tower, Mont -	18
Croc point - - -	104
Cul de l'Autel - -	26
Danger rock - -	91
——— passage -	98
——— rocks -	47
Dasher rock - -	45
De Pas tower - -	94
Delancy mill - -	17
Demie Balmée - -	36
——— de Pas - -	104
——— rocks, Grande -	20
——— Jeffrey -	124
Demies - -	125, 128
——— du Nord -	26
Dents rocks - -	39
Deroute channel -	5, 133
——— stream -	5
Desormes bank -	78
Diamond rock -	92
Dogs nest, rock and beacon -	103
Dover tide - -	5
Doyle's column -	2
Doyle fort - -	10
Drouilles channel -	79, 130
——— rocks -	130
——— Platte rock -	129
——— Grunes -	130
Eastern passage -	99
Echiquelez rock -	104
Ecréhos - -	126
Ecrevière bank -	4, 127
——— rock -	127
Ecureuil rock and beacon -	111

	Page
Eight-fathoms ledge -	45
Elizabeth castle - -	87
——— college - -	17
Ellis rock - -	55
Emprone reef - -	53
Engineers' barrack -	100
Epissures rock - -	38
Equerrière rock and beacon -	111
Equet rocks - -	46
Erée tower - -	1
Essex castle - -	62
——— hill - -	62
——— nunnery -	64
Etac point - -	1, 80
——— reef - -	80
——— rock - -	21
Etacs - -	59
——— banks - -	54
Etacre rock - -	28
——— , Grande -	22
Etat, Gros - -	22
——— , Petit -	22
Etoc fort - -	62
——— pass - -	130
——— rock - -	130
Eureka rock - -	119
Fara, or St. Catherine bank and rocks - -	119
——— , Petite - -	120
Fauconnière Grande -	32
——— Petite -	32
Ferico rock - -	17
Fermain point and beacon -	10
Ferrières - -	25
Fierco rock - -	131
Firs house - -	97
Flabet - -	22
Flamanville - -	1
Fliquet bay - -	120
——— tower -	128
Florains fort - -	62
Folie, Grande -	64
Fossé Malières -	66
Founiais rock -	60
Four rocks - -	89
——— Grande -	90, 108
——— Petit -	106
Fourché rocks -	85
Fournier du Hâvre -	85
——— rock -	85

	Page
Fourquie rock, Guernsey - -	24
————— near Casquets -	46
————— Haut -	23
Fourquies rocks - - -	31
Fourquie, Plateau de la -	105
Fremont point - -	124
Fret bank - - -	85
—— point - - -	84
Frettes - - -	16
Frouquie - - -	104, 129
————— Aubert rock -	107
————— de la Grève rock and beacon - -	111
————— Grande -	104
————— pass and rock -	82
Gabrielle - - -	17
Galere, Grand - -	127
Gales - - -	3
Galeu - - -	26
George, St., tower - -	22
Giffard bay - -	123
———— rocks - -	111
Givaude rock - -	32
Goudin islet - -	26
Gorey church - -	114
——— harbour entrance -	115
——— pier - -	110
——— road, north channel -	114
——— road, south channel -	115
——— tower - -	106
Gorge - - -	36
Goubinière rock in the Great Russel	27
————— Jersey -	107
Goulet pass - -	35
Gouliôt pass - -	33
Government moorings -	67
Grande Boue - -	37
Granville - -	7
Great bank - - -	81
——— road - -	13
——— Russel - -	13
Green rock - - -	83
Grese rock - -	129
Grève au Lancon bay -	125
————— anchorage -	125
——— d'Azette white patch -	90
——— de Lecq bay -	125
————— anchorage -	125
——— de la Ville -	37
———, La Grande -	39

	Page
Grey bank - - - -	81
——, Fort - - - -	1
Gripe rock- - - -	36
Grois rock - - -	61
Gros du Chateau rock -	92
—— Etac - - -	111
—— Pont - -	16
Grosnez bluff and cape -	36, 125
———— fort - -	57
———— point - -	79
Grosse Moie - -	120
——— Tête - -	84, 126
——— rock - -	88
——— rock, Rocquaine bay -	23
———, Alderney -	61
——— Ferrière - -	32
Grouville bay - -	110
———— anchorage -	113
———— directions -	114
———— great road -	113
———— inner road -	114
———— road rocks -	114
———— rocks and dangers in -	111
———— through Violet channel	117
———— to South-eastward -	116
——— church - -	110
——— mill - -	113
Grunes - - -	8, 89
——— rock - -	32
———, La - -	37
——— au Rouge - -	30
——— aux Dards - -	91
———, Bonne - -	31
——— de Becquet -	125
——— de Douet -	125
——— de Gouliot -	38
——— de Jerbourg -	18
——— de Lecq - -	79
——— de l'Ouest, or du Nord-Ouai -	11
——— de Vicq - -	125
——— de Vicard -	123
——— du Nord -	119
——— du N.W. -	131
——— du port -	112
——— du S.W. -	130
——— Grande - -	89
——— la Fosse - -	31
——— le Feuvre -	108
——— Moulet rock and beacon -	93
——— Petite - -	89
——— Pierre - -	31

	Page
Grunes St. Michel	91
——— Vaudin	90
Grunette rock	20
Guernsey	7
Guet du Câtel	16
—— du Tielle	17
Guillaumez rock	38
Guillimots rocks	111
Haisse rocks, Grande	111
Hanois bank	16
——— Grand	23
——— Petit	23
——— rock light	1, 10
Harbour of refuge	57, 66
Hau rock	129
Hauch rock	108
Haule house	88
Hautes Boues	39
Hautnez	7
Havre, Grand	20
——— Petit	43
Hayes rock	23
—— channel	26
Helier, St.	87
——— anchorage	95
——— coast eastward of	103
——— harbours	87
——— harbour light	88
——— little road	100
Henry fort	114
Herm island	25
—— mill	18
Hermetier	27
Hermitage rocks	100
——— false rock	91
Herpin rock	16
Hiaux rock	122
Hinguette passage	99
——— reef	91
Hoffets	21
Hogue à la Pierre tower	29
Homeaux Florains reef	62
Houmet de Câtel	63
——— de Longy	62
——— fort	22
——— Herbe	63
Honoré	62
Horn rock and beacon	111
Hougue Bic	2

	Page
Hubaut rocks	89
Huchon, Mount	116
Hurd deep	4
Icart bay	25
—— point	16
Icho tower	103
—— bank	105
Inner road rock	112
Ivy castle	29
Janvrin tower	86
Jerbourg point	18
Jersey	76
——— appearance from the westward	79
——— approaches to	78, 132, 134
——— aspect of	2
——— exports	77
——— imports	77
——— language	77
——— legislature	76
——— outlying rocks and dangers	78
——— pilots	77
——— population	77
——— tides	134
Jethou island	25
Jeu point	40
Jinquet rock	104
Joli rock	129
Jolicot rock	37
Jumelles rocks	61
Jument rock	84
Junée rocks	92
Kaines rocks	84
——— d'Amont	17
Karamé rock	103
Kosem	130
La Hague, Cape de	5
L'Etac de la Quoire	64
——— de Serk	35
Le Marchant, Fort	20
Lieuses	17
Lihou island	16
Longue Pierre rock	10
Longy	63
—— bay	56
Lower heads rocks	10
——— buoy	10

	Page
Main rock - - - -	21
Maitu isle - - - -	126
Malassise rock - - -	57
Malo, St., gulf - - -	5
Mangeuse rock, Grande -	94
Mannez - - - -	56
——— quarries - -	62
Manor tower - - -	39
Maquereaux rocks - -	52
Marin reef - - -	108
Mark's, St., church - -	90
Marmotier - - -	126
Martin's, St., church -	118
——— point - -	2
Mary, St., church - -	2
Matthew, St., church -	22, 97
Mauve rock - - -	23
Messellettes - - -	22
Meulet point - - -	123
Middle bank - - -	112
——— passage - -	98
——— rock - - -	73
Millbrook - - -	90
——— mill - -	99
Minquiers - - -	78, 133
Moie de Batardes - -	35
——— de la Bretagne -	35
——— de la Fontaine -	35
——— du Port Goury -	35
——— Grande - -	26
——— Petite - -	35
Mont Mado windmill -	124
——— Plaisir house -	91
Moorings - - -	58
Motte, La, islet - -	86
Mouette rock - - -	27
Mouillière - - -	22
Moulinet, Guernsey, beacon	17
——— Serk - -	37
Mousionnière rocks - -	27
Moye high land - -	83
——— point - -	16, 84
——— signal post - -	78
Mulet rock - - -	27
Nannels reef - - -	52
Narrows, Alderney - -	55
Nez du Guet - -	114, 121
——— fort - -	122
Nianaise - - -	52

	Page
Nicolle tower - - -	90
Nine feet rock - - -	92
Nipple rock, Guernsey -	24
——— Jersey - -	128
Noir Pute rock - -	31
Noire Houmet - -	54
——, La - - -	111
——— Pierre - -	35
——— Petite - -	128
——— Roque -	44, 130
——— ledge - -	44
Noires Putes - - -	65
Noirmont house - -	21
——— point and tower -	84
Noirmontaise reef - -	83
Nord-Ouai - - -	11
North channel, Grouville bay	114
——— rock - - -	54
——— sand ridge - -	112
North-west passage - -	95
Old harbour - - -	100
Orboue rock - - -	49
Orbouée bank - - -	66
——— rock - - -	65
Orgueil castle - - -	105
——— Mount, bluff and point	103
Ortac channel - - -	45
——— ledge - -	44
——— rock - - -	48
Ouen, St., bay - -	1, 80
——, anchorage -	82
——— dangers in and off	80
——— church - -	82
——— mill - -	80
Outer rock - - -	93
Oyster rocks - -	17, 93, 123
——— beacon - -	74
——— ground - -	74
Ozard rock - - -	60
Pacquet rock - - -	112
Passe de la Percée - -	26
Pas point - - -	104
Pater Nosters or Pierres de Lecq	79
Pavlaison rock - - -	37
Pécheresse rock - - -	37
Pendante - - -	16
Percée rock - - -	23
——— Ile - - -	91

	Page
Perelle bay - - - -	22
Peter, St., barracks - - -	80
———— church - - -	2, 80
———— port - - -	8
———————— harbours - -	8
———————— light - -	11
———————— road - -	10
Petit Port - - - -	11
———— banc du - - -	25
———— bay - - -	25
Pezerie point - - -	23
Picnic Hotel - - -	97
Pierre au Norman - - -	40
———— au Vraic - - -	54
———— aux Rats - - -	27
———— Carrée rock - - -	35
———— de Bût - - -	53
———— des Enfans rock - -	97
———— de la Moue - - -	26
———— du Cours - - -	35
———— de Lecq or Pater Noster rocks	79
———— St., du Bois - - -	16
———— Mouillée - - -	118
Pignonet rock and beacon - -	92
Pillon rock - - -	119
Pilotage - - -	11, 77
Plaine point - - -	125
Plat Boue rock of Herm - -	26
———————— of Alderney -	60
———— Saline - - -	56
Platte Fougére - - -	28
———— Houmet - - -	85
———— rock - ·· -	61, 94
———— Roque - - -	29, 39
———————— tower - -	105
———— Rousse rocks - -	106
Pleinmont, bluff land - -	79
———————— guard-house -	1
———————— Guet - -	16
———————— ledge - -	16
———————— point - -	10
Plèmont point - - -	124
Poches-à-suie - - -	90
Pommier banks - - -	47
Porpoise rock - - -	108
Port du Moulin - - -	34
Portelet bay - - -	86
———————— anchorage -	86
———————— ledge - -	86
Princes tower - - -	2, 89

	Page
Quenard fort - - -	62
Quenvais - - - -	80
Querouelles - - - -	60
Queslingue rock - - -	64
Race channel - - -	5
———— of Alderney - -	43
———— rock - - -	67
Raz island flagstaff - -	62
Refraction - - -	2
Regent fort - - -	77
Renonquet reef - - -	52
Richards rock - - -	55
Richmont fort - - -	22
Rigdon bank - - -	80
———— swatchway - -	81
Road rock - - -	112
Robert point - - -	38
Rocco fort and tower - -	80
Roches Douvres - - -	5
———————— light -	134
———————— de l'Ouest -	16
Rocquain bay - - -	23
Rocque Poisson - - -	86
Ronde Selliere - - -	128
Ronez point - - -	124
Roque au Nord - - -	31
———— de Braye - -	28
———— Noire rocks - -	21
———— Pendante - -	64
———— point - -	103
———— tower - -	114
———————— , Grand - -	16
Roselle point - - -	58
Rosiere anchorage - -	27
Rouaudière rock - -	91
Rouget rock - - -	104
Round rock, Burhou island -	53
———————— Rocquaine bay -	23
Rouquet reef - - -	128
Rousse de Mer - - -	20
———— Frouquie - -	89
———— Platte rock - -	107
———— point - -	20
———— rock, Alderney -	29
———————— Jersey -	89
———————— , Grande -	129
———————— Petite -	129
Rousset rock - - -	64

	Page
Roustel rock - - -	29
Route en Ville rocks -	105
Rozel - - -	76
—— bay - - -	121
—— harbour - -	122
—— hotel - -	122
—— manor-house -	107
—— Tour de -	79, 122
—— windmill -	79
Russel channel - -	3
——————— Great -	27
——————— Little -	28
Ruau channel - -	126, 130
Sabloniere - - -	127
Salerie point and battery -	18
Sambule rock - -	15
Sambues rocks - -	123
Sampson, St., harbour -	19
Sardinière rock - -	41
Sardrette rock and beacon -	10
Sardrière rock - -	32
Sauquet - - -	62
Saut Roquier rocks -	21
Saviour, St., Church -	16, 91
Schole, Banc de la -	4, 74
Schue bay - -	64
S. E. rock - -	100
Seals rocks - -	107
Seamen - - -	77
Selle Roque - -	32
Sept Boues - -	17
Sercul - - -	41
Serk - - -	33
—— church - -	18
—— mill - -	74
—— Little - -	33
——— mill -	39
Seven Grunes rocks -	117
Seymour little rock and beacon -	111
——— tower -	2, 103
Shamrock bank -	124
Sharp rock - -	94
Ship building - -	77
Speedy rock - -	48
Sillette passage - -	97
——— rocks -	90
Square fort - -	82
Sommeilleuse guard-house -	18

	Page
Sorel point - - -	124
Soufleuresse - -	15
Soundings - -	4
South channel, Grouville bay -	115
—— hill - -	107
—— passage -	99
——————— rock -	54
—— sand ridge -	113
South-west passage -	97
Supplies, St. Helier -	77
Susanne - -	22
Swatchway - -	81
Swinge channel -	5, 53
Tabor chapel - -	85
Tas de Pez - -	126
Tas de Pois - -	17, 104, 128
——————— d'Aval -	23
Tautenay - -	29
——— ledge -	27
Taxé rock - -	106
Telegraph cable -	121
Terrible point -	37
Têtards rocks -	92
Tête Petite -	126
Têtes Champignons	58
—— d'Aval rocks -	32
—— de la Conchée	36
Tides - -	5, 134
—— around Serk -	40
——, Casquet -	50
——, Swinge -	55
Tidal Streams -	12
——————— Alderney -	69
Tinker rocks -	27
Tongue banks -	113
Tonnage - -	77
Torquetil rock -	24
Torteval church -	1, 16
Tour islet - -	40
Tourgis beacon -	54
—— fort -	49
Traiffe rocks -	26
Tres Grunes -	112
Tremies - -	17
Trois Grunes -	29
—— Pères bank -	23
Troupeurs - -	123

	Page
Vale castle - - - -	32
—— church - -	- 2, 16
—— mill - - -	- 32
Variation - - -	- 1
Vauville bay - -	- 132
Vazon bay - - -	22
—— tower - -	- 16
Verclut guard-house -	- 2
—— pier and light -	- 118
—— point and bluff -	- 109
—— house - -	- 117
Vermerette rock - -	- 27
Verte Tête reef - -	- 51
Vesté rock - - -	- 32
Vicard point - -	- 123
Victoria college - -	- 91
—— harbour -	- 100
—— new South pier and light -	88
—— terrace - -	- 93
—— tower - -	- 2, 10

	Page
Violet banks and reef -	2, 103
—— channel - -	- 105
—— directions -	- 109
—— rocks and dangers in -	106
Vielle - - -	- 126
Ville, La - - -	- 34
Vingt Clos - - -	- 36
Vrachères rock - -	- 89
—— Frouquie -	- 89
Vraic - - -	- 31
Water, fresh, St. Aubin bay	- 88
West rock - - -	- 81
Western passage - -	- 96
White rock - - -	- 52
—— or Tas de Pois -	- 104
William fort - -	- 114
Winds and Weather -	- 3

LONDON:
Printed by George E. Eyre and William Spottiswoode,
Printers to the Queen's most Excellent Majesty.
For Her Majesty's Stationery Office.

[.—250—]
[P.   .—250—} 4/70.]